THE DIGITAL PULPIT

The Digital Pulpit

Preaching in the Revolutionary Era of Online Technology and Social Media

EDITED BY
SUNGGU A. YANG

foreword by
O. Wesley Allen Jr.

CASCADE *Books* • Eugene, Oregon

THE DIGITAL PULPIT
Preaching in the Revolutionary Era of Online Technology and Social Media

Copyright © 2024 Wipf and Stock Publishers. All rights reserved. Except for brief quotations in critical publications or reviews, no part of this book may be reproduced in any manner without prior written permission from the publisher. Write: Permissions, Wipf and Stock Publishers, 199 W. 8th Ave., Suite 3, Eugene, OR 97401.

Cascade Books
An Imprint of Wipf and Stock Publishers
199 W. 8th Ave., Suite 3
Eugene, OR 97401

www.wipfandstock.com

PAPERBACK ISBN: 978-1-6667-8397-1
HARDCOVER ISBN: 978-1-6667-8398-8
EBOOK ISBN: 978-1-6667-8399-5

Cataloguing-in-Publication data:

Names: Yang, Sunggu A., 1980–, editor. | Allen, O. Wesley, Jr., 1965–, foreword.

Title: The digital pulpit : preaching in the revolutionary era of online technology and social media / edited by Sunggu A. Yang ; foreword by O. Wesley Allen Jr.

Description: Eugene, OR : Cascade Books, 2024 | Includes bibliographical references and index.

Identifiers: ISBN 978-1-6667-8397-1 (paperback) | ISBN 978-1-6667-8398-8 (hardcover) | ISBN 978-1-6667-8399-5 (ebook)

Subjects: LCSH: Online preaching. | Webcasting—Religious aspects—Christianity.

Classification: BV4235.O5 .D53 2024 (paperback) | BV4235.O5 .D53 (ebook)

12/10/24

Scripture quotations marked (NRSV) are from New Revised Standard Version Bible, copyright © 1989 National Council of the Churches of Christ in the United States of America. Used by permission. All rights reserved worldwide.

Scripture quotations marked (RSV) are taken from Revised Standard Version of the Bible, copyright © 1946, 1952, and 1971 National Council of the Churches of Christ in the United States of America. Used by permission. All rights reserved worldwide.

To All Preachers and Homileticians
Pioneering the Digital World for the Sacred Practice of Preaching

Contents

Foreword by O. Wesley Allen Jr. | ix

Preface | xv

Contributors | xvii

1. The Digital Media Sermon: Definitions, Evaluations, Considerations | 1
   ROB O'LYNN

2. Understanding the Paradox of (Im)Perfection: An Actor-Network Approach to Digitally Mediated Preaching | 23
   TONE S. KAUFMAN AND FRIDA MANNERFELT

3. Co-preaching: The Effects of Religious Digital Creatives' Engagement in the Preaching Event | 52
   FRIDA MANNERFELT

4. Symbol Preaching in the Digital Age: From Symbol Recognition to Symbol Interpretation in Facebook Ads | 85
   PIERRE HEGY

5. Metaverse Preaching | 105
   JEAWOONG JUNG

6. Being There Even When You Are Not: Presence in Distance Preaching | 125
   TIM SENSING

7   E-Word?: McLuhan, Baudrillard, and Verisimilitude
    in Preaching | 144
    MICHAEL P. KNOWLES

8   Resolution and Remote Real Presence: How Does Preaching
    Relate to the Eucharist in Remote Worship? | 173
    TIMOTHY A. LEITZKE

Index | 189

Foreword

O. WESLEY ALLEN JR.

Given my age, I may not be the best person to write a foreword for a book concerned with *the digital pulpit*. I barely made the cut of being Gen X instead of a Baby Boomer. Streaming, pre-recorded, and virtual reality homiletical concerns should really be a young preacher's game. But, of course, the COVID-19 pandemic changed that for all of us. It made online worship everyone's game. The problem, however, is that no one knows the rules of the game.

The mass move to online worship brought on by the pandemic follows a long trajectory of evolving forms of media and communication across distance. In terms of participatory, give-and-take communication (in contrast to communication that involves performers and an audience), most of human history required a messenger to physically carry a message from one party to another. This message would have been in the form of a written letter or an oral repetition of a message memorized. Either way, this form of communication was primarily available only to the wealthy elite who were literate and/or could afford servants who delivered such messages.

The modern age changed this. First, mail systems were developed that allowed for much more affordable ways to correspond with people across a distance. This development was followed in the mid-nineteenth century by the telegraph. Still, snail mail (as we now call it) and telegrams (the first version of emails) were occasional for most people.

The telephone changed this. Again, at first this was an invention only available to the wealthy, but the landline telephone became a household feature in all homes and businesses. Pay phones were available everywhere (remember phone booths?!). Late in the twentieth century, the cell phone followed the same path. And with the internet, so came email, texting, and video conferencing, the likes of which previously had only been imagined in James Bond movies and *The Jetsons*. Indeed, had the coronavirus pandemic occurred just a few decades earlier, online worship would not have been a possibility.

Communication in the form of a performance before an audience has followed a parallel trajectory to that of participatory communication across distance. For most of human history, performance required in-person attendance. There was no technology that allowed otherwise. Someone stood up on a stage before a gathered crowd speaking, acting, or singing. Then came movies, but of course these were originally silent films. The performers were not physically present (only images on the screen), but the audience was still required to gather in person to watch (and later hear) a film performance.

Only with the rise of radio could performances (and worship) involve performers or preachers speaking in one place with their audience scattered in different places around radios in homes, businesses, and automobiles. Television and then the internet followed in the radio's wake, allowing for performative communication across distance, while seemingly collapsing that distance. Again, at first each of these technologies were only available to elite, but they would all eventually become household items, at least in the so-called "first world."

My professional entry into this communication/technology history begins back in early 1985 when I was appointed to serve my first congregation as a part-time student licensed pastor. Village Falls United Methodist Church was a tiny church in Mulga, Alabama, a tiny town left behind after a coal mine had closed down. I began writing my sermons out by hand on lined notebook paper, only getting a large, monochromatic desktop computer with a five-and-a-quarter floppy disk a year or so into my pastorate. Obviously, I had no cell phone either—this did not come until a couple more congregations into my ministry. Indeed, it was a year into my ministry before I even got an answering machine with one cassette tape for the outgoing greeting and one for incoming messages. The church and my ministry were low tech, indeed.

Village Falls had as many, if not more, homebound members of the church as there were ones who were able to attend in person regularly. I spent many an hour each week visiting in homes, hearing stories about children, grandchildren, and great-grandchildren, and sharing Holy Communion. Often in these homes I would find the television tuned to *The*

700 Club, a calendar from Jimmy Swaggart hanging on the refrigerator, an anointed prayer cloth from Jim and Tammy Faye Bakker hanging with the dish towels, and/or a "free" book from Jerry Falwell sitting on the recliner's side table next to the leftovers from a lunch provided by Meals on Wheels. The use of "free" in quotation marks intended to be understood as expressing snarky sarcasm because I knew these types of items were sent only to patrons who mailed in donations. While my ministry was low-tech, these people were using the technology of the day to invade my parish.

They not only offered my parishioners theology that conflicted with my mainline denominational tradition, it was a theology that I saw as benefitting the preacher more than the hearer—theology that was often intended to "scare the hell out of" potential converts or which presented a God who eternally rewarded those who gave to God, either of which translated into contributions for the televangelists' ministries. I saw these televangelists as nothing more than con artists scamming my poor, older members of some of the few resources they had to live on in the final days. The best I could do was use a dual cassette boom box to record sermons poorly in worship and then to re-record sermons (one at a time . . . in real time) so these people could listen to them on small cassette players the church provided for them. But the age of radio had passed, and my efforts lost in competition with the glitz of television ministry, whose production quality rivaled that of network television.

For me, ministry was incarnate. In my head, I would challenge my people to ask one of these celebrities to visit them in their home or in the hospital, to hold their hand while praying with them, to place the host in their hand and say, "The body of Christ given *for you*," or to trim their toenails when they could no longer bend over to reach their feet. See what answer you get, then, I would protest silently. To be sure, these people showed me great appreciation for the care I and other members of the church offered them, but they continued to watch and send their money to those two-dimensional preachers who were on the screen any time they desired.

Years later when the context of my preaching ministry had shifted from the sanctuary to the classroom, my disdain for televangelists evolved into a similar contempt for internet preachers. Televangelists at least had to pay for airtime, but anyone with a dial-up modem and a camcorder that could be connected to a computer could post a video made in their basement online with little cost, no one jurying the sermons, and no judiciary authorizing them. I warned my students not to waste time watching them, but they did not listen. Indeed, they would ask me which preacher online was my favorite. "None!" I would scream silently in my head, while out loud I calmly made my argument against internet sermons for the twelve hundred twenty-sixth time.

Then came the pandemic, with social distancing and isolation. I found myself temporarily homebound with the rest of the world. Yes, I longed for contact (incarnate ministry), but when it was not possible, I longed even more for a word. Thank heavens preachers out there did not share, or at least overcame, the sentiments I had held in the past. It was not only the preachers with large A/V budgets who answered the call. Every pastor with a smartphone propped up on hymnals in front of their pulpit tried to speak the gospel into the situation of illness, anxiety, death, and grief.

As a scholar of preaching, I wandered all over the web looking to see what different preachers were doing. As a person of faith, I tuned into the Facebook live stream of the congregation I regularly attended, greeting others in the comments, and clicking on heart emojis during the liturgy and sermon. I was filled with humility in the face of the risks they were taking and with gratitude for each and every one of them. The word God spoke through them did not return to God empty.

Initially, these faithful heralds simply had to scramble to get online. Is the Wi-Fi signal strong enough? Is the lighting bright enough and the right tone for the screen? Where do I make "eye contact" with the camera lens? Do I use Zoom, Facebook, or YouTube? There was lots of experimentation occurring.[1]

They had no time to take historical account of how this moment related to past forms of proclamation. No chance to debate whether preaching should move online. No time to develop a homiletical theology of digital preaching. No opportunity to create a taxonomy of different approaches to online preaching. No time to ponder best homiletical practices for this virtual medium in contrast to face-to-face preaching.

Now, however, there is time. To be clear, such reflection is no academic exercise related only to understanding the past. Yes, the numbers of people attending worship and listening to sermons online have decreased since isolation ended and in-person worship restarted. But once the digital

---

1 While Hollywood was in pandemic isolation with the rest of the world, *Saturday Night Live* actors from their homes did a wonderful sketch parodying an early attempt at online worship (see Saturday Night Live, "Zoom Church," YouTube, May 9, 2020. https://youtu.be/AYP1mXqiwqc?si=DY_1z5YMDTyKWawe).

FOREWORD

Mentos were dropped into the homiletical bottle, there was no getting the soda pop back in. Or, to mix metaphors, we might recall Franz Kafka's parable, "Leopards break into the temple and drink all the sacrificial vessels dry; it keeps happening; in the end, it can be calculated in advance and is incorporated into the ritual."[2] The digital pulpit is here to stay. In it now part of the church's ritual. Its future is assured.

The nature of that future, however, is less clear. Just because we can and have embraced the digital pulpit out of necessity and it has now a regular role in church life and ministry does not mean the future of such preaching is necessarily bright. The practice needs to be shaped positively by critical exegetical, theological, ethical, liturgical, rhetorical, technological, and practical study.

The length of the above list of needed types of study is daunting, especially given that it is surely not exhaustive. But following in the wake of faithful preachers who moved online are faithful scholars like those who have essays in this book stepping in to guide us in reflecting on that move—reflecting on what we have been doing, what we could possibly do, and what we should and should not do when it comes to preaching online. Reading this book is like signing into a Zoom meeting and getting to participate in an initial conversation about a new homiletical practice with a diverse group of thoughtful homiletical scholars utilizing different and sometimes disagreeing perspectives. The conversation moves richly beyond questions of the best place to mount a webcam in a traditional worship space. Deep analyses into the why and what and how of the diverse and quickly evolving modes of online homiletical practices are found in the pages that follow. This collection will fund many conversations to follow. And this old preacher could not be more thankful.

---

2 Franz Kafka, *Parables and Paradoxes*, 93 (New York: Schocken, 1961).

Preface

In human history, technology has invariably served as both a blessing and a curse. This duality rings particularly true for Christianity, as exemplified by the invention of the Gutenberg press. This breakthrough facilitated the widespread dissemination of the Bible in hard copy, thereby promoting the democratization of ecclesial authority and enhancing the theological knowledge of the laity. Conversely, it also amplified the potential for the propagation of erroneous teachings and misinformation. In the twenty-first century, we are acutely aware of this historical irony, as the advent of digital and online technologies, alongside social media, has recapitulated this pattern; fostering a more egalitarian access to knowledge on one hand, and on the other, facilitating the dissemination of false representations, misinformation, and unjustifiable claims, including but not limited to sexism, racism, ableism, classism, and genocidal ideologies.

The focus of this edited volume is the practice of preaching as it evolves and is performed within the revolutionary milieu of digital technology and social media. Throughout the twentieth century, the Christian pulpit adeptly incorporated these tools through television, radio, film, cassette tapes, and CD-ROMs. The twenty-first century's technological revolution demands a new theological and methodological assessment, particularly regarding preaching. Contributors to this volume will address pivotal questions: What technologies are at our disposal, and which can be synergized with preaching? Is there a robust homiletical theology of digital technology and social media? What constitutes the best practices in preaching within the current digital and social media landscape? What benefits and detriments—pertaining to what is stated above and beyond—have been observed in these practices? What novel homiletical strategies are emerging within this context?

Contributors may consider various scenarios, forms, and styles of technology-enhanced or social media–integrated preaching with these

PREFACE

questions in mind: ranging from live-streamed traditional pulpit preaching, to streaming prerecorded sermons, to live preaching via platforms like Zoom or YouTube, and even to VR (virtual reality) preaching. The dual objectives of this volume are to complete a homiletical evaluation of contemporary preaching practices and to advance constructive homiletical theologies, theories, and strategies. Each chapter may address one or both objectives within the scope of the author's specific topic.

I am profoundly grateful for the international collaboration that has made this volume possible, with esteemed contributors hailing from various parts of the world. Such diversity ensures a rich array of theological and technical insights, reflecting the global nature of the topic; homiletical impacts of digital technology and social media vary worldwide, a phenomenon that merits comprehensive examination in scholarly works such as this. Readers will discover that the present volume indeed offers such a global perspective.

Once again, we are reminded that technology, through human history, has consistently been a double-edged sword. The field of Christian preaching must confront this two-faced technological entity—akin to the Janus of ancient lore. The imperative is clear, undeniably simple, yet profoundly crucial; preaching now, as in the past, makes use of technology, for better or for worse. It is time to engage with and learn from the insights that the authors of this volume offer on this subject. You are warmly invited to do so.

In the wake of the season of Epiphany 2024,
Sunggu A. Yang

Contributors

Pierre Hegy, PhD
Professor emeritus, department of sociology, Adelphi University, USA

Jaewoong Jung, PhD
Assistant professor of homiletics, Seoul Theological University, South Korea

Michael P. Knowles, PhD
George Franklin Hurlburt Chair of Preaching, McMaster Divinity College, Canada

Timothy Leitzke, PhD
Pastor of Trinity Lutheran Church of Valparaiso, adjunct instructor in theology at Valparaiso University, USA

Frida Mannerfelt, PhD
Visiting research fellow, Lund University, Sweden

Tim Sensing, PhD
Professor of practical theology at the Graduate School of Theology, Abilene Christian University, USA

Tone Stangeland Kaufman, PhD
Professor of practical theology, Norwegian School of Theology, Norway

Rob O'Lynn, DMin
Dean of distance education, associate professor of preaching and ministry, Kentucky Christian University, USA

1

The Digital Media Sermon
Definitions, Evaluations, Considerations

ROB O'LYNN

INTRODUCTION

In many ways, conversations related to all things "digital" have become the hot topic, especially in subdisciplines connected to the metadiscipline of communication. Studies in rhetoric, media, writing, information technology, creativity, and even homiletics are circling the concept of "digital," primarily in light of the continuing effects of the culturally seismic COVID-19 pandemic. Generally thought of as a conversation for junior scholars, those working to establish a niche for themselves in academic discourse, this collection features contributions from senior scholars who are seeking to understand preaching in the digital frontier. For example, Tim Sensing explores how pastoral presence can be achieved through online preaching.[1] Also, Michael P. Knowles explores how foundational voices of media theory provide guardrails against losing authentic pastoral *ethos* on the digital frontier, a topic that will also be addressed below.[2] The question driving this particular essay is how to understand the place of the sermon on the digital frontier. In hopes of accomplishing this rather abstract task, this essay will begin with an analysis of the concept of digital rhetoric. Next, this essay will review dissertation literature published since 2013 that address preaching

---

1. Sensing, chapter 6 of this book.
2. Knowles, chapter 7 of this book.

and technology. Then, this essay will address "best practices" research on preaching and technology published since 2019 to see what influence the dissertation research is having on functional conversations. Finally, a proposal for capturing the concept of "digital homiletics" will be articulated.

DEFINING "DIGITAL MEDIA"

The phrase "digital media" has had an evolutionary journey to this point in history, as much of its development has taken place in the field of rhetoric, which itself has experienced something of an ongoing revisioning over the last three decades. The phrase was first coined by noted University of California at Los Angeles rhetorician Richard A. Lanham in a 1989 essay on the digital revolution in literary studies. These were still the early days of digital media, as commonly understood today. Research still needed to be conducted in libraries, often still using microfilm and microfiche. The personal computer was still a dream for many, and access to the World Wide Web was still a full high school or college experience away. Yet, Lanham argued that a time when one could read books in "pixeled print" was closer than commonly imagined.[3] Lanham further argued that "Digitized communication is forcing a radical realignment of the alphabetic and graphic components of ordinary textual communication," something he saw as becoming a collaborative process between author and reader.[4] This, in his estimation, would lead to a general revolution of the concept of a "fixed text," thus accelerating the oscillation of interpretations that a given reader could make about the text under consideration.[5] Not only this, however, there would also be a sharpening of constructive and deconstructive approaches to literary and rhetorical interpretation. In what now seems like prophecy, Lanham postulated our current ability to access numerous editions and renderings of classic texts like *Paradise Lost* on a single reading device while also envisioning the director's cut approach to releasing films after their theatrical run. To be specific, what Lanham envisioned is more akin to the "dangerous precedent" of Zack Snyder's director's cut of *Justice League*, which repurposed the film into "narrative acts" that can be viewed continuously or independently and provides nearly two additional hours of

---

3. Lanham, "The Electronic Word," 265.
4. Lanham, "The Electronic Word," 265.
5. Lanham, "The Electronic Word," 268.

content,[6] than it is to the simple adding of edited footage, such as in *True Romance* or *Kingdom of Heaven*—which are considered two of the best director's cut films of all time.[7] "Digital media," then, is the "metaphysical adjustment" that all media—print, music, art, film, etc.—will eventually evolve into, as technology continues to expand the boundaries of what is possible, what Lanham refers to as "the relentless *dramaticality*."[8]

The next major definition of "digital media" comes in a 2005 essay from James P. Zappen. Rather than the abstract postulating of Lanham, Zappen takes a more functional, more technical approach. He refers to "digital media" as "digital rhetoric" and notes that the study of this subject "is at once exciting and troublesome."[9] It is exciting because it opens new possibilities for the nature and function of rhetoric. However, it is troublesome because rhetoric brings over two millennia of cognitive baggage with it to the emerging digital frontier. Yet, a way of explaining traditional models of rhetoric in digital spaces is needed. In what ultimately functions as a literature review, Zappen notes the common characteristics that are emerging with digital media. In terms of characteristics, digital media provides speed, reach, anonymity, and interactivity. Speed goes without saying. The existence of digital media facilitates access to content much quicker. Even in a 5G world, dial-up internet is still faster than spending hours combing through newspapers and reference books at the library. Reach also goes without saying. As I have noted elsewhere, one of the intrinsic values of digital media (or social media, specifically) is that it builds relationships (relational), expands the capacity for doing good (influential), and shares what we have with others (generous).[10] Reach is only determined by the platform chosen. Digital media also offers anonymity, which allows freedom of expression yet also causes problems when it comes to ownership of content and expressions of anger, hatred, and abuse. Interactivity relates to reach in that it allows for persons to engage with the spectrum of humanity, although it brings concerns of personal privacy more to the forefront of ongoing conversations. And while epistemological debates about how one even defines digital and interactivity continue, Zappen noted that digital rhetoric (media) would move beyond the simple goal

6. Dockterman, "Snyder Cut."
7. Hanley, "20 Director's Cuts."
8. Lanham, "Electronic Word," 275.
9. Zappen, "Digital Rhetoric," 319.
10. O'Lynn, "Social Media and Preaching."

of persuasion to the exploration of identity (what has colloquially become known as truth-telling) and community building (also known as creative collaboration). Finally, Zappen envisioned that digital rhetoric (media) would become "an amalgam of more-or-less discrete components rather than a complete and integrated theory in its own right."[11] Ultimately, it would become the medium or context in which conversation and exploration would occur rather than a model to be applied.

The third major definition of "digital media" comes from Douglas Eyman in his book *Digital Rhetoric: Theory, Method, Practice*. Here, Eyman seeks to demonstrate the interdisciplinary nature of rhetoric, and digital rhetoric specifically, as the study of rhetoric is both performative and conceptual in nature. It bleeds over into disciplines other than just communication or grammar. It influences a number of disciplines, such as political science, education, and, for our purposes, religion broadly speaking. As such, digital rhetoric requires a holistic approach to its study as it is becoming its own field of study rather than a discipline within another field of study.[12] This is where the notion of "digital media" comes into the picture, presented by Eyman more as the vehicle for digital rhetoric than as a synonymous or interchangeable concept. Specifically, in contrasting analog and digital, where analog is "based on the principles of similarity, proportion, and resemblance,"[13] digital functions in coded differences and dissimilarities. In so doing, digital media "can be articulated and rearticulated, reshaped or recreated as (nearly) perfect copies, carrying with those copies and ancillary works an apparent cohesiveness, but digital work is also composed of discrete bits (individual binary digits)—these components enable reconstruction, but they can also be susceptible to fragmentation."[14] As such, digital media becomes a metaphor for postmodern thought, as it represents both construction and deconstruction (and even reconstruction) simultaneously—a development from Lanham's original concept. The articulation of rhetoric through digital media takes on a "hyper" quality, borrowing from Heba who saw rhetoric taking on a continuously reinventive nature through ongoing use by the various users involved in multimedia practice.[15] Eyman notes that the emergence of postmodern thought

11. Zappen, "Digital Rhetoric," 323.
12. Eyman, *Digital Rhetoric*, 9.
13. Pawlett, *Jean Baudrillard*, 79.
14. Eyman, *Digital Rhetoric*, 20.
15. Heba, "Hyperrhetoric," 19–44.

in mainstream content discussions brought about major shifts in concept and methodology, specifically such as how "persuasion" is understood, now seen as more collaborative than unidirectional. Digital media, according to Eyman, is more than a vehicle, such as watching a sermon on YouTube as opposed to reading it in a printed collection. Digital relates to the foundational concept of literacy, as digital media becomes the new framework through which we discern meaning through communication. This will lead to a synergism both in development of content and interpretation of meaning, as competency in use of the media will determine efficacy in interpretive practice.

The final major definition of "digital media" comes from a 2018 essay by Angela M. Hass. For Haas, rhetoric offers a cultural framework, one that outlines accepted values as well as norms that foster conversations and methodologies. Haas thus defines digital rhetoric as follows:

> Digital rhetoric is the digital negotiation of information—and its historical, social, economic, and political contexts and influences—to affect change. By digital negotiation, we can think in terms of the role(s) of digital media in relation to invention, arrangement, style, memory, and delivery. Further, we might consider the rhetorical work of digitality as key to digital rhetoric.... No matter which approach, digital cultural rhetoricians typically agree that digital rhetoric requires a negotiation—an interfacing—between bodies, identities, rhetoric, and technology.[16]

On one hand, Haas's concept of rhetoric does offer a cultural framework, as noted above. Rhetoric not only provides the language of virtue and ethics (more on this below), it also offers the vehicle for communicating virtue and ethics through digital media. On the other hand, Haas's concept of rhetoric brings the problematic issue of power systems to the surface. Given that the goal of classical rhetoric is persuasion, the concern of philosophical colonization is very real.[17] We have seen and continue to see this dysfunctional application of power in modern American politics.[18] Either way we approach this, this is what Haas further defines as "interface," the practice of engaging digital media for epistemological expression.[19] Thus, and

---

16. Haas, "Toward a Digital Cultural Rhetoric," 412.

17. Neal offers a thorough and stinging critique of rhetoric, especially more exclusionary applications of rhetoric; Neal, *Overshadowed Preaching*, 24–54.

18. See Bail, *Breaking the Social Media Prism*.

19. Haas, "Toward a Digital Cultural Rhetoric," 413.

something that will course as a thread through the remainder of this essay, is that rhetoric—and the ways in which we communicate—is *not* morally neutral. Regardless of whether the information and media are employed to emancipate the oppressed or oppress the emancipated, the rhetorical form takes on moral currency. For example, a politician standing in front of a church and holding up a Bible holds negative moral currency due to its semblance of US President #45's action at Lafayette Park during the Black Lives Matter demonstrations in May 2020. With this in mind, communicators, and preachers specifically for our purposes, must give attention not only to what they communicate but also through what media they communicate. Preaching on the digital frontier must continue to imagine how it will "foster and sustain more ethical, positive, and just relationships between rhetoric, bodies, cultures, communities, and technologies in our disciplines, organizations, communities, and the world."[20]

The question that comes after this survey of roughly thirty years of conceptual development is how one defines "digital media." Initially conceptualized by Lanham, "digital media" would be the move of traditional forms of media into digital forms, such as reading a print book on a digital reader such as a Kindle. This has happened, and continues to happen, as more and more digital applications are developed. What came after Lanham with Zappen and Eyman is the move toward "digital media" as a practical function. With Zappen, "digital media" evolves into the medium for rhetorical communication. With Eyman, "digital media" is itself the framework for literacy. Together, we see the advent of media as both message and messenger. Finally, through Haas, we see "digital media" as providing the framework for understanding the culture in which we exist. It provides us with our interface for meaning and existence. Thus, the journey has progressed from media as tool to media as existential space. As homileticians and preachers, it is imperative to discern how "digital media" impacts the communication of the gospel.

EVALUATING RELEVANT HOMILETICAL RESEARCH

The conversation regarding the move toward digital is not new or unexpected. This conversation has been brewing below the surface of homiletics for the better part of the last three decades—perhaps four, depending on how one assesses the influence of televangelism on rhetoric and media.

---

20. Haas, "Toward a Digital Cultural Rhetoric," 420.

Back then, the conversations were labeled "multimedia," which would encompass everything from using projectors to displaying images on a screen to visual aids. One of the first to enter this emerging conversation was Thomas H. Troeger. In his book *Ten Strategies for Preaching in a Multimedia Culture*, Troeger offers more of a defense for creativity in preaching than explicitly engaging with multimedia or digital culture.[21] Some of his strategies include "create a parable," "use a flashback," and "reframe a sacrament." Each chapter then ends with a sample sermon where the creative application is incorporated into the sermon. The strategies are more static than they are dynamic and remain largely oral in delivery. However, it does demonstrate an awareness of the need to include more than just the spoken word.

As a quick aside, Daniel Overdorf and Karyn L. Wiseman offer solid updates to Troeger's groundbreaking effort, although their focus on multimedia and digital media is limited. In *One Year to Better Preaching: 52 Exercises to Hone Your Skills*, Overdorf includes chapters entitled "Illustrate with Video," "Conduct E-Interviews," and "Show Websites."[22] In *I Refuse to Preach a Boring Sermon! Engaging the 21st Century Listeners*, Wiseman discusses creativity in preaching more explicitly. Some of her chapters discuss using visual aids like Play-Doh and social media like TikTok as avenues through which to engage hearers.[23] One noticeable difference between Wiseman's book and the others discussed is that she includes a chapter on the process of selecting and using audio and visual equipment.

Between the publication of Troeger's book and those written by Overdorf and Wiseman, Rick Blackwood published his dissertation. Entitled *The Power of Multi-Sensory Preaching and Teaching*, Blackwood ramped up the conversation from preaching being a strictly or, at least, largely oral event to one that could be fully immersive sensationally. However, this was not engaging the senses of touch, taste, smell, sight, and hearing just for the sake of engaging the senses. It was for the sake of discipleship, of growing faith in those who gave ear to the sermon. Engaging more with learning theories than with homiletic theories, Blackwood developed his master template for designing creative and engaging sermons and worship services, including the REEKS (Relevant, Excellence, Engaging, Kreative,

---

21. Troeger, *Ten Strategies*.
22. Overdorf, *One Year to Better Preaching*.
23. Wiseman, *I Refuse to Preach*.

and Seamless) model.²⁴ Out of all of this construction emerges a model that leads to improved "attention, comprehension, and retention."²⁵ From this, an equally niche conversation has emerged—the role of neuroscience and learning theory on preaching and discipleship, seen in the work of Richard Cox,²⁶ J. Ellsworth Kalas,²⁷ Julius J. Kim,²⁸ and Richard W. Voelz,²⁹ as well as my own dissertation research.³⁰ As we will see below, the ongoing conversation regarding the intersection of theories of creativity and learning will continue to seed future conversations about preaching.

We now turn to evaluating literature relevant to our discussion of preaching and digital media. Specifically, we will examine four doctoral dissertations, two PhD and two DMin, published since 2013. Two notes about criteria. First, doctoral dissertations were selected due to the concentrated nature of dissertation work. Rather than selecting established scholars who may or may not be invested in this topic long-term, the emerging scholars chosen demonstrated commitment to not only engaging this conversation but also expanding it. Second, it is assumed that dissertations on preaching and digital media were published prior to 2013. However, the date coincides with the dates listed above of works from established scholars who have written on the subject. Dissertation work in coming years on the intersection of the topics of preaching, technology, media, rhetoric, and discipleship, then, will seek to validate the more established opinions rather than be validated by them. This will be demonstrated through the use of essays published since 2013, many of them by the doctoral students whose dissertation work is being evaluated.

The first dissertation considered is from Alison C. Witte. Submitted in May 2013, Witte was a PhD student at Bowling Green State University who authored a dissertation entitled "Preaching and Technology: A Study of Attitudes and Practices." The focus of Witte's research is how Christian congregations adopt and implement various technologies for the purpose of communicating the gospel. Witte argues that "understanding genre expectations, which are steeped in the traditions and values of a community,

---

24. Blackwood, *Power of Multi-Sensory Preaching*, 121–24.
25. Blackwood, *Power of Multi-Sensory Preaching*, 15.
26. Cox, *Rewiring Your Preaching*.
27. Kalas, *Preaching in an Age*.
28. Kim, *Preaching the Whole Counsel*.
29. Voelz, *Preaching to Teach*.
30. O'Lynn, "Transformative Homiletic."

is key to understanding how and why digital technologies are used in particular ways and further, how those uses shape or fail to shape the preacher's *ethos*."[31] As her research demonstrates, most Christians—whether in the pulpit or in the pew—prefer oral communication of preaching and, therefore, use technology in supplemental roles. In some cases, technology is perceived as a necessary evil, something that is expected by contemporary worshippers. As such, pastoral and ecclesiastical *ethos* is restricted to what occurs in the worship hour, promoting exclusionary tendencies such as establishing boundaries to liturgical and pastoral access and isolating the congregation from the larger community. In conclusion, Witte argues that how preaching is both heard and perceived is fluctuating due to the presence and use of technology, specifically digital technology. If preaching is to remain effective, Witte argues, preachers must acquaint themselves with appropriate methods of engaging "an increasingly digital culture."[32]

The second dissertation considered is from Bryce Ashlin-Mayo. Submitted in September 2013, Ashlin-Mayo was a DMin student at George Fox Evangelical Seminary who authored a dissertation entitled "Shift: Expanding Preaching for a Social Media Sermon." The focus of Ashlin-Mayo's research is how the introduction of various modes of information technology has drastically shifted how humans communicate and relate to one another in social settings. Based on the foundational rhetorical theories of Ong and McLuhan, Ashlin-Mao argues that "people are using old tools in new environments."[33] As such, well-worn approaches to preaching are losing their connectivity to contemporary listeners. Attention and comprehension are declining and discipleship is waning. Preaching itself, in terms of its rhetorical and theological nature, is not the problem. The problem is a question of methodology, *how* preaching is communicated. Thus, Ashlin-Mayo argues that preaching, in its contemporary state, has lost its "north star" and needs to realign itself with the "constellations" of relevance, Christocentric theology, participation, and responsiveness.[34] Using the metaphor of one who repairs stringed musical instruments (luthier), Ashlin-Mayo crafts a more pedagogical and narrative approach to preaching that connects with social networks that are perpetuated through social media.

31. Witte, "Preaching and Technology," iii.
32. Witte, "Preaching and Technology," iv.
33. Ashlin-Mayo, "Shift," vii.
34. Ashlin-Mayo, "Shift," 12–13.

The third dissertation considered is from Casey Thornburgh Sigmon. Submitted in May 2017, Sigmon was a PhD student at Vanderbilt University who authored a dissertation entitled "Engaging the Gadfly: A Process Homilecclesiology for a Digital Age." The focus of Sigmon's research is that preaching needs to undergo a significant transformation in order to engage the growing influence of postmodernity. The ever-growing number of new methods for preaching both demonstrates this reality while also noting the very lack of ability for homiletic thought to do so. The digital age is ever evolving and responsible preaching and ecclesiastical practice must address this. Drawing on Whitehead's concept of novelty—what Whitehead termed as a "gadfly"—Sigmon argues against the binary approaches to defining reality.[35] This concept of novelty, then, offers preaching and homiletical practice a needed avenue for engaging the digital age in which we find ourselves. As such, Sigmon proposes that preaching adopt more conversational and dialogical models of homiletical design and delivery. Sigmon offers a theological method she termed homilecclesiology that centers its delivery in touch, here defined as "a full-bodied sensation of coming into contact with another in ways that are mutually affirming."[36] Whereas technology has a tendency to disconnect and isolate (a common complaint against traditional forms of preaching), Sigmon's approach seeks to connect and embrace through the preaching moment and our continued engagement in the digital culture. In her final analysis, Sigmon argues that preaching done in this way restores humanity as created in God's image (*imago Dei*) as we engage in the homiletic and missional work of discipleship. Additionally, Sigmon's research presents a significant shift in research, not only related to this project specifically but in regards to homiletics broadly speaking. Whereas the other projects focused on one specific area of preaching, Sigmon envisions a substantive revision to both the art and science of preaching, both how to understand preaching and how preaching is accomplished. It will be interesting to see how Sigmon's work ripples through the homiletics community in coming years.

The final dissertation considered is from Ramona Hays. Submitted in May 2018, Hays was a DMin student at Luther Seminary who authored a dissertation entitled "Digital and Analog: Preaching in a Multi-Media World." The focus of Hays's research is how sermons are heard by two different listening groups—"analog" listeners and "digital" listeners. Analog

---

35. Sigmon, "Engaging the Gadfly," 4.
36. Sigmon, "Engaging the Gadfly," 175.

listeners are those who have been formed rhetorically by more traditional forms of communication and process information in a linear fashion. Digital listeners are those who have been formed rhetorically by more technological forms of communication and process information through disconnected excerpts. More practical in nature, Hays provides an analysis of her own preaching to these two listening groups through delivering five sermons crafted and delivered in different ways—a traditional manuscript, an integrated worship service, a TED Talk, a participatory sermon, and implementing multiple learning styles. Unlike the other research projects analyzed here, Hays's project is more personal, more of an estimation of her own preaching as a self-described analog who preaches in a digital world.[37] However, by the end of the project, she admits that any effective preacher must learn to lean in to the digital world.[38] What this project confirms more personally is that the conversation regarding preaching in a digital context is a locked component of any rhetorical or theological conversation.

CONSIDERING DIGITAL MEDIA "BEST PRACTICES"

What this dissertation research demonstrates is that the homiletical community, in general, is unprepared to engage the digital world through effective rhetorical practice. At best, the use of technology and the ability to engage the digital frontier are secondary or tertiary concerns at best. This reality has only been compounded by the recent COVID-19 pandemic, where houses of worship were closed for extended periods of time and much of the liturgical and pastoral work moved to digital spaces out of necessity. As I have noted elsewhere, even those of us who considered ourselves conversant and competent with technology were caught off-guard when we stepped into our digital pulpits in March 2020.[39] While it would be impossible to have expected those who engaged in the above research to have divined for the need for technological competence that could have navigated the shift to virtual preaching and worship—and the further shift to continuing forms of homiletic and liturgical hybridity—this research does demonstrate that a needed partner has been missing from ongoing homiletic and liturgical conversations. As Peterson noted nearly twenty-five years ago, we who declare the good news of God do so in a "wired

---

37. Hays, "Digital and Analog," 1.
38. Hays, "Digital and Analog," 94.
39. O'Lynn, *Digital Jazz*, 5–6.

world."⁴⁰ However, as Yang has astutely noted, there has been a "paucity of theological reflection related" to preaching and digital media.⁴¹ While that has changed some due to the COVID pandemic, what has emerged is more akin to individual "things learned while preaching to a camera." I will even admit to doing this.

What is needed is an exploration of the consistent wins discovered from preaching in digital and hybrid spaces. As was noted in Ashlin-Mayo's research above, contemporary approaches to preaching have continued "using old tools in new environments."⁴² This is not to say that tools that have served preaching well in the past cannot be repurposed for digital and hybrid environments. What it does mean is that a new wave of invention needs to crash through the discipline of homiletics, washing away what is no longer useful and reshaping the landscape of the conversation of what is considered responsible and competent preaching. However, more on this below. We are getting ahead of ourselves.

Since Yang's essay cited above was published in 2021, a number of articles, essays, and book chapters on preaching in digital spaces have been published (many of them in recent special issues published by the international journal *Religions*), and full-length book projects are starting to pop up on the literary horizon. Eventually, enough content will be produced that similarity and consistency of thought will emerge. New "best practices" for the digital sermon will distinguish themselves from more rudimentary or less effective practices. This is the very nature of invention in any practice, especially more creative practices. And preaching is a creative practice. This leads to the question of what is emerging now. What practices are setting the tone now? Who are the voices shaping and contributing to the conversation?

To answer this question, an extensive search of essays published on the themes of "preaching online," "digital preaching," and "preaching and digital media" was conducted. The search produced six essays by five different authors. One essay predates the COVID-19 pandemic by a few months. Also, the essays published in this collection were not discovered in this search, as they were in the process of being authored. The discovered essays will now be analyzed in publication order to determine if any "best practices" are emerging. First, Hudgins, writing before the COVID

40. Peterson, "Preaching Technique," 47–56.
41. Yang, "Word Digitalized," 75.
42. Ashlin-Mayo, "Shift," vii.

pandemic, argues that the mass dispensing of content "across social media platforms completely disrupted the information marketplace."[43] Whereas people once turned to static outlets such as newspapers or news broadcasts to discern what was happening in the world, people can now open an app on their phone and find out not only what has happened that day but what is happening *at that moment*. As such, people now feel that they are more informed and, therefore, seek out more connection to content providers. Yet, are people wiser? The jury seems out on this, which is where preaching comes into play. Hudgins here argues that thoughtful exegesis of Scripture remains the starting place for effective preaching in such a context. Then, he offers three examples of digital preaching. First, there is the *social media platform sermon*. Here, the preacher preaches her sermon in the traditional setting of the gathered worship service. Then, thoughts from the sermon are posted to social media in a thread. This allows listeners (followers) to engage with both the preacher's process of crafting the sermon as well as the preached sermon. Second, there is the *live from the pulpit sermon*. Here, the preacher preaches the sermon to a camera. The sermon is communicated with the same verbal and nonverbal notes that a traditionally preached sermon is preached with. However, here, listeners are not present in the sanctuary but are gathered around their computers or smartphones. Third, there is the *online sermon for the online church*. Here, the preacher preaches the sermon in real time with the service being broadcast (a.k.a., live streaming). The intention here is to reach more listeners than those who have gathered physically for worship. Prior to the COVID pandemic, these options, at least the second and third, were used by "resource rich" congregations—congregations that invested resources and funds into how technology is used for missional purposes.[44] Yet, they also demonstrated where the conversation about preaching in digital spaces was moving in its beginning phase. Much of what Hudgins saw as outlier practices became—and have remained—staple approaches to preaching during and after the COVID pandemic.

Second, Yang, as noted above, seeks to address the scarcity of homiletic scholarship that focused on preaching in digital spaces. Yang begins with a reexamination of Barth's "threefold" dimensions of God's Word—written, revealed, preached. Then, he offers an innovative concept—a fourth dimension of the Word *digitalized*. Here, the written Word (the Bible) is digitized

43. Hudgins, "Preaching Online," 79.
44. O'Lynn, "Fair Use Sermon," 28.

for accessibility. The revealed Word (Jesus) is digitized by "cross-cultural ubiquity" for connectivity.[45] The preached Word (the sermon) is digitized for spontaneous and sharable interaction. These traits of digital preaching are then used to envision eight creative approaches to preaching online: *lecture style* (live streamed from traditional worship service), *conversation style* (recorded sermon from behind a desk), *reporter style* (removed from pulpit or desk and presented as real-time presentation), *interview style* (situated in a comfortable setting to promote interaction between preacher and listener), *drama style* (presented theatrically, possibly with props), *Zoom/chat style* (like conversation style but presented informally to decenter authority/power and promote equality between the preacher and listener), *rock concert style* (portrayed as an engaged presentation between preacher and listener), and *film (or vidpod) style* (filmed in a cinematic or documentary style). While not each of Yang's styles addresses every trait, we see options that are available for creative homiletic use in digital spaces.

Third, Chan seeks to discern a set of "best practices" rather than new models for preaching digitally.[46] These practices may resonate as common sense to even the novice preacher. However, as discourse continues its demise in some religious and political circles, these practices are offered as a remembrance of what should undergird effective preaching rather than a propping up of what Ashlin-Mayo referred to as "old tools."[47] First, Chan reminds the preacher to know their audience. This means that preachers must not only know the names and faces of those who give ear to the sermon but should also be qualitatively and quantitatively adept sociologically. Preachers should learn how social media works and how to engage their members through social media. Also, it means that preachers should learn the concerns that are swimming in the cultural ethos and how preaching can address these concerns. Second, Chan reminds the preacher to engage the text. In addition to traditional print resources such as original language translations and commentaries, Chan encourages preachers to take advantage of the plethora of online resources such as digital lectionaries from Working Preacher and Preaching Today as well as podcasts from biblical scholars and pay-to-play academic sites such as Logos and Oxford Biblical Studies Online. All of this content opens the preacher up to the rich and beautiful diversity that is Christian scholarship. Finally, Chan reminds the

---

45. Yang, "Word Digitalized," 79.
46. Chan, "Digital Resources," 100–105.
47. Ashlin-Mayo, "Shift," vii.

preacher of the need to cultivate empathy and understanding. As noted above, dysfunctional uses of power continue to manipulate and distort views held by those who adhere to Christian faith. Caught in what Bail calls "echo chambers," most are not even aware of the distorted and potentially destructive views that they hold.[48] Authentic pastoral authority is not demonstrated in equalizing all opinions, especially those that contradict the mission of God. Instead, authentic pastoral authority addresses these doctrinal discrepancies with considerate compassion in the hope that God can redeem them.

Fourth, Sigmon offers an apologetic for the connectivity that digital media provides, especially when isolation is mandated to ensure safety.[49] Forced indoors, people of all kinds turned to digital forms of community building in order to assuage social disruption, the anxiety and loneliness being felt due to the uncertainty of the COVID pandemic. Sigmon talks about hosting social events via Zoom while also noting the concerns with relying on technology to maintain human connection. Sigmon quotes Kranzberg who noted, "Technology is neither good nor bad; nor is it neutral."[50] From here, Sigmon argues against the commonly held poles of thought regarding technology—technopilia (the worship of technology) and technophobia (the fear of technology). Appropriate use of technology, Sigmon further argues, is a matter of discipleship and spiritual maturity. Here, Sigmon turns to *Reaching Out*, Henri Nouwen's classic study of spiritual formation. Written during the early days of significant digital technological advancement, Nouwen addressed the spiritual concerns of loneliness, hostility, and illusion—concerns still felt deeply by many today—with the disciplines of solitude, hospitality, and prayer. Sigmon, then, builds an ecclesiastical approach from Nouwen's model that can be applied to digital preaching and worship. She notes the obvious concern about missionally engaging in digital spaces—clickbaiting. Homiletic and liturgical engagement is about proclaiming the gospel, not securing followers and getting likes. Therefore, although not fully discussed by Sigmon, pastoral *ethos* returns to the forefront of the conversation. Do we offer solitude, hospitality, and prayer, or are we simply looking for clicks? Sigmon concludes by offering a number of examples of those who sought to develop Nouwen-like communities of

---

48. Bail, *Breaking the Social Media Prism*, 3–6.

49. Sigmon, "Reaching Out for Community," 164–72.

50. Kranzberg, "Technology and History," 545, quoted in Sigmon, "Reaching Out for Community," 165.

belonging amidst a time of loneliness and isolation. These examples are intended to demonstrate how Nouwen's model can be applied homiletically.

Finally, Schatzle, in a two-part essay, examines the digital ecology in which preaching occurs, building primarily on Ong, McLuhan, and Postman, and then offers six practices for effectively engaging this ecology.[51] Much of what Schatzle addresses in his section on digital ecology has been covered elsewhere in this essay. First, Schatzle encourages preachers to be captivating, not only entertaining. Second, Schatzle encourages preachers to be succinct, not only shallow. Third, Schatzle encourages preachers to be narrative, not only illustrative. Fourth, Schatzle encourages preachers to be savvy, not only trendy. Fifth, Schatzle encourages preachers to be deep, not only content-driven. Finally, Schatzle encourages preachers to be imaginative, not only intellectual. In conclusion, Schatzle postulates that the application of these practices brings preaching full circle, as many of these practices have been adopted time and time again throughout the history of the Christian mission.

PROPOSING "DIGITAL HOMILETICS"

To begin bringing our conversation to a close, this final section will proceed in the following fashion. First, a summary of the above discussions will be offered. Second, John McClure's concept of theological invention will be analyzed and evaluated, especially as it relates to preaching. Finally, a proposal for "digital homiletics" will be articulated. To begin, we should assess and summarize the two previous sections—the review of relevant dissertation research and the discussion of "best practices." These two collections of research unintentionally collaborate to form an important track that will lead us through this final main section. To be more specific, it will be argued that the above discussions are the paving stones for all future conversations about preaching and digital media. First, from Witte's research, the importance of *ethos* in preaching is reaffirmed. This discussion has always remained integral to any discussion of contemporary homiletics, with significant studies on the topic emerging from Resner,[52]

---

51. Schatzle, "How Then Shall We Preach: Proclamation in a Digital Age—Part 1"; and Schatzle, "How Then Shall We Preach: Proclamation in a Digital Age—Part 2."

52. Resner, *Preacher and Cross*.

Reid and Hogan,[53] Schultze,[54] and McClure.[55] Ever since the days of Aristotle, authenticity of character has been accepted as a foundation element of effective communication. Does the personality presented on stage match the person encountered off stage? As Schultze notes, "One aspect of ethos is *virtue*—intrinsically good qualities of character. Virtuous persons habitually display an authentic, positive ethos. As a result, others generally like and trust them."[56] The opposite practice is to craft a *persona*, a false projection that is rooted in dishonesty. In a highly digitized world, this is an ever-growing concern as the use of a *persona* (a.k.a., avatar) is a commonly accepted—if not, encouraged—practice of social media usage, video game playing, and content-creation culture.

Second, from both Ashlin-Mayo and Sigmon's research, we need an intentional shift toward more pedagogical and dialogical models of preaching. Although still a niche topic in homiletics, the work mentioned above—especially that of Rick Blackwood, Julius Kim, and Richard Voelz—deserves special attention. Preachers simply can no longer expect for spiritual growth or missional engagement to simply happen because we have preached the sermon. This does not remove divine authority from inspired texts such as Isaiah 55 or Romans 10. However, it does mean that preachers should give more attention to effective modes of learning and homiletical pedagogy. An excellent example is Sigmon's essay in this collection. In it, Sigmon applies the pedagogical method of master educator Parker Palmer, à la his classic work *The Courage to Teach*, to homiletical practice.[57] Additionally, preachers must give more attention to measured forms of discipleship that are rooted in developmental theory. Recent work from Lisa Lamb[58] and Luke Powery,[59] as well as the trauma-informed work of such homileticians as Joni S. Sancken,[60] Sarah Travis,[61] and Kimberly Wagner,[62] are addressing this developing area. However, more work is needed.

53. Reid and Hogan, *Six Deadly Sins*.
54. Schultze, *Communicating with Grace*.
55. McClure, *Ethical Approaches to Preaching*.
56. Schultze, *Communicating with Grace*, 102.
57. Sigmon, "Courage to Preach," 551–62.
58. Lamb, *Resonate*.
59. Powery, *Becoming Human*.
60. Sancken, *Words That Heal*.
61. Travis, *Unspeakable*.
62. Wagner, *Fractured Ground*.

Third, from both Hays and each of the "best practices" essays reviewed above, the reminder to be creative is reaffirmed. One of the continued blessings of the New Homiletic movement is the plethora of new sermon development and delivery models that have emerged over the past forty-five years. However, like the more deductive and topical models that preceded it, the New Homiletic has stagnated as it has remained locked to the physical pulpit. As will be proposed below, digital preaching will need to be creative both in content as well as delivery. However, this creativity will be applied to nontraditional worship spaces.

What is needed is a moment of invention, a moment where imagination becomes the philosophical currency and epistemological capital. Invention, according to McClure, is the process of play applied to meaning-making. Theologically speaking, creation is the activity of taking nothing and making something out of it. Since humans are incapable of literal creation, humans, instead, invent. We take tools and materials already in existence and invent the chair, light bulb, and computer chip. Specifically, McClure looks to music as his heuristic, specifically the "mash-up." The mash-up is a kind of song where a musician mashes two (or more) different songs in order to produce a new song for a new listening audience. A classic example is Wyclef Jean's, formerly of the Fugees, mash-up of Queen's rock song "Another One Bites the Dust" (originally recorded with David Bowie), where Jean sampled the original recording's chorus, remixed Freddie Mercury's vocals, recorded new instrumentation with the remaining original band members, and wrote new lyrics to give the song an updated sound that mixed classic rock and hip-hop. While there was certainly a familiarity to the song, it was fresh and funky. McClure suggests the same be applied to theological invention—or, in our case, preaching: "Whereas some theologians use newer technologies to spruce up the presentation of traditional ideas, they do not use them to aid in the invention of new ideas."[63] To engage in this concept of invention, preachers should engage in four contexts. First, preachers should *decide what to say*, meaning preachers should explore new ideas both rhetorically and theologically. Second, preachers should *engage in discovery*, meaning preachers should venture out from traditionally held norms in order to explore the grand diversity of theological thought. Third, preachers should *push toward stylistic morphing*, meaning preachers should discontinue methods of rhetorical and theological imitation and engage in methods of cross-cultural contextualization. Finally, preachers should

---

63. McClure, *Mashup Religion*, 2.

participate in ideological legitimation, meaning preaching should engage in crowdsourcing, fan networks, and movement development. Although the connections to homiletics may not be readily evident, McClure's "inventive practices" provide a context for fostering encouraging conversations regarding preaching, creativity, and digital rhetoric.[64] McClure's focus on musical techniques such as sampling and remixing speak deeply to how new ideas are formed and articulated. As such, the preacher can approach the task of sermon design much the same way as a musician approach the crafting of an album. While we hear and are guided by Scripture, we sample from other theological voices and then mix these perspectives together, along with how these ideas will be presented, into the sermon.

Finally, what would "digital homiletics" look like? It should be noted here that what is proposed in the following sentences is done so in the abstract. This is a conversation that we are still on the emerging cusp of. Habituating the digital frontier requires both patience and zealous ambition, patience for discerning movement from trend and zealous ambition for tapping the pulse of culture in order to resist stagnation. At this point, the following are proposed as starting points for articulating the course of the conversation. First, "digital homiletics" will require an authentic practice of *ethos*. In a culture where *persona* is encouraged, preachers must live in the pew in the same way as they do when communicating from the pulpit. Second, "digital homiletics" will demonstrate an intentional focus on pedagogy and discipleship, preaching for intentional spiritual growth and missional engagement rather than simple cognitive assent. Dominique A. Robinson's iHomiletic program serves as a good example of this concept, as she focuses on training ministry leaders to develop pedagogically and technologically competent approaches to preaching and discipleship through digital media.[65] Finally, "digital homiletics" will foster creativity in both content and delivery, not in that the method will dictate the message but that the method will not be restricted to traditional avenues and will strive to discover creative ways to deliver the message. Melva Sampson's *Pink Robe Chronicles* serves as a good example of this concept, as she focuses on using nontraditional approaches that are influenced by historic methods of truth-telling to proclaim the gospel and engage in discipleship.[66]

64. McClure, *Mashup Religion*, 8.

65. Please see Robinson's website for more information: https://www.dominiquearobinson.com.

66. Please see Sampson's website for more information: https://www.drmelvasampson.com/pink-robe-chronicles.

CONCLUSION

As mentioned in the introduction, the conversation about the digital nature of preaching is not going away. It can no longer be ignored. It is now part of the larger meta-conversation of preaching and homiletics. Yet, the conversation revolves not only around how technology and media is used in preaching. The conversation will now consider embodiment, presence, creativity, digital rhetoric, and media theory alongside more traditional topics such interpretation, *ethos*, and delivery methods. It is hoped that this will foster more robust articulations of homiletical theory and practice as we continue moving into the digital frontier.

BIBLIOGRAPHY

Ashlin-Mayo, Bryce. "Shift: Expanding Preaching for a Social Media World." DMin diss., George Fox Theological Seminary, 2013.

Bail, Chris. *Breaking the Social Media Prism: How to Make Our Platforms Less Polarizing*. Princeton: Princeton University Press, 2021.

Blackwood, Rick. *The Power of Multi-Sensory Preaching and Teaching: Increase Attention, Comprehension, and Retention*. Grand Rapids: Zondervan, 2008.

Chan, Michael J. "Digital Resources for Teaching and Preaching: A Review Article." *Word and World* 42.1 (2022) 100–105.

Cox, Richard H. *Rewiring Your Preaching: How the Brain Processes Sermons*. Downers Grove, IL: IVP, 2012.

Dockterman, Eliana. "The Snyder Cut Is a Better Version of *Justice League*. But It Sets a Dangerous Precedent." *Time*, March 15, 2021. https://time.com/5946917/snyder-cut-justice-league-fans/.

Eyman, Douglas. *Digital Rhetoric: Theory, Method, Practice*. Ann Arbor: University of Michigan Press, 2015.

Haas, Angela M. "Toward a Digital Cultural Rhetoric." In *The Routledge Handbook of Digital Writing and Rhetoric*, edited by Jonathan Alexander and Jacqueline Rhodes, 412–22. New York: Routledge, 2018.

Hanley, Dan W. "20 Director's Cuts That Outshine the Original Versions." *BuzzFeed*, May 11, 2022. https://www.buzzfeed.com/kenwhanley/directors-cuts-better-than-the-original-films.

Hays, Ramona. "Digital and Analog: Preaching in a Multi-Media World." DMin diss., Luther Seminary, 2018.

Heba, Gary. "Hyperrhetoric: Multimedia, Literacy, and the Future of Composition." *Computers and Composition* 14.1 (1997) 19–44.

Hudgins, Tripp. "Preaching Online." *Anglican Theological Review* 10.1 (2019) 79–88.

Kalas, J. Ellsworth. *Preaching in an Age of Distraction*. Downers Grove, IL: IVP, 2014.

Kim, Julius J. *Preaching the Whole Counsel of God: Design and Deliver Gospel-Centered Sermons*. Grand Rapids: Zondervan, 2015.

Knowles, Michael P. "E-Word? McLuhan, Baudrillard, and Verisimilitude in Preaching." *Religions* 13.12 (2022) 1131–46. https://www.mdpi.com/2077-1444/13/12/1131.

Lamb, Lisa Washington. *Resonate: How to Preach for Deep Connection*. Eugene, OR: Cascade, 2022.

Lanham, Richard A. "The Electronic Word: Literary Study and the Digital Revolution." *New Literary History* 20.2 (1989) 265–90.

McClure, John S. *Ethical Approaches to Preaching: Choosing the Best Way to Preach About Difficult Issues*. Eugene, OR: Cascade, 2021.

———. *Mashup Religion: Pop Music and Theological Invention*. Waco: Baylor University Press, 2011.

Neal, Jerusha Matsen. *The Overshadowed Preaching: Mary, the Spirit, and the Labor of Proclamation*. Grand Rapids: Eerdmans, 2020.

O'Lynn, Rob. *Digital Jazz: Preaching, Media, and Technology*. Grand Rapids: Working Preacher, 2023.

———. "The Fair Use Sermon: When Verbal and Visual Borrowing Cross the Line." *Homiletic* 47.1 (2022) 23–31.

———. "Social Media and Preaching: A Primer (Part 1 of 2)." *Working Preacher* (blog), July 1, 2014. https://www.workingpreacher.org/culture/social-media-and-preaching-a-primer-part-1-of-2.

———. "A Transformative Homiletic." DMin diss., Harding School of Theology, 2015.

Overdorf, Daniel. *One Year to Better Preaching: 52 Exercises to Hone Your Skills*. Grand Rapids: Kregel Ministry, 2013.

Pawlett, William. *Jean Baudrillard: Against Banality*. New York: Routledge, 2007.

Peterson, Jeffrey. "Preaching Technique: The Ministry of the Word in a Wired World." *Christian Studies* 17 (1999) 47–56.

Powery, Luke A. *Becoming Human: The Holy Spirit and the Rhetoric of Race*. Louisville: Westminster John Knox, 2022.

Reid, Robert Stephen, and Lucy Lind Hogan. *The Six Deadly Sins of Preaching: Becoming Responsible for the Faith We Proclaim*. Nashville: Abingdon, 2012.

Resner, Andre. *Preacher and Cross: Person and Message in Theology and Rhetoric*. Grand Rapids: Eerdmans, 1999.

Sancken, Joni S. *Words That Heal: Preaching Hope to Wounded Souls*. Artistry of Preaching Series. Nashville: Abingdon, 2019.

Schatzle, Joshua. "How Then Shall We Preach: Proclamation in a Digital Age—Part 1." Covenant Theological Seminary, January 20, 2023. https://www.covenantseminary.edu/theology/how-then-shall-we-preach-part1.

———. "How Then Shall We Preach: Proclamation in a Digital Age—Part 2." Covenant Theological Seminary, January 30, 2023. https://www.covenantseminary.edu/theology/how-then-shall-we-preach-part2.

Schultze, Quentin J. *Communicating with Grace and Virtue: Learning to Listen, Speak, Text, and Interact as a Christian*. Grand Rapids: Baker Academic, 2020.

Sensing, Tim. "Being There Even When You Are Not: Presence in Distance Preaching." *Religions* 14.3 (2023) 347–58. https://www.mdpi.com/2077-1444/14/3/347.

Sigmon, Casey Thornburg. "The Courage to Preach in a Digital Age," *Religions* 14.4 (2023) 551–62. https://www.mdpi.com/2077-1444/14/4/551.

———. "Engaging the Gadfly: A Process Homilecclesiology for a Digital Age." PhD diss., Vanderbilt University, 2017.

———. "Reaching Out for Community in a Digital World: Problems and Possibilities." *Word and World* 42.2 (2022) 164–72.
Travis, Sarah. *Unspeakable: Preaching and Trauma-Informed Theology*. New Studies in Theology and Trauma. Eugene, OR: Cascade, 2021.
Troeger, Thomas H. *Ten Strategies for Preaching in a Multimedia Culture*. Nashville: Abingdon, 1996.
Voelz, Richard W. *Preaching to Teach: Inspire People to Think and Act*. Artistry of Preaching Series. Nashville: Abingdon, 2019.
Wagner, Kimberly R. *Fractured Ground: Preaching in the Wake of Mass Trauma*. Louisville: Westminster John Knox, 2023.
Wiseman, Karyn L. *I Refuse to Preach a Boring Sermon! Engaging the 21st Century Listener*. Cleveland: Pilgrim, 2013.
Witte, Alison C. "Preaching and Technology: A Study of Attitudes and Practices." PhD diss., Bowling Green State University, 2013.
Yang Sunggu A. "The Word Digitalized: A Tehno-Theological Reflection on Online Preaching and Its Types." *Homiletic* 46.1 (2021) 75–90.
Zappen, James P. "Digital Rhetoric: Toward an Integrated Theory." *Technical Communication Quarterly* 14.3 (2005) 319–25.

2

Understanding the Paradox of (Im)Perfection

An Actor-Network Approach to Digitally Mediated Preaching

TONE S. KAUFMAN AND FRIDA MANNERFELT

INTRODUCTION

How do we, as homileticians, engage with the *study* of digitally mediated preaching? Before the COVID-19 pandemic, homiletical research that dealt with the practice of preaching in digital culture was scarce.[1] The pandemic changed all of that. As churches underwent a variety of digital transitions in response to a patchwork of pandemic-era government regulations and restrictions, homiletical interest naturally followed. The present chapter hopes to add to this growing body of literature by offering a sociomaterial approach to describe and discuss what we call "the paradox of (im)perfection." This phenomenon first emerged for us in an empirical study of what "being church" meant in digital spaces, specifically in the diocese of Stockholm, Sweden, and in the period when preachers and other church practitioners were thrown online overnight en masse by the pandemic.

The chapter proceeds as follows. We begin by briefly outlining three approaches to the study of digitally mediated preaching, followed by methodological reflections (Section 1). Next, we introduce our theoretical

1. Yang, "Word Digitalized," 75.

lenses: actor-network theory (ANT) and, to a somewhat lesser extent, media theorist Amanda Lagerkvist's work on the nature of digital media (Section 2). Then, we analyze "the paradox of (im)perfection" by means of two strategically sampled cases from our empirical study, which constitutes the bulk of the chapter (Section 3). Finally, we draw both on Lagerkvist and Lutheran theologian Deanna A. Thompson, particularly her conceptualization of the church as "the virtual body of the suffering Christ," to argue for a *nondichotomous approach* to the homiletical discussion of digitally mediated preaching (Section 4).

Three Trajectories for Digitally Mediated Preaching

According to Frida Mannerfelt, three of the most common paradigms for engaging in an analysis of digitally mediated preaching each tend to rely and reinforce certain unhelpful binaries.[2] While these paradigms are contiguous with those that have been applied to on-site preaching, and have contributed to essential insights about the practice of preaching as a whole, the unprecedented pandemic-era mass transition to digital contexts has only served to further reveal inherent problems in each approach. However, before we analyze these trajectories further, it behooves us to briefly outline them.

First is the *message-oriented trajectory*. Homiletician Lisa K. Cressman paradigmatically embodies this approach, downplaying the role of media, formats, and methods when she writes: "The reasons we preach and the components that constitute a sermon are unaffected by the medium. The word of God is transmitted just as efficiently whether told as a story in ancient times, read silently in a Bible a hundred years ago, or listened to in a podcast today."[3] For Cressman, the core components and purposes of a sermon—that is, to liberate the listener to praise, gratitude, celebration, and action—are not dependent on the medium. The message-oriented approach, then, focuses on human agency, with the result being that the medium is made invisible, or relegated to a bit part in the preaching event.

Second, at the other end of the scale, we find *the media-oriented trajectory*, in which communication or media theories are the most critical aspect of the analysis, sometimes overshadowing all other factors. This approach focuses on how the various affordances of different types of

2. See Mannerfelt, "Online Preaching."
3. Cressman, "B.C. and A.C.," 46–47.

digital media, and different platforms, affect preaching, often including podcasts,[4] WhatsApp,[5] Instagram,[6] or Twitter[7] in its purview. In contrast to the message-oriented trajectory, then, this paradigm is at risk of paying too much attention to media and medium, ending up in what Pink and colleagues call "a media-centric approach."[8]

Third is *the ontological trajectory*. As homiletician Casey Thornburgh Sigmon has emphasized, the close connection between the word and the table, as elaborated in twentieth-century theological thinking, has ensnared digitally mediated preaching, as well as transcribing well-trodden discussions about theological ontology and real presence into the new key of online communion.[9] Often, this results in digitally mediated preaching being dismissed as unreal and disembodied. One example is Luke A. Powery's discussion about the advantages and challenges of online preaching, in which he fears the "loss of incarnational preaching" as a real risk. Referencing the doctrine of the incarnation, he contrasts "real" and "virtual," stating that "real human bodies, as opposed to virtual realities and bodies, are essential for the preaching ministry. . . . Jesus was the Word incarnate, a person, an enfleshed sermon, not a text."[10]

As theologian Katherine G. Schmidt has noted in her overview of theological discourse on virtual ecclesiology and liturgical practices, most theological accounts of the internet are undergirded by such opposites and binaries.[11] According to Schmidt's analysis, this tendency toward dichotomic thinking stems from the idea that digitally mediated interactions draw people away from what is real, and somehow does not involve bodies or other kinds of materiality. For these reasons, many theologians argue that digitally mediated social action, communal gatherings, or preaching events can never measure up to their on-site counterparts. In fact, they might even lure people away from what is truly real: God. Accordingly, the

---

4. Plüss, "Dialogue Form."
5. Masoga, "Effectiveness of WhatsApp."
6. Lienau, "Kommunikation des Evangeliums"; Menzel, "More Than the Argument."
7. Cheong, "Tweet the Message?"; Codone, "Megachurch Pastor Twitter"; Burge and Williams, "Is Social Media a Digital Pulpit?"; Mannerfelt, "From the Amphitheatre to Twitter."
8. Pink et al., *Digital Ethnography*, 41–58.
9. Sigmon, "Engaging the Gadfly."
10. Powery, "Preaching and Teaching," 215.
11. Schmidt, *Virtual Communion*, 15–18.

coin of the realm in this theological discourse is the oppositional, contrasting terms of virtual and real—with the "real" being separate and superior from the virtual.

There are a few notable exceptions to this in the homiletical discourse. One is theologian Ilona Nord, who sees the virtual as a continuation of the real—a consequence of the fact that being itself is mediated. Pointing to particular passages in Scripture that describe revelations of God and the nature of reality as mediated, Nord argues that there is no such thing as "an unmediated experience with reality."[12] While this position is common among scholars who specialize in digital media and religion, it is not yet particularly common in the field of homiletics, the discipline at issue in the present chapter.[13] As such, the ontological approach is still more common among homileticians, and may thus dismiss digitally mediated preaching based on a presumed, arguably unjustified, dichotomy between real/virtual.

However, what if there were another approach available to us? We aim to supplement the three trajectories outlined above, each valuable in its own right, with a fourth trajectory: *a sociomaterial trajectory*, in which the message/media and virtual/real binaries are made more nuanced and even collapsed. Here, the paradox of (im)perfection will come to the fore as an observed phenomenon that further complicates and illuminates the range of merits and harms available to digitally mediated preaching in its context of related church practices.

Methodological Reflections

However, before moving on to a fuller analysis of this paradox and the sociomaterial trajectory it elucidates, a few methodological considerations are needed. The project Church in Digital Space (CiDS), from which the following empirical case studies are drawn, was initiated by the Church of Sweden (CofS), implemented by the bishop of Stockholm diocese, and spearheaded by his theological advisor, Sara Garpe, and Jonas Idestrőm, a professor of practical theology. The project took place from January 2021 to September 2022, and intentionally drew on the experiences of church leadership and laity during the widespread digital transition churches underwent as a result of the COVID-19 pandemic. It is probably not coincidental that such a project was conducted in Stockholm and CofS, as

---

12. Nord, "Experiment with Freedom," 31–37.
13. See, for example, Campbell and Tsuria, *Digital Religion*.

Sweden is one of the most digitalized societies in the world,[14] and the CofS is an unusually affluent church. In most local CofS parishes, for instance, there is typically a director of communication on staff, and very often paid A/V technicians.

The aim of the CiDS study was to find sustainable and theologically informed ways to keep church doors open online, even when the lockdown of on-site church locations ended. The project was designed as an "action research project"[15] organized into four subprojects, involving a total of seven congregations in the Diocese of Stockholm, the diocese employees, the CofS national research unit, and five researchers. As in most action research projects, the empirical material was generated and analyzed through an intense collaboration between researchers and practitioners.[16]

The analysis of the paradox of (im)perfection in this chapter takes as its point of departure two cases from one of the subprojects found in this greater CiDS study, conducted by Jonas Ideström and Tone Stangeland Kaufman together with the practitioners in two parishes.[17] However, as the phenomenon in question also occurred in the subproject conducted by Frida Mannerfelt and Rikard Roitto in conjunction with practitioners in two other parishes, we briefly compare findings from it in our analysis of the former.[18]

Our analysis is built from individual interviews with church employees and volunteers, recordings of worship and devotions, and group interviews. Notably, the group interviews were conducted as four successive workshops with each group,[19] in which church employees (hereafter called "practitioners")[20] contributed to planning the research process, including the research question, and discussed various aspects of "being church" in digital space by looking at websites, Facebook pages, recordings of digitally

---

14. See Digital Economy and Society Index.

15. The research project was inspired by Theological Action Research (TAR). See, for example, Cameron et al., *Talking about God*; Watkins, *Disclosing Church*.

16. Garpe et al., "Att vara kyrka i digitala rum," 6–18.

17. Ideström and Kaufman, "Hållbar närvaro" and "Hur framträder kyrkan?"

18. Mannerfelt and Roitto, "Mellan rit och reklam del 1" and "Mellan rit och reklam del 2." In the original project, the seven congregations were studied and analyzed separately. In this article, though, such a distinction is not made.

19. In one of the groups the second workshop turned into individual interviews due to illness. The third workshop took place as a common workshop and group interview with practitioners from both parishes.

20. For a similar use of terminology, see Cameron et al., *Talking about God*.

mediated preaching, and more. The researchers recorded and transcribed parts of the workshops, and also took notes. They also presented relevant theories for the practitioners to consider in relation to their own digitally mediated practices, and encouraged the practitioners to reflect on them.[21] This means that some, though not all, of the theoretical perspectives used in the analysis here were part of the discussions conducted in the subproject. The practitioners in question are employees of the CofS: pastors, musicians, religious educators, technicians, communications directors, and deacons.

Finally, the practice of preaching is analyzed as part of the larger context of liturgical and congregational life. As Kaufman et al. notes in a study of intergenerational preaching, which concluded by including the entire worship service in its purview, we, too, found it impossible to separate the practice of preaching from its context, particularly when applying a sociomaterial lens.[22] Similarly, Theo Pleizier finds that listeners often experience preaching and worship as an inseparable whole, a finding that corresponds with Frida Mannerfelt's own recent study on listeners listening to digitally mediated preaching.[23] To better understand the paradox of (im)perfection, our analysis attends to more than just the bare words of the sermon, but intentionally expands its scope to religious practices that border the practice of preaching, such as digitally mediated intercession and other digital features and practices that inform the larger themes of visibility, performance, and intimacy.

THEORETICAL LENSES

A number of theoretical lenses have inspired our analysis, namely actor-network theory and Lagerkvist's work on the nature of digital media, to which we now turn.

---

21. For a detailed account of methods and theories, see Garpe and Ideström, *Kyrka i digitala rum*, and in particular Ideström and Kaufman, "Hållbar närvaro," 18–20. The two most important theoretical perspectives introduced in this subproject were a sociomaterial sensibility (ANT) in a very simplified fashion and Lindgren's use of Girard's theory of mimesis; see Lindgren, *Ekko*.

22. Kaufman, "Forkynnelse for barn og voksne," 11–13.

23. Pleizier, *Religious Involvement*, 165; Mannerfelt, "Listening to Listeners."

Actor-Network Theory

Actor-network theory (ANT), as outlined for example by Bruno Latour and John Law,[24] is a sociomaterial approach from which we draw our own understanding of digitally mediated preaching. Despite having its origin in studies of science and technology (STS), ANT has recently been employed in several fields adjacent to homiletics to analyze various religious practices, including the fields of theology and pastoral learning.[25]

The present chapter takes a similar approach, using ANT as a heuristic device to create an analytical distance from a familiar field of study (in our case, homiletics). Applying ANT in this way provides several salutatory benefits to the field of homiletics. Firstly, it introduces ANT to this academic field, as literature searches show that ANT is an underutilized theoretical resource in homiletics.[26] While employing ANT as one analytical tool in their study of intergenerational preaching, the framework is not used extensively for in-depth analysis, as is being explored in this chapter.[27] Secondly, ANT has not been applied to digitally mediated preaching before, as far as we know—a lacuna in the literature that this chapter seeks to fill.

Although there are considerable incoherences and tensions between scholars affiliated with ANT—even between Latour and Law—it is possible to identify some shared key characteristics relevant to our analysis. Contra structuralism, ANT thinkers tend to dismiss explanations for human behavior that take the underlying structures of society as their starting point. Instead, according to ANT, the world consists of bits and pieces that are ordered and connected in various ways, but which are often invisible and

---

24. While there are differences between Latour and Law in their approaches to ANT, they also share some of the most profound characteristics of ANT, and we do not distinguish between them in this chapter.

25. Reite, "Between Blackboxing and Unfolding"; Reite, "Pastors and the Perpetuum Mobile"; Holmqvist, "Material Logics of Confirmation"; Johnsen, "Teologi som ulike biter og deler"; Holtedahl, "Community"; Ideström, "Mediators of Tradition"; Kaufman and Ideström, "Why Matter Matters"; Gregersen, "Exploring the Atmosphere"; Kaufman and Mosdøl, "More than Words"; Johnsen and Afdal, "Practice Theory"; Ledstam and Afdal, "Negotiating Purity."

26. We have conducted literature searches in databases such as JSTOR, ORIA; homiletical journals such as *Homiletic*, *International Journal of Homiletics*; and in practical theological journals such as the *International Journal of Practical Theology* and *Tidsskrift for praktisk teologi*.

27. Kaufman and Mosdøl, "More than Words."

taken for granted.[28] The processes of acquiring knowledge and the generation of "facts" are, as ANT puts it, "black-boxed"—that is, hidden.[29] The establishment of Christian doctrines is no exception. Once doctrines are approved as ecclesial and orthodox (widely understood), the controversies that led to their establishment, including the sometimes ugly interactions between ecclesial actors in the process of coming to an agreement, tend to be quickly forgotten.[30] Take, for example, the doctrine of the Trinity, and the many attendant councils, treatises, and bitterly contested arguments behind its formalization in the historical record—much of which is not widely known by your average contemporary Christian, or taught in a given local parish. ANT has an analytical interest in opening the black box, and exploring the unfolding, often previously "invisible" network that results.

A second key characteristic of ANT is the idea that agency is not restricted to humans.[31] On the contrary—pathogens and natural events (such as viruses or pandemics), material objects (books, Bibles, guitars, pianos, sanctuaries, pulpits, hymnals, iPads, smartphones, social media, cameras, microphones, projectors, cords, and websites), and other less visible nonhuman actors (i.e., algorithms and electricity), all play a prominent role as actors in enacting dynamic, ever-changing networks of relations. Human actors (such as practitioners and participants in digitally mediated worship services) are equally significant parts of such networks, relating to and interacting with other humans and nonhuman actors alike. ANT thus maintains a symmetry between human and nonhuman actors, with both bringing resources and constraints to situations in which they define and act upon each other.[32]

An actor, also called a "mediator" in ANT terminology, is "anything that does modify a state of affairs by making a difference."[33] Actors "transform, translate, distort, and modify the meaning or the elements they are supposed to carry."[34] Moreover, they themselves are not left unchanged by the process. Two examples not too far afield from homiletics are the

28. Law, "Actor Network Theory."
29. Latour, *Science in Action*.
30. Kaufman and Ideström, "Why Matter Matters," 101.
31. Gaining this insight from laboratory studies, a microscope, for example, emerged as a significant actor in the knowledge construction of the laboratory.
32. Fenwick et al., *Emerging Approaches*.
33. Latour, *Reassembling*, 71.
34. Latour, *Reassembling*, 39.

enactment of liturgical reforms, and the embodiment of doctrines in local church contexts. Ingrid C. Reite Christensen[35] shows how liturgical reforms are not simply "implemented," but rather "enacted into being" by professional learning networks of pastors.[36] The reform itself is not left unchanged by these networks, either, as they recreate, replace, or ignore it—and thus can be said to translate it.[37] The importance of translators and mediators surfaces again in the work of Jonas Ideström, who describes how doctrines are embodied in the practices of local church life, such as the Eucharist, and how these embodiments serve as mediators of the Christian tradition.[38] These doctrinal embodiments carry the Christian tradition into new networks and situations, with neither the doctrines themselves, nor the Christian tradition, left unchanged by the process. The opposite of *actors/mediators* would be so-called *intermediaries*—empty vessels, which only transport meaning or message, leaving no impact on the message and remaining themselves unchanged by it.

ANT understands the world to be profoundly relational. Everything in the social and natural worlds is enacted in webs or networks of relations. ANT "tells stories about 'how' relations assemble or don't."[39] According to Law, ANT can be "understood as a toolkit for telling interesting stories and interfering in those stories," offering "a sensibility to the messy practices of materiality and relationality of the world."[40] As an analytical toolkit, one which we seek to employ here, ANT is able to trace networks of interactions and connections between various actors or mediators, studying the way in which they relate to one another and what they do to each other in looser or more stable networks.[41] Law terms this "modes of ordering," and the highly relational, network-enmeshed lens of ANT means even material objects, such as Bibles, digital platforms, or technology, are not to be regarded as static or reified.[42] Rather, they are dynamic, entangled in our practices, and ordered in various and ever-variable ways.

---

35. Ingrid C. Reite Christensen changed her name after the publications referred to here. They are listed as "Reite."
36. Reite, "Pastors and the Perpetuum Mobile," 405.
37. Reite, "Pastors and the Perpetuum Mobile," 405.
38. Ideström, "Mediators of Tradition."
39. Law, "Actor Network Theory," 2.
40. Law, "Actor Network Theory," 2.
41. Latour, *Reassembling*, 8.
42. Law, *Organizing Modernity*.

A fifth key feature of ANT concerns ontology. In ANT the "real" is neither constructed in our minds (constructivism) nor a fixed *a priori* reality (realism). Instead, the real is enacted in dynamic, ever-changing networks of relations. Notably, this position does not reduce reality to a mere plurality of subjective viewpoints. Rather, it claims that things and situations are real *in their consequences* and *in their relations*, as they are *enacted into being*. Not surprisingly, this rather controversial ontology has prompted criticism. Graham Harman has written at length on Latour, and points to the problem of reducing material objects to their potential as actors, thereby limiting an object's existence to its possibility for engaging in interactions and translations.[43] Other critics object to the weight given to ANT's symmetry between human and nonhuman actors, and instead prefer to speak of the latter as "artifacts" rather than actors, agents, or actants.[44] Another line of critique comes from the sociology of knowledge tradition, of which David Bloor's famous paper "Anti-Latour," is an example.[45] Critics have also foregrounded the lack of substantial political critique yet apparent in ANT studies, referring to the promise of such developments as "ANT and After."[46] Despite these critiques, we still find ANT to be a helpful analytical tool kit, especially when it is supplemented by the modulating perspectives of media theory and theology.

Digital Media as Metric Media and Caring Media

ANT allows us to scrutinize digital media as a central actor in networks, but it is less helpful in analyzing the ethical and theological consequences of such networks and the various actors who take part in them. Supplementing ANT with ethical, moral, and theologically informed approaches, such as those found in Amanda Lagerkvist's and Deanna Thompson's works, helps to better foreground crucial theological issues—such as vulnerability—and enables us to discuss critically what Lagerkvist terms "metric media."

Building on philosopher Karl Jasper's concept of *the limit situation* as a framing device to understand media, Lagerkvist draws attention to the

---

43. Harman, *Prince of Networks*.
44. Schatzki, *Social Change*.
45. Bloor, "Anti-Latour."
46. Alcadipani and Hassard, "Actor-Network Theory." For a helpful introduction to how ANT can be used in an anthropological study and some of ANT's critics, see Chambon, *Making Christ Present*, 6–10.

precise existential and ethical perspectives of media. She foregrounds the importance of materiality: media are considered materiality, and to some extent, all materiality is conceived of as media. Media are embedded into existence as the very building blocks of existence itself. Being is enacted in and through the entanglement of media. For Lagerkvist, new materialism and its thinkers often miss an important implication that flows from this ontology. If being is enacted in relation to materiality and others, the result is radical *interdependence*, and since both the humans and the media involved are themselves limited, bounded, and finite, they are also *vulnerable*.

Lagerkvist, therefore, approaches digital media as enabling possibilities for relationality and connection in vulnerable situations, with the upshot that digital media can become a literal lifeline for the suffering.[47] She calls this dimension of digital media *caring media*.

Lagerkvist also identifies *metric media* as a feature of digital mediation, which exists in tension with the caring dimension described above. Metric media often fosters a culture based around an ontology of numbers in which numbers confirm existence, validate importance, and communicate care. Lagerkvist describes the resulting ethos of quantification as an ideology in which numbers reveal hidden truths about value, being, selfhood, and body. However, while digital media might amplify the ontology of numbers and *ethos of quantification*, these are not new phenomena but ongoing features of modernity.[48] In Lagerkvist's argument, digital media's metric dimension is closely connected to the idea that digitality itself promotes limitlessness, creativity, and the belief that anything is possible—with vulnerability, suffering, and limitation often rendered invisible.[49]

THE PARADOX OF (IM)PERFECTION

This precise paradox—whereby one dimension of digital media supports the building of connection and intimacy via vulnerability and imperfection, while another dimension races toward perfection and quantified visibility—lies at the heart of what we observed practitioners and preachers grappling with as their church communities underwent sometimes wrenching digital transitions in our empirical study. To describe and analyze the paradox of (im)perfection, we must trace the networks of digitally

---

47. Lagerkvist, *Existential Media*, 38–47.
48. Lagerkvist, *Existential Media*, 120–46.
49. Lagerkvist, *Existential Media*, 1–12, 107–9.

mediated preaching, focusing on the ways in which various mediators relate to one another and what they do to each other, and studying the modes of ordering that structure this network. What are the significant actors in this network and how are they connected? What modes are enacted? What are the salient features of these modes?

Toward a Mode of Visibility and Perfection

> It ended up as a contest. There was so much creativity. Everyone was supposed to be visible! It was like competing in the Olympics without having prepared for it! (Group interview)

Thrown into a Visibility Contest

The notion of a "visibility contest" first surfaced in a group interview, an attempt by practitioners to describe the difference between being church in "the old way," as they expressed it, and being church online. To some, the "new way" of being church was like "competing in the Olympics without having prepared for it," and furthermore was often tinged by failure: "It ended up not reaching the level of the Olympics!" The term "contest" or "competition" was repeated several times in the same group interview, as was the notion of "being visible" as a constitutive part of that competition. Church staff were expected to participate in this visibility contest, they felt, with one communication director in particular emphasizing the outsized significance of being visible in online church. A group of practitioners in the subproject conducted by Mannerfelt and Roitto described their feelings of frustration and shame when their digitally mediated worship services did not garner as much interaction as the practitioners had hoped for.[50] To them, the number of views, comments, and likes—the amount of visibility, or quantified visibility, that a sermon or a posting from the church or preacher accrued—indicated whether their efforts to proclaim the gospel were heard and appreciated. They counted and compared themselves with other preachers in the congregation and with preachers in other churches. Visibility, as quantified by the metric of social media interactions, also

---

50. Mannerfelt and Roitto "Rit och reklam del 2," 70–71. See also Mannerfelt, "Co-preaching" in this volume.

functioned as evidence to congregational leadership of whether it was worth continuing with digitally mediated worship at all.

The first group of practitioners also connected visibility to value within the ecclesiastical workplace. One of them mentioned the fear of future layoffs: "It is important to be visible in order to survive [in the organization]. If you are not visible, you might disappear!" One of the directors of communication shared that she felt this "visibility contest" even when opening Facebook on vacation and scrolling through what other parishes and congregations had posted online.

Digital Media and Algorithms as an Actor

The sudden transition to digital spaces, and the subsequent visibility contest church practitioners felt they were newly enmeshed in, was prompted by the COVID-19 pandemic. Expressed from the perspective of ANT, a strong nonhuman actor, a *virus*, traveled all over the world, leading to *a pandemic* with immense consequences as it engaged in *translations* with innumerable other actors, with the consequence that many churches had to close their onsite church doors for often indefinite periods of time. Most churches (sometimes reluctantly) had little choice but to go online on short notice. Lockdowns thus paved the way for another key nonhuman actor, *digital media*, to take the stage. It is important to note that digital media is by its nature characterized by multiplicity, with possible variations in hardware and software, and the countless different ways humans can interact with both, contributing to myriad possibilities. Hence, from a strictly held ANT perspective, digital media would of course not be considered one *singular* actor. Digital media are, after all, an entanglement of different kinds of hardware and software that all contribute to the assemblage experienced as "digital media." However, while we seek to open this black box and demonstrate its complexity, we also close it at times for the sake of clarity and generalization, relating to digital media as one key actor significantly acting on other actors in the network of digitally mediated preaching and worship.

The complexity of digital media as a mediator is important, not least in relation to algorithms. Although invisible to most human end-users in the digital media assemblage, algorithms are a crucial nonhuman actor. Consider the following quote from an interview with a director of communications:

Interviewer (I): Do you think in algorithms?

Informant: Yes, all the time.

I: Could you please give us an example of this?

Informant: I need to hit it right. When it comes to thinking about algorithms, it is like, as soon as you have understood it, then they have changed it. And it is . . . you cannot plan, only try and test. Put out things and see what happens, put out things and see what happens. . . . It was right after the summer this year. After the summer. Why don't people look at our stuff. People were tired [of the digital church experience]. Because we had so many hits during spring, the algorithms liked us. They caught an eye on us. In order to become popular again, we must be visible. We went out and told everyone to publish more of what they are doing [on social media]. If you don't click on stuff from CofS, you won't get that kind of stuff in your social media flow. It is a bit revealing when the chair of the parish board asks why we have not published stuff. Yes, but we have. But you don't click enough [on CofS content]. They [the algorithms] have interpreted [it] as if you are not interested [in CofS content].

Note how algorithms are given agency and are personified in terms of "liking us," "having their eyes opened to us," and "have interpreted it." At the same time it is obvious they do not act alone but are deeply entangled in networks in which algorithms and other actors mutually act on each other, whether that be the chair of the parish board, who obviously did not spend enough time looking at posts from CofS; communications directors considering what and when to post and strategizing about how to boost visibility; or everyday people and parishioners who do or do not click on CofS posts, view them, or engage with them. Algorithms, then, are mediators that translate and change whatever other actors they are connected to or interact with. These actors include everything and everyone including: those designing websites and platforms to give algorithms a prominent role or those who "game" the algorithmic system to increase their own content's visibility; website users who accept cookies, thereby opening up their personal preferences and information to algorithmic use; and directors of communication who spend money on the creation of digital content, including the use of "paid media" strategies to increase publicity and visibility on digital platforms. Moreover, algorithms are clearly mediators in the ongoing performance and reshaping of the collective, as they participate in a process of translation, and push content into personalized feeds.[51] Thus, they play an outsized role in digital spaces, carrying meaning by and through their very coexistence and interaction with other mediators. Church practitioners might discover, for instance, that a prerecorded devotion is all of a sudden widely spread online, receiving numerous likes (to their delight!)—while other practitioners are disappointed, wondering why *their* prerecorded messages, films, or worship services have only accrued a handful of likes. The network, then, extends to the bodies and emotions of the human actors involved, causing joy, fueling rivalry, and prompting disappointment. In this way the line between online and offline is blurred: the network is simultaneously at work online and on-site.

While we are aware of this complexity, and do not seek to flatten the multiplicity inherent to digitality in all its multifarious permutations, we will still for the sake of analytical clarity use the concept "digital media" to refer to these assemblages. The plural form of the word—"media"—helpfully serves as a reminder of the true nature of the actor here called *digital media*. To the wonder and sometimes bafflement of practitioners in our study, this new actor, digital media, meant that human and nonhuman actors became connected in new and complex ways. They used "digital media" as an umbrella term for this new actor, while at the same time being clear that they also recognized, paradoxically, this term contained within it multiple actors. This was evident not least in their use of the terms "new" and "old" digital media. Some digital media, such as Zoom, Teams, and other digital platforms used to record devotions and worship services, were new to them. Other kinds of digital media were "old": the use of smartphones and iPads for filming videos or taking pictures, and the creation of posts on Facebook, Instagram, YouTube, etc. And yet, while these latter platforms were familiar to them from the prepandemic, on-site-first church world, they felt they had to interact with these "old" digital media in new ways, and to a considerably greater extent, than before the pandemic. The entry of digital media into the network of this parish, then, translated church life. It is no wonder, then, that the practitioners involved described this as a transition from "being church the old way to being church online," that is, "the new way."

---

51. Latour uses the word translation to describe "a relation that does not transport causality but induces two mediators into coexisting" (Latour, *Reassembling*, 108).

Digital Media as a Mimetic Toolbox and Mimetic Rivalry

Once this notion of a "visibility contest" was advanced by the study practitioners, we as researchers sought to understand it better via Norwegian author Lena Lindgren's description of social media platforms as a mimetic toolbox, and introduced this concept to the practitioners in the group interviews. Lindgren draws on René Girard's theory of mimetic desire and mimetic rivalry to ask whether technology strengthens the mimetic nature of human beings, and if social media in particular is inherently mimetic by its very nature.[52] She writes:

> Social media platforms are created by means of mimetic principles. A framework for precisely mediated desire, in which *everyone can behold each other* as imitators and models at the same time. Additionally, everyone is equipped with a *mimetic toolbox* (sharing, reposting, retweeting), *which enables the distribution of visibility*.[53]

Lindgren here helps illuminate the experiences described by the practitioners we interviewed. With every other parish's social media footprint visible to everyone with an internet connection, and the "mimetic toolbox (sharing, reposting, retweeting)," with its *distribution of visibility* quantifying and empowering engagement, a comparison between the practitioners' own parishes and others emerged. It was not just church leadership; digital platforms made it possible for various congregations within the parish to compete with each other as well. Without these social media platforms, the network would be completely altered, alongside the mode of visibility being enacted.

Most practitioners confirmed that Lindgren's concepts made sense to them, especially those who had brought the language of contest and visibility up in the first place. Notably, this parish had a history marked by competition between its various units and congregations. As the lead pastor reflected:

> I can recognize the narrative of competition. Not towards other parishes [but among the congregations within *our* parish]. Yet, this fear-driven need of being visible. We do not quite keep up. . . .

---

52. Lindgren, *Ekko*, 55. These observations from the material sparked the idea of drawing on René Girard's theory of mimesis, and mimetic desire in particular, Girard, *Things Hidden*, as an analytic device.

53. Lindgren, *Ekko*, 63, our emphasis.

> We have a history of internal competition between four different districts/congregations [within the parish]. The contagious mimesis of snowballing. Especially at the beginning of the pandemic. I experienced a great sense of competition.... We had to be visible.

However, some of the practitioners from the parish (who had *not* brought these issues up for discussion previously) spontaneously replied, when introduced to the concept of *mimetic rivalry*, "I did not recognize this rivalry mindset. I have not thought about it at all. Not within the parish, not between parishes. Perhaps I have been too visible!" Another practitioner from the same parish then chimed in to emphasize how she would rather find *inspiration* from looking at other parishes' online presence: "It can be generous. We don't have to compete!" However, later in the conversations, these same practitioners appeared to change their minds:

> But actually, the number of views. I have felt rivalry in that area. Why does this parish have 5,000 views while we have only had 300? Views are interesting from a psychological perspective. What a lot of people like, you [automatically] think you ought to like.

Here, the practitioner seems to confirm the theory of mimetic desire and mimetic rivalry afforded by social media platforms. Lindgren's concepts are thus a good illustration of the agency nonhuman actors bring to bear on digital media, and the influence they have on the networks that enmesh practitioners.

Digital Media as an Ethos of Quantification

Beyond the mimetic rivalry of Lindgren's account, there is a further dimension to the network logic of digital media, which Lagerkvist identifies. She describes how the actors involved in social media networks are deeply embedded in an *ontology of numbers*, and characterized by an *ethos of quantification*. In Lagerkvist's argument, this dimension of *metric media* is closely connected to the belief that digital media promotes limitlessness, creativity, and unfettered possibility—with the resulting networks assembled or ordered toward a *mode of visibility* and *perfection*.

As opposed to this ordering toward perfection and limitlessness, qualities such as vulnerability, suffering, and limitation are often made invisible.[54] Practitioners of both parishes voiced strikingly similar critiques

---

54. Lagerkvist, *Existential Media*, 1–12, 107–9.

against the mode of visibility they perceived churches were participating in online. They questioned the church's participation in a competition for people's attention:

> What does it mean for the church to use social media platforms when they can also be considered "a mimetic toolbox"? To what extent should the church contribute to amplifying "an economy of attention" in which various actors compete for people's attention?

Another one added: "Given this reality, what should the role of the church be?" The practitioners, then, called for critical theological reflection to guide the church in dealing with this phenomenon in a responsible way. They discussed the tension that emerges between what the church would like to convey and preach and what is enacted and mediated in digital spaces:

> It concerns how to view the church and what kind of church we would like to be. We want to be a church open to everyone . . . and that it [life] does not always end up as we had imagined it to be, and that is what we would like to communicate. At the same time, the carefully prerecorded devotions and services that the congregation publishes can easily end up being "perfect" for better and for worse.

Practitioners agreed that they were hesitant to share recordings that were deficient or "not good enough." As one of them remarked: "I don't want it to be on Facebook for all eternity if I make a mistake when reciting The Lord's Prayer."

Here, we find expressed a conundrum: the paradox of (im)perfection. To be human, to be a church, requires an openness to imperfection, according to these parishioners. Intimacy and fellowship are enacted in concrete ways via the recognition of vulnerability and limitation. At the same time, the very logic of digital media and social media platforms tends to reward perfection, or the appearance of perfection. Lagerkvist's analysis of digital media as *limitless* and therefore affording *perfection* might help us understand why this network assembles toward such a paradox, where a mode of visibility and perfection dominates despite the human actors' ideal of vulnerability as a display of *im*perfection.

In the last workshop discussion, an insight emerged among the practitioners. They came to the conclusion that the visibility contest afforded by the new actor of digital media was not really anything new:

Marketing and competition. We have talked quite a lot about competition, and this potential . . . in digital media. We have also talked about statistics, but not so much about how it is exactly the same thing. How many people do you have in your youth ministry? It [numbers] becomes a measurement of how good things are. Now we have many confirmands . . . it would not be so good if we were only 15. That is also a comparison and is clearly related to what we talked about earlier.

Another one commented: "Yes, digital media makes numbers visible in a new way. But statistics are also important." This practitioner foregrounded how statistics are used as a tool in the distribution of resources: "After two years of using digital media this way it is possible to detect patterns of what is being spread/shared. When I [as a leader] am going to make decisions about how to prioritize our work, we need to be wise."

Rivalry between colleagues, competitors, and even congregations is nothing new, to be sure, but digital and social media are nevertheless significant actors that act on, and make visible, these age-old dynamics of rivalry and competition in new ways. The increased focus on digital media and its attendant metrics have made visible the already existing significance of statistics and numbers as a sign of success—a logic that, too, is nothing new. Nevertheless, this new actor, digital media, has contributed to an opening up of the black box of an ontology of numbers, in which the online visibility contest described by church practitioners above can be understood as an extension and an amplification of an existing ethos of quantification—an ethos has been at work before the pandemic, but perhaps in different, less extensive, and less visible ways.

However, digital media are not static actors. Following Lagerkvist, we believe these qualities of *metric media* are not fixed—that is, digital media do not *necessarily* have to move the networks they enact toward modes of visibility and perfection. Instead, the possibility exists for digital media to be *caring media*—enacting a network that moves toward a mode of authenticity and imperfection. To this possibility we turn now.

Toward a Mode of Authenticity and Imperfection

[The evening devotions] mean something. It is the most important part of my ministry. . . . I don't approach devotion as a production but as worship. We worship together despite being in different places.... It is also something continual. Every Thursday evening until Christmas. At the same time. Continuity. (Kristian, pastor)

Kristian, as we call him, is a pastor and preacher who offered digitally mediated evening devotions once a week during the pandemic. He works in the same parish as the parishioners above, who first surfaced the issue of a "visibility contest." By exploring the network in which Kristian is entangled, and his interactions with other actors in it, our analysis uncovered a remarkable countertendency. The same analytical questions drove our work: what are significant actors in this network and how are they connected? What modes are enacted? What are salient features of these modes?

Here, we found evidence of translations that assembled the larger network in which Kristian played a small part toward, not the modes of visibility and perfection outlined earlier, but rather a mode of authenticity and imperfection—allowing for a caring, anonymous, spiritual intimacy and, ultimately, the creation of an ethos of care.

Enacting Simplicity, Authenticity, and Imperfection

Kristian was experienced with digital media and had previously been engaged in work with local television. He was used to interacting with actors (human and nonhuman) in digital media networks in their various constellations. Given his experience, he became a significant actor in the parish's digitally mediated presence and digital strategy during the pandemic.

To Kristian, the evening devotions he facilitated did not require much planning and preparation. They were unpretentious and down-to-earth, characteristics expressed in the choice of nonhuman actors he chose to employ, including everyday things such as the hymnal, a Bible, the lectionary text from the previous Sunday, a text on baptism, a prayer book, and a guitar. In one recording, he tunes the guitar on camera and selects the hymns to sing in "real time," chatting with listeners as he does so. Even though he often had to multitask, doing so did not stress him out, which Kristian attested to in individual interviews we conducted with him. His "see how the sausage is made" approach and unassuming demeanor created a climate of authenticity—a model of *imperfection*.

The digitally mediated network that was enacted by Kristian and the evening devotions he led contained another crucial actor: the *structure* of the devotions themselves. They took place at the same time in the evening, on the same weekday, week in and week out, and were live streamed from the same physical space. Despite being an invisible part of this network, this stable structure is still a salient actor, without which the community of worshippers who gathered for devotions (see below) would have been different, or even nonexistent. The repetitive structure lent itself to the everyday; the rhythmic nature of it precluded Kristian from the perceived necessity of having to preach the "best sermon ever" every time. Its difference from a prerecorded, professional production that aims for perfection is striking.

The digitally mediated devotions were live streamed on Facebook and Instagram from Kristian's living room by means of his own smartphone and iPad—a setup that did not allow for retakes or edits. It was neither a professional Swedish television production broadcasting a worship service from the cathedral, nor the typical prerecorded devotion or worship service from a CofS congregation during the pandemic, all of which required significantly more sophisticated technical equipment and human resources. On the contrary, these devotions made minimal demands on the human and nonhuman actors involved. Consequently, the obvious *absence* of advanced technical equipment (and the attendant team of professionals often required to operate such equipment!), became an actor in and of itself, thus affording simplicity, authenticity, and imperfection.

Enacting Anonymous Spiritual Intimacy and an Ethos of Care

Notably, Kristian's digital setup also allowed for a higher degree of interaction from the participants. In an interview, Kristian commented: "This small format . . . is more fun to live stream. Then it is happening now." This orientation to the *now* reflects Kristian's emphasis that digitally mediated worship is *a communal practice*. Digital media emerges as a salient actor again—but this time affording *interaction* instead of an ontology of numbers. Kristian himself explicitly foregrounds the importance of interaction, especially through intercession:

> It is interaction. They can send in prayer requests, [a feature] which was added as we went along. They send them in as they write their comments. They are not so many, 20–25 persons. . . . They comment on one another's prayer requests. There is more interaction here than when being on-site. It is part of the format. . . . I respond to comments. One space. On the one hand, *it is intimate*. Greater proximity than in a sanctuary. Everyone sees the conversations [in the comments]. One is visible. On the other hand, though,

> [being] anonymous and [safeguarding one's] integrity. It happens that I am bombarded with prayer requests. "I feel so calm with you," they might comment. It is the intimate format that people are mostly attracted to. (Kristian, our emphasis)

In this quote, the caring dimension of digital media as an actor, itself intimately connected to the ability to comment and interact while engaging in the online devotional experience, comes to the fore. Simply removing digital media as an actor, by returning to on-site-only evening devotions, for example, would significantly change the network and its affordance. Nevertheless, despite the interactivity afforded by the devotion's digital platform, the most important actor here is undoubtedly Kristian. He functions as a mediator without whom the network would collapse. In one of the devotions we watched, he nudges the actor that is digital media into functioning as caring media—with an act as simple as encouraging the participants to write prayer requests in the chat, and then offering to pray for them.

Following, perhaps, Kristian's example, the devotional participants themselves engaged with digital media tools as caring media, too—by commenting on each other's prayer requests and offering encouragement, despite not knowing one another. Here, another key actor emerges: the *community* of listeners and the preacher who synchronically participate in the digitally mediated act of worship. This community consists of several human and nonhuman actors (Kristian and the listeners with their phones, iPads, computers, and Facebook app or browser, each placed in various geographically distinct spaces all over the country, though most of them were local to Kristian's parish) who act upon one another, most typically by inviting, writing, and commenting on comments.

In sum, *digital media*, then, appears as a mediator that typically "modif[ies] a state of affairs by making a difference." The resulting changes typically relate to visibility, as we have seen. However, in this network with Kristian as a key actor, the use of digital media did not assemble actors toward perfection. Instead, the network is ordered in such a way that imperfection is enacted and made visible—including imperfections that are not usually visible in on-site Sunday morning worship in CofS, at least not intentionally. As opposed to a regular CofS worship service, which often takes place in a large sanctuary with people who are, more or less, strangers, digital media in Kristian's network creates a space characterized by intimacy and proximity, while nevertheless maintaining the possibility of anonymity, thus safeguarding the integrity of the participants. As opposed to the network described above, in which digital media assembled the network toward a mode of visibility and perfection, this network is ordered toward a mode of authenticity and imperfection. As a result, the visibility contest is replaced by an anonymous spiritual intimacy, characterized not primarily by an ethos of quantification but by an ethos of care.

A NONDICHOTOMOUS APPROACH TO DIGITALLY MEDIATED PREACHING

The discussion in this section is twofold. Firstly, we discuss how the results of the analysis can be understood theoretically, drawing on Lagerkvist's media theory of limits, and theologically, in relation to Deanna A. Thompson's work on "the virtual body of the suffering Christ." Secondly, we turn to the question raised in the introduction of the chapter: how can we, as homileticians, engage more effectively with digitally mediated preaching?

Between Perfection and Imperfection

How might the results of our analysis be understood theoretically and theologically? One might argue that Kristian's conscious interaction with digital media should rather be understood in terms of a "tactical vulnerability," a strategy, perhaps even a cynical one, that shares vulnerability on social media only in order to gain likes and visibility—and thus we have only snuck in a logic of metric media and an ontology of numbers through the back door. According to Lagerkvist, vulnerability can become a trademark or commodity used to manipulate and generate attention and sales.[55] While we take seriously this possibility, we nevertheless find it more likely to interpret Kristian's case as a straightforward example of authenticity through imperfection. Our argument is based on his emphasis on how important the digitally mediated devotions are to him personally and as a pastor, foregrounding it as "worshipping together." He expresses no worry about the relatively low number of participants. His priority is on interaction, pastoring, and care, rather than displaying a perfect performance that attracts a large viewership.

---

55. Lagerkvist, *Existential Media*, 94–97.

Theologically, this mode of authenticity and imperfection can be understood as the "virtual body of the suffering Christ," in the words of Thompson.[56] Drawing on Martin Luther's theology of the cross, Thompson argues that theologians ought to begin their theologizing at the foot of the cross, where they would discover that God is present where God is least expected to be—a call to pay attention to God's hidden presence in pain and suffering and witness how God works *in unexpected places* to bring redemption and healing. She applies this to virtual settings, specifically calling upon the church to embody a *cruciform media ethic*.[57] We argue that the network assembled around Kristian is such a cruciform media ethic at play. It constitutes "the virtual body of the suffering Christ."

Thompson also points to the possible advantages of "the virtual" in the church's calling to tend to the suffering. For example, a sick or disabled person might find it easier to interact with others in digital spaces, where the affliction of her body is not the center of attention. Likewise, the other worshippers in Kristian's network seemed to be aided by the virtuality of the setting. Digital media allowed them to show vulnerability and participate in intimate prayer in ways they would most likely neither be able nor willing to do in a typical on-site CofS worship service.

Beyond the Virtual/Real and Message/Media Divides

What, then, are the implications for homiletical engagement with digitally mediated preaching? From an ANT perspective, the divide between virtual and real does not exist. As previously mentioned, ANT views the real as enacted in the relations and interactions between human and nonhuman actors in *dynamic ever-changing networks of relations*. Both the visibility contest described by church practitioners and the spiritual intimacy of Kristian's evening devotions, as enacted in their respective networks, involve bodies and emotions as well as material objects and spaces. Based on our analysis, then, we follow Thompson in making the case that "virtual" is not in contrast to "real." Instead, the virtual is a continuation of the real since we engage in it with our bodies, which are situated in the material world. Virtual worlds impact us and shape our embodied lives.[58] In opposition to ontology-oriented homileticians who claim that digitally mediated

---

56. Thompson, *Virtual Body*.
57. Thompson, *Virtual Body*, 70–71; Thompson, "Christ Is Really Present," 20.
58. Thompson, *Virtual Body*, 25.

preaching is called into question by the incarnation, and that "real" human bodies are opposed to "virtual" realities and/or bodies, we argue with Thompson that "real, embodied reality and virtual reality are always inextricably intertwined."[59] Indeed, real and virtual are different ways of being embodied as part of one unified creation.

Moreover, as Thompson holds, the continuity between real and virtual reflects Paul's understanding of the relationship between the local and universal church. Paul describes the church as the body of Christ. It is local, just like the local congregation in Corinth, where Paul spent a great deal of time forming "networks." And yet, as he moved on physically to other geographic regions, he claimed in his letters to still be a part of this network that he calls the body of Christ, affirming in his writings that this "virtual" body, despite his physical absence from the Corinthians, is nonetheless a continuation of the real.[60] Similarly, the community that gathers to participate in the weekly digitally mediated devotions is an enactment of "the virtual body of Christ," spread out in space (though not, in this case, time).

Sociomaterial sensibilities, such as the ANT, move the discussion beyond dichotomies of real/virtual. As such, it offers a theoretically and theologically informed way forward for homileticians who are not ready to dismiss digitally mediated preaching as "less" incarnational than on-site preaching in the local church.

Furthermore, a sociomaterial lens, such as that of ANT, offers other advantages. Message- and media-oriented approaches to digitally mediated preaching, which are common trajectories taken by many homileticians who write about digitality, both tend to understate certain key aspects of digital media. Firstly, the message-oriented trajectory often neglects important actors in a network, rendering them intermediaries, or vessels, simply transporting a meaning or a message but not impacting the contents or the network itself. In contradistinction, ANT attends to the role nonhuman actors such as digital media play in nudging a network toward a certain mode, thereby changing the network, its actors, and the messages contained therein.

In contrast, the media-oriented trajectory pays too much attention to only *one* actor, the medium or format, while downplaying the influence of human actors, such as Kristian, and denying them considerable agency in any given network, precluding their ability to nudge the network toward

59. Thompson, "Christ Is Really Present," 19.
60. Thompson, *Virtual Body*, 43.

a different mode. Using ANT as an analytical lens, then, enables a non-media-centric approach that balances agency, actors, media, and message. This approach avoids the lure of attributing too much significance to the affordances of media, while simultaneously drawing attention to hidden material actors within digital media, such as various social media platforms and their specific products and features, and including invisible actors such as algorithms. Instead, ANT allows for fine-grained analyses of the multifarious interactions between various human and nonhuman actors assembled in networks, as we hope to have demonstrated in our analysis. We make the case that such a sociomaterial approach is a helpful contribution to the field of digital homiletics.

BIBLIOGRAPHY

Alcadipani, Rafael, and John Hassard. "Actor-Network Theory, Organizations and Critique: Towards a Politics of Organizing." *Organization* 17 (2010) 419–35.

Bloor, David. "Anti-Latour." *Studies in History and Philosophy of Science* 30 (1999) 81–112.

Burge, Ryan P., and Miles D. Williams. "Is Social Media a Digital Pulpit? How Evangelical Leaders Use Twitter to Encourage the Faithful and Publicize Their Work." *Journal of Religion, Media & Digital Culture* 8 (2019) 309–39.

Cameron, Helen, et al. *Talking about God in Practice: Theological Action Research and Practical Theology.* London: SCM, 2010.

Campbell, Heidi, and Ruth Tsuria, eds. *Digital Religion: Understanding Religious Practice in Digital Media.* New York: Routledge, 2022.

Chambon, Michel. *Making Christ Present in China: Actor-Network Theory and the Anthropology of Christianity.* Cham, Switzerland: Springer, 2020.

Cheong, Pauline. "Tweet the Message? Religious Authority and Social Media Innovation." *Journal of Religion, Media and Digital Culture* 3 (2014) 1–19.

Codone, Susan. "Megachurch Pastor Twitter: An Analysis of Rick Warren and Andy Stanley, Two of America's Social Pastors." *Journal of Religion, Media and Digital Culture* 3 (2014) 1–32.

Cressman, Lisa K. "B.C. and A.C.: Preaching and Worship Before COVID and After COVID." *Journal for Preachers* 44 (2021) 46–52.

"Digital Economy and Society Index (DESI)." European Commission, 2022. https://digital-strategy.ec.europa.eu/en/policies/desi.

Fenwick, Tara J., et al. *Emerging Approaches to Educational Research: Tracing the Sociomaterial.* London: Routledge, 2011.

Garpe, Sara, and Jonas Ideström, eds. Kyrka i digitala rum: Ett aktionsforskningsprojekt om församlingsliv online. Uppsala: Svenska kyrkan, 2022.

Garpe, Sara, et al. "Att vara kyrka i digitala rum." In *Kyrka i digitala rum: Ett aktionsforskningsprojekt om församlingsliv online*, edited by Sara Garpe and Jonas Ideström, 5–17. Uppsala: Svenska kyrkan, 2022.

Girard, Renè. *Things Hidden Since the Foundation of the World.* Stanford: Stanford University Press, 1987.

Gregersen, Andreas M. "Exploring the Atmosphere Inside a Liturgical Laboratory." *Material Religion: The Journal of Objects, Art and Belief* 17 (2021) 627–50.

Harman, Graham. *Prince of Networks: Bruno Latour and Metaphysics*. Melbourne: Re.Press, 2009.

Holmqvist, Morten. "The Material Logics of Confirmation." *International Journal of Actor-Network Theory and Technological Innovation* 6 (2014) 26–37.

Holtedahl, Øivind K. "Community: God from above and God from below: An Ethnographic Study of Religious Knowledge Practices in Two Youth Ministries in the Church of Norway." PhD diss., VID Specialized University, 2017.

Ideström, Jonas. "Mediators of Tradition: Embodiment of Doctrine in Rural Swedish Parish Life. Ecclesial Practices." *Journal of Ecclesiology and Ethnography* 3 (2016) 53–69.

Ideström, Jonas, and Tone S. Kaufman. "Hållbar närvaro i digitala rum: Mellan omsorgskultur och synlighetstävling." In *Kyrka i digitala rum: Ett aktionsforskningsprojekt om församlingsliv online*, edited by Sara Garpe and Jonas Ideström, 18–29. Uppsala: Svenska kyrkan, 2022.

———. "Hur framträder kyrkan i de digitala rummen? Kommunikation, teologi och folkyrkotankar." In *Kyrka i digitala rum: Ett aktionsforskningsprojekt om församlingsliv online*, edited by Sara Garpe and Jonas Ideström, 30–42. Uppsala: Svenska kyrkan, 2022.

Johnsen, Elisabeth T. "Teologi som ulike biter og deler: Ti år med trosopplæring i Den norske kirke." *Prismet* 66 (2015) 125–44.

Johnsen, Elisabeth T., and Geir Afdal. "Practice Theory in Empirical Practical Theological Research the Scientific Contribution of LETRA." *Tidsskrift for Praktisk Teologi* 57 (2020) 58–76.

Kaufman, Tone S. "Forkynnelse for barn og voksne." In *Forkynnelse for Barn og Voksne. En Studie av sju Gudstjenester i Trosopplæringen*, edited by Tone S. Kaufman, 8–18. Oslo: IKO, 2021.

Kaufman, Tone S., and Hallvard O. Mosdøl. "More than Words: A Multimodal and Sociomaterial Approach to Understanding the Preaching Event." In *Preaching Promises within the Paradoxes of Life*, edited by Cilliers, Johan and Len Hansen, 123–33. Studia Homiletica 11. Stellenbosch: African Sun Media, 2018.

Kaufman, Tone S., and Jonas Ideström. "Why Matter Matters in Theological Action Research: Attending to the Voices of Tradition." *International Journal of Practical Theology* 22 (2018) 84–102.

Lagerkvist, Amanda. *Existential Media: A Media Theory of the Limit Situation*. Oxford: Oxford University Press, 2022.

Latour, Bruno. *Science in Action: How to Follow Scientists and Engineers through Society*. Milton Keynes: Open University Press, 1987.

———. *Reassembling the Social: An Introduction to Actor-Network-Theory*. Clarendon Lectures in Management Studies. Oxford: Oxford University Press, 2005.

Law, John. *Organizing Modernity*. Oxford: Blackwell, 1994.

———. "Actor Network Theory and Material Semiotics" Center for Science Studies and Department of Sociology, Lancaster University, 2007. http://www.heterogeneities.net/publications/Law2007ANTandMaterialSemiotics.pdf.

Ledstam, Maria, and Geir Afdal. "Negotiating Purity and Impurity of Religion and Economy: An Empirical Contribution to Kathryn Tanner's Christianity and the New Spirit of Capitalism." *Religions* 11 (2020) 588.

Lienau, Anna-Katharina. "Kommunikation des Evangeliums in social media." *Zeitschrift für Theologie und Kirche (ZThK)* 117 (2020) 489–522.
Lindgren, Lena. *Ekko: Et Essay om Algoritmer og Begjær.* Oslo: Gyldendal, 2020.
Mannerfelt, Frida. "From the Amphitheatre to Twitter: Cultivating Secondary Orality in Dialogue with Female Preachers." *Studies in World Christianity* 28 (2022) 6–27.
———. "Listening to Listeners in a Digital Culture: The Practice of Listening to Digitally-Mediated Sermons." *Homiletic* 48 (2023) 1.
———. "Online Preaching." In *The Oxford Handbook of Digital Theology*, edited by Alexander Chow, Jonas Kurlberg, and Peter M. Phillips. Oxford: Oxford University Press, forthcoming.
Mannerfelt, Frida, and Rikard Roitto. "Mellan rit och reklam del 1: Berättelsen om två församlingars utveckling." In *Kyrka i digitala rum: Ett aktionsforskningsprojekt om församlingsliv online*, edited by Sara Garpe and Jonas Ideström, 47–60. Uppsala: Svenska kyrkan, 2022.
———. "Mellan rit och reklam del 2: Interaktion, synkronicitet och integritet i förinspelade digitalt förmedlade andakter." In *Kyrka i digitala rum: Ett aktionsforskningsprojekt om församlingsliv online*, edited by Sara Garpe and Jonas Ideström, 61–79. Uppsala: Svenska kyrkan, 2022.
Masoga, Mogomme A. "Effectiveness of WhatsApp Homiletics in the Era of COVID-19 in South Africa." *Pharos Journal of Theology* 101 (2020) 1–16.
Menzel, Kerstin. "More than the Argument of Experience? Preaching with Episodes from Everyday Life on Instagram." Paper presented at the Societas Homiletica 2022 Conference Preaching towards Truth, Budapest, Hungary, August 12–17, 2022.
Nord, Ilona. "Experiment with Freedom Every Day: Regarding the Virtual Dimension of Homiletics." *Homiletic* 36 (2011) 31–37.
Pink, Sarah, et al. *Digital Ethnography: Principles and Practice.* London: Sage, 2016.
Pleizier, Theo. *Religious Involvement in Hearing Sermons.* Delft: Eburon Academic Publishers, 2010.
Plüss, David. "The Dialogue Form of Online Preaching. Case Studies." Paper presented at the Societas Homiletica 2022 Conference Preaching towards Truth, Budapest, Hungary, August 12–17, 2022.
Powery, Luke A. "Preaching and Technology." In *Ways of the Word: Learning to Preach for Your Time and Place*, edited by Luke A. Powery and Sally A. Brown, 209–34. Minneapolis: Fortress, 2016.
Reite, Ingrid. "Between Blackboxing and Unfolding: Professional Learning Networks of Pastors." *International Journal of ActorNetwork Theory and Technological Innovation* 5 (2013) 47–64.
———. "Pastors and the Perpetuum Mobile: The Dynamics of Professional Learning in Times of Reform." *Pedagogy, Culture & Society* 53 (2015) 389–409.
Schatzki, Theodore. *Social Change in a Material World.* London: Routledge, 2019.
Schmidt, Katherine G. *Virtual Communion: Theology of the Internet and the Catholic Sacramental Imagination.* London: Lexington, 2020.
Sigmon, Casey T. "Engaging the Gadfly: A Process Homilecclesiology for a Digital Age." PhD diss., Vanderbilt University, 2017.
Thompson, Deanna A. *The Virtual Body of the Suffering Christ.* Nashville: Abingdon, 2016.
———. "Christ Is Really Present, Even in Holy Communion via Online Worship." *Liturgy* 35 (2020) 18–24.

Watkins, Clare. *Disclosing Church: An Ecclesiology Learned from Conversations in Practice.* London: Routledge, 2020.

Yang, Sunggu A. "The Word Digitalized: A Techno-Theological Reflection on Online Preaching and Its Types." *Homiletic* 46 (2020) 75–90.

3

Co-preaching

The Effects of Religious Digital Creatives' Engagement in the Preaching Event

FRIDA MANNERFELT

INTRODUCTION

The preaching event is a complex thing.[1] As Wilfrid Engemann has shown, the preaching event is a process of comprehension and communication

---

1. "Preaching event" is a concept that has become increasingly common in homiletical discourse. But just like the term "practice of preaching" (Rystad, "Overestimated and Underestimated," 19), it is not always clear what is meant by "preaching event," since the term has been used in a variety of ways over time. John Claypool, one of the first to invoke the term, understands a preaching event as the event when the human utterances of the preacher become God's living words to the listeners (Claypool, *Preaching Event*). To other homileticians, it designates the situation (oral event) when the preacher is speaking to the listeners (Bruce, "Vital Importance"; Maddock, "'Like One of the Old Apostles'"). The concept preaching event could also be understood as the event that occurs in performative situations where the preacher, listeners, and message interact (Fahlgren, *Predikantskap*, 43–47). Finally, the concept could also be employed like Wilfrid Engemann, who argues that since it is not entirely clear when the sermon actually becomes a sermon, it is important to keep all the parts of the process together in the analysis. The concept "preaching event" is therefore used to designate everything from the preparation phase to the moment the audience listens (Engemann, *Homiletics*, xix–xx). In this chapter, I draw on Engemann's broad understanding of the concept. As Linn Sæbø Rystad has argued, there are several benefits to conceiving of preaching as an event. It allows for understanding preaching as a practice, which in turn sheds light on how preaching is both "processual, performative and emerging" and radically relational.

that consists of several phases of text interpretations and text introductions that involve the interaction between the authors of the Bible text, the Bible, preacher, sermon manuscript, the delivered sermon, listener, and the "auredit" (what the listener has heard), each in their specific context.[2] Therefore, Carina Sundberg has argued, the preaching event—as the product of very complex situated interactions between multiple actors[3] like preacher, listener, architecture, liturgy, artifacts, and so on—is characterized by "polyagency."[4]

While the preacher, word, and listener are usually the foci of attention in the preaching event, with a few notable exceptions scant attention has been paid to materiality as an actor in the communication and meaning-making process.[5] However, as practice theorists like Theodore Schatzki has pointed out, all social phenomena are constituted by the entanglement of human practices and material entities, such as bodies and artifacts, and material arrangements like buildings and technology.[6]

In her article "Preaching at the Thresholds—Bakhtinian Polyphony in Preaching for Children," Linn Sæbø Rystad argues that materiality is a dimension of preaching that must not be overlooked. She underlines that: "Focusing on materiality might highlight what preaching from a pulpit does or does not do in the communication situation, or which body it is that is preaching."[7] In the article, she discusses the use of "mediational means" (the biblical narrative, costumes, and objects) in preaching for children. Drawing on James Wertsch, Rystad argues that access to the world is always mediated. For this reason, a scholar should not limit her scope to what humans are doing, but must look into how humans interact with mediating materiality.[8]

The term also highlights the importance of material entities like architecture, art, artifacts, and other visual aids for the meaning-making process (Rystad, "Underestimated and Overestimated," 122–23).

2. Engemann, *Homiletics*, 3–4.

3. In this chapter, I use the concept "actor" in the same sense as it is used by Bruno Latour in his Actor-Network Theory: an actor is something that acts or to which activity is granted by others. Latour, "Technology Is Society," 120–23.

4. Sundberg, "Här är rymlig plats," 195–99.

5. For example, Kaufman and Mosdøl, "More than Words," 123–32.

6. Schatzki, *Social Change*, 19–22.

7. Rystad, "Overestimated and Underestimated," 122–23.

8. Rystad, "Overestimated and Underestimated," 45–46, 108–25.

This chapter will explore and analyze what happens when yet another actor is brought into the complexity of the preaching event: digital technology. According to Schatzki, human practice has become increasingly dependent on material arrangements enabled by technology, in particular digital technology.[9] Clearly, digital devices are deeply embedded in our daily lives, including worship. In a sociomaterial perspective, digital technology could be said to be an actor in its own right. However, this chapter will focus on the new human actors that digital technology brings into the preaching event. Dubbed religious digital creatives (RDCs), these are the "individuals whose digital media work and skills grant them unique status and influence within their religious communities."[10]

In her book *Digital Creatives and the Rethinking of Religious Authority* (2021), Heidi Campbell argues that religious authority is transformed by digital media and technology. This transformation is due not only to the transition of established religious authorities (like priests and pastors) from physical spaces into digital environments, but also to the occurrence of new actors (like technicians or social media ministers). They present religious content online and have become religious authorities in their own right. The purpose of this chapter is to explore and discuss what happens when RDCs engage in a preaching event. This is achieved through a case study of the preaching event in prerecorded digitally mediated worship services in two Stockholm congregations in the Church of Sweden (CofS).

The research questions guiding this chapter are: (1) When and how do RDCs engage in the preaching event? (2) How can the effects of RDC engagement in the preaching event be understood? I will argue that the RDCs can be understood as "co-preachers," as they all contribute significantly to the sermon and thus to the preaching event. The effects of co-preaching will be discussed in the light of homiletical theory that focuses on the concept of polyphony.

The chapter is structured as follows: first, I will present the methodology, material, and the theoretical frameworks employed. In doing so, I will discuss both the concept of RDCs—what it is and how it is applied in the analysis of the article's source material—and the concept of polyphonic preaching invoked in the results discussion. Next, I will describe when and how the RDCs engage in the preaching event. Finally, I will conclude with a discussion of the results in the light of polyphonic preaching, an

---

9. Schatzki, *Social Change*, 19–22, 36–37.
10. Campbell, *Religious Creatives*, 4–5.

umbrella term for the Scandinavian line of homileticians inspired by the communication theories of Mikhail Bakhtin.

METHODS, MATERIALS, AND THEORETICAL FRAMEWORKS

The case study's source material was gathered within the framework of the action research project Church in Digital Space.[11] As part of the project, I collaborated with the New Testament scholar and pastor Rikard Roitto to follow two congregations in the CofS Diocese of Stockholm, Järfälla and Täby, as they developed short, prerecorded, digitally mediated worship services.[12]

The subject material was created from August 2021 to February 2022, well into the COVID-19 pandemic, and involves six preaching events, three for each congregation. During the period, researchers and practitioners met once a month. The researchers observed the practitioners' preparation for and recording of the worship services, made individual interviews with all practitioners involved, and gathered recordings and screenshots of publication in social media. A month later, practitioners and researchers met for focus group conversations in which the researchers presented an analysis of what they had seen and heard, and theories that could aid in understanding. The researchers also facilitated a discussion in which the practitioners responded to the analysis and reflected on their own practices. Next month, there was a new round of observations and interviews, and so on.

This chapter, however, uses an ethnographical case study approach to the sources instead of the highly collaborative practices of action research we initially applied.[13] In other words, the practitioners were not involved

11. Church in Digital Space was a collaboration between the CofS Diocese of Stockholm and University College Stockholm. It involved five researchers and seven congregations, and it was led by professor of practical theology Jonas Ideström and the bishop's theological advisor, Sara Garpe. The project took place between January 2021 and September 2022 (Garpe et al., "Inledning"). The research project was inspired by Theological Action Research (TAR) (see for example Watkins, *Disclosing Church*), as well as the methods and concepts developed by Jonas Ideström (Ideström, "Implicit Ecclesiology") and the bishop of the CofS Diocese of Stockholm, Andreas Holmberg, *Kyrka i Nytt Landskap*. There are very few action research projects that focuses on homiletics, Boyd, *Naked Preacher*, being an exception.

12. Mannerfelt and Roitto, "Mellan rit och reklam del 1"; Mannerfelt and Roitto, "Mellan rit och reklam del 2."

13. As stated in the introduction to the research report, the starting point of action

in the negotiation of research questions or the analysis and presentation of the research except for an opportunity to reflect on the validity of the RDC theory.

The source material thus consists of six observation protocols, transcriptions of eighteen individual and six focus group interviews, six edited recordings of the services, and eighteen screen shots of how the recordings were presented on the congregation's websites and social media platforms (YouTube, Facebook, and Instagram).[14] In analyzing the source material, I have drawn on Heidi Campbell's work on authority and religious digital creatives.

Religious Digital Creatives

As Campbell and Tsuria point out in the introduction to *Digital Religion: Understanding Religion in a Digital Age*, authority is one of the key research areas and questions in the field of digital religion.[15] In one of her recent books, *Digital Creatives and the Rethinking of Religious Authority*, Campbell pursues the question of what religious authority looks like in an age of digital media. She states that the typical conclusion in scholarly studies of religious authority and new media is that, since digital culture and technology is characterized by features like freedom and a lack of hierarchy, established religious authorities are challenged. In an effort to turn the tables, Campbell asks instead what religious authority looks like and how it is established in a digital context. Her hypothesis is that internet technology and digital culture both facilitate and empower new religious actors, and their wielding of authority creates hybrid structures that over time may change their religious institutions.[16]

---

research consists of two ideas: (1) research can contribute to solving actual problems and develop knowledge and skills; (2) participants possess knowledge that could significantly contribute to the research process. Research is therefore carried out in collaboration between researchers and practitioners, who come together in a process of interpretation and reflection. Practitioners contribute with their experience and knowledge, while researchers contribute resources like methods, theories, and research from other contexts (Garpe et al., "Inledning," 13–16).

14. For a detailed description of how the source material was created, see (Mannerfelt and Roitto "Mellan rit och reklam del 1").

15. Campbell and Tsuria, "Introduction," 7–12.

16. Campbell, *Digital Creatives*, 1–21. Although not its primary purpose, the book does contribute to confirming Campbell's hypothesis by giving concrete examples of how

To examine how religious authority is structured in a digital culture, Campbell interviewed 120 individuals, all of whom had been active for at least four years and renowned for their digital work for and in Christian churches.[17] While these interviews took place between 2011 and 2016, well before the pandemic and the subsequent radical—and rapid—digital transition of churches, they provided a foundational framework for analyzing future digital mediation. Campbell's analysis of the interviews yielded three categories of actors:

1. Digital entrepreneurs, who create digital resources—platforms or content—for their communities in their free time.
2. Digital spokespersons, who are employed to manage a religious community's digital presence.
3. Digital strategists, who already have an official position (e.g., as pastors and deacons), but who use digital media to do their work more effectively.

Common to all three groups is that they possess skills and experience in digital media work—they are "digital creatives"—which gives them unique influence and status in their religious communities. Hence, they are religious digital creatives, RDCs.[18]

The RDCs in question in this study are employed in congregations in Täby and Järfälla, two communities within the CofS's Stockholm diocese. The team in Järfälla consists of a pastor, a religious educator, two technicians (responsible for recording and editing audio and video), and a communications director (responsible for publishing content on digital platforms). The team in Täby consists of a pastor, a deacon, a musician, and a communications director (who records, edits, and publishes content).[19] In other words, the preaching events in this case study included both digital spokespersons (the communications director and tech team) and digital strategists of the online-minister type.

These particular congregations in this study were chosen for several reasons. For starters, the congregations and RDCs are in Sweden, one of

religious institutions are, in fact, changed by their adoption of new media.
17. Campbell, *Digital Creatives*, 14, 53.
18. Campbell, *Digital Creatives*, 49–53.
19. In the following, I will refer to them with professional title and congregation, for example "pastor in Täby" or "technician in Järfälla."

the world's most digitalized societies.[20] In addition, the CofS is also one of the world's wealthiest churches, which has allowed congregations to hire employees such as dedicated A/V technicians. In Campbell and Osteen's study on how churches digitized during the COVID-19 pandemic, the digital transition was often carried out by either a single pastor (i.e., what Campbell would call "digital strategist") or a small group of volunteers ("digital entrepreneurs").[21] In this study, we get a glimpse of churches' digital transformation through collaboration between different groups of RDCs. Finally, the RDCs in Campbell's study were mainly focused on missional or educational activities in their digital work. The RDCs in this study are engaged in online worship services and digitally mediated preaching events.

The digital team members at both congregations in this study will be analyzed as RDCs, i.e., people wielding religious authority through their use of digital technology. The analysis will focus on describing what they do, how they understand their work in relation to the digitally mediated preaching event, and what kind of authority they perform through their words and actions.

According to Campbell, RDCs' use of authority may be described through four categories:

1. Authority as role based (as in the works of Weber)
2. Authority as power struggle (as in the works of Foucault)
3. Authority as relational—where authority is seen as negotiated and mutually beneficial, as described by, for example, Mia Lövheim, in her study on the authority of bloggers.
4. Algorithmic authority—where algorithms "tells us what voices to listen to, which topics are important and which structures to give weight to in evaluating credibility."[22] Algorithmic authority comes from statistics and figures like number of followers, hits and rankings from search engines, or—in an academic setting—the number of publications.[23]

---

20. "Sweden in the Digital Economy."
21. Campbell and Osteen, *When Pastors Put on the "Tech Hat."*
22. Campbell, *Digital Creatives*, 31.
23. Campbell, *Digital Creatives*, 18–37.

Digital spokespersons tend to describe themselves as institutional identity curators whose task is to present and represent the identity of the community in media, particularly on digital platforms. Sometimes they relate to algorithmic authority, but more often on role-based authority, in particular what Weber called rational-legal authority. In other words, they see themselves as part of a structure with particular rules that they support. Within churches, they do their job to serve the church's greater mission. However, in this service they are often caught in something of a contradiction: the same institutions that hired them to do digital media work are reluctant about the use of digital technology. When these digital strategists are called upon by the church's leadership to contribute with their expertise, the shift in power dynamic is not always welcome. Therefore, they tend to be very cautious, and emphasize that their work is not about theological interpretation but about making the message of the church accessible.[24]

Digital strategists view themselves as missional media negotiators. They work in institutions that claim they do not need digital technology, but the strategists believe the institutions can do their work more efficiently and creatively with the aid of digital media. They continuously blend online and offline ministry, and see digital platforms as an extension of their local work. In this position, they are bridge-builders who often negotiate. This means that they tend to view authority as relational, as something that is created and negotiated between different parties through communicative interaction. Or, as Campbell summarizes it, "Authority comes to the leader through creating a balanced or interdependent relationship."[25]

It is worth noting that the digital strategists in this case study differ slightly from Campbell's category because they have not chosen the hybrid role themselves. That is, they were given the task to provide digitally mediated worship services during the COVID-19 pandemic, and they state that they would not have taken on this task if they could avoid it. Over time, however, they have grown into the role as bridge builders between on-site and online church. The fact that their work was sanctioned by the leadership and necessitated by the pandemic might explain why stories of "technological apologetics," the justification narratives that were such a prominent feature of Campbell's pre-pandemic RDCs, are virtually absent from the narratives of these CofS strategists.

---

24. Campbell, *Digital Creatives*, 110–29, 157–62.
25. Campbell, *Digital Creatives*, 133–53, 162–66.

These conditions also affect the digital spokespersons in this study. Absent are the narratives so common to digital spokespersons in Campbell's study, namely that the same leadership that hired them to do digital work is also suspicious of digital technology. Also missing are Campbell's accounts of grudges stemming from the shift in authority when the spokespeople are called upon to work as media mentors to, for example, pastors.

Instead, the strategists in this study express a profound gratitude and trust toward the spokespersons. For example, when asked about one of the recording sessions in which the spokesperson (communications director) clearly was in charge of what, when, and how every part of the worship service should be recorded, the strategist (pastor) said that "in that case, it is [the communications director] who does his thing, he is completely in charge. I gladly let him decide what is best." When asked about this, the communications director himself compared it to the local worship service:

> (Interviewee):"[Laughs] If I were to participate in a physical worship service, I would turn to the pastor and musician and ask: "What should I do? Is this right? In what order should this be done?" In the same way, I think they give me more responsibility because they are not at home in this area, even if they have been involved in planning the order of the worship....
>
> (Interviewer): All right. So in this church space, your "sixth church" [an expression frequently used by the team in Täby about online church as an addition to their five local churches], you are more in charge?
>
> (Interviewee): Yes, you could say that. [Smiles] It is quite exiting that I should know more about a church space in that way.

These quotes are not just examples of how the shifting power dynamics between the usual leaders and the digital spokespersons do not seem to cause unease. They are also examples of the spokespersons' use of relational authority. In Campbell's study, her spokespersons often downplayed their autonomy and personal contribution to the messages and underlined their loyalty towards the theological message of their institutions. In other words, they favored a role-based authority. While the spokespersons in this study in some instances did relate to role-based authority, they also commonly performed and spoke about relational authority.

Polyphonic Preaching

This study's results build on the Scandinavian homiletical discussion that draws on the theories of the Russian philosopher and literary critic Mikhail Bakhtin to describe and understand the communication going on in the preaching event. Since the concept of polyphony is central in several of these discussions, I will use the shorthand term "polyphonic preaching" to refer to them.

A landmark volume in the discussion on polyphonic preaching is Marlene Ringgaard Lorensen's *Dialogical Preaching: Bakhtin, Otherness and Homiletics* in which she explores how preachers expose their preaching to interactions with various "others" of preaching, and how a Bakhtinian understanding of communication might be incorporated into homiletical theories.[26] While Lorensen herself mainly focuses on Bakhtin's theories of dialogue and carnivalization, the concept of polyphony is intrinsically related to them, and she introduces the concept to offer a theological model of communication for the homiletical strand of "other-wise preaching."[27]

Bakhtin developed the concept of polyphony in his work on Dostoevsky and Rabelais. According to Bakhtin, their novels are dialogical since the characters possess and interact with their own consciousness and voices. As such, the reader does not just hear the author's voice, she also hears the characters' voices and is thus drawn into her own dialogue with them, creating a polyphony. This dialogical polyphony is contrasted with a monological authorship in which the author is omniscient and has the final word on interpretation. To Lorensen, "the role of the preacher in contemporary preaching practices has striking similarities to the polyphonic author-position."[28]

In Bakhtin's thinking, communication is thus relational and collaborative. Conversation partners (local and distant) always play a constitutive part in how the speaker develops and shapes his or her utterance. With the aid of Bakhtin's theories, Lorensen pleads for a collaborative preaching practice, in which preachers act as hosts who invite others into the conversation and,

---

26. Before Lorensen, there are other Scandinavian theologians who have used Bakhtin in their homiletical reflection. See Karlsson, *Predikans Samtal*, and Bjerg and Lynglund, "Den karnevalesque praediken." In addition, it is not just Scandinavian homileticians who have drawn on Bakhtin. See Harris, *Word Made Plain*.
27. See McClure, *Other-Wise Preaching*.
28. Lorensen, *Dialogical Preaching*, 66–67.

in the process, become guests themselves.[29] She underlines the importance of the preacher not ventriloquizing different voices, arguing, "If preaching, in spite of its monological appearance, is to function as a dialogical encounter, one of the most important tasks for the preacher, from a Bakhtinian perspective, is to avoid conflating the voices of the listener, preacher, and Scripture into one and instead let the polyphony of voices interact in a way that let them transform and enrich each other mutually." To Lorensen, this means that Bakhtin may provide the homiletical movement with "the beginnings of a polyphonic theology of communication."[30]

In the article "Listeners as Authors in Preaching," Gaarden and Lorensen use Bakhtinian perspectives to discuss the empirical findings in Gaarden's study of the listener's meaning-making processes. They argue for a reversed perspective in the analysis of preaching, and challenge fellow homileticians to understand listeners as primary authors of the sermon. They make this rather surprising move in relation to Bakhtin's idea that meaning emerges in interaction with dialogue partners. According to Bakhtin, the addressees of an oral or written discourse always play an implicit and explicit part as coauthors, and in this sense the "listener becomes the speaker." Instead of discussing how preachers invite listeners as coauthors in sermon preparation, they want to discuss how listeners invite preachers to be coauthors of their inner reflections during the preaching event.[31] Lorensen elaborates further on this idea in an article written with Gitte Buch-Hansen. They argue that the refugees in a Danish church acted as coauthors of practical theology, since they provoked adjustments to the traditional theory of human capital. Furthermore, the refugees' understanding of the ritual challenged traditional Danish Lutheran understandings of the Eucharist and the church.[32] It is this notion of interplay between authors/coauthors that has inspired the concept of "co-preacher" that is found in this study.

In her previously mentioned article, Rystad employs Bahktin's concept of polyphony to analyze two sermons directed to children. Through her discussion about analytical concepts, it becomes clear how communication is tied to authority in Bakhtin's thinking. In delineating both the monological and dialogical, Bakhtin makes a distinction between scaffolding (words

---

29. Lorensen, "Carnivalized Preaching," 26–45; Lorensen, *Dialogical Preaching*, 66–67.

30. Lorensen, "Carnivalized Preaching," 44.

31. Gaarden and Lorensen, "Listeners as Authors," 28–45. See especially p. 32.

32. Lorensen and Buch-Hansen, "Listening to the Voices," 29–41.

that are used to build up a monological discourse) and architectonic whole (words that are allowed to influence a dialogical discourse in a way that may lead to transformation and new perspectives). He also makes a distinction between, on the one hand, words that are part of an authoritative discourse that creates monologue, and, on the other, words that are part of an internally persuasive discourse that creates dialogue. In Rystad's interpretation of Bakhtin, authoritative words are words spoken from a distance, which gives an impression of their being more important than our own words, possessing a meaning that must either be accepted or rejected. An inner persuasive word "does not have status or authority and is tightly interwoven with our own words." It is creative and interacts with other inner discourses to cause change.[33]

However, Rystad draws on Olga Dysthe to nuance Bakhtin's notion of authority. Alongside both an authoritarian discourse based on power and tradition, and an inner persuasive discourse free from authority, there is a third discourse of authority based on trust and respect. According to Rystad, preachers often aim for the latter. In her case study, Rystad found that while the sermons started out as polyphonic—particularly through the aid of the mediational means—both sermons ended up as monologues when the preacher stepped in at the end with authoritative words and proclaimed the message of what "all of this truly meant."[34] Rystad concludes that "polyphony is the most important consideration when laying the groundwork for dialogical interaction with a preaching event. Polyphony helps create a threshold space in which authoritarian discourses are challenged and narratives re-interpreted."[35]

It is no wonder that Rystad makes this move. Authority is not just a key research area in the field of digital religion. Ever since Fred B. Craddock's *As One without Authority* (1971), the question of authority has been at the forefront of homiletics.[36] The issue of authority has been particularly

---

33. Rystad, "Overestimated and Underestimated," 111.
34. Rystad, "Overestimated and Underestimated," 45.
35. Rystad, "Overestimated and Underestimated," 124.
36. Homileticians suggest various reasons for this. It could be a matter of hermeneutics—for example historical-critical Bible studies who challenged the idea of the biblical text as a source of absolute truth and authority—or general societal developments like secularization, pluralism, or postmodernism (Mervin, "Preaching with Authority"; Brueggemann, "Preacher"; Tornfelt, "Preaching with Authority"; Davies, "New Teaching"). Interestingly, digitalization is never mentioned as a reason for changes in the understanding of authority.

important to homileticians who argue for conversational and/or dialogical approaches, like polyphonic preaching. These scholars tend to trace the development of homiletics and build their argument in relation to authority. As for example the homiletical contribution of John McClure (2001) in his landmark book *Other-Wise Preaching*. According to McClure,

> preaching is exiting itself through the doors of many deconstructions or gradual otherings. Among these are deconstructions of self, culture, scripture, reason, language, metaphysics, tradition, even of the word itself. Most specifically . . . preaching is exiting through the deconstructions of the four overlapping authorities that have bequeathed preaching to us: the authority of the Bible, the authority of tradition, the authority of experience, and the authority of reason.[37]

McClure not only launches his homiletical theory in relation to changes in the understanding of authority, but he also writes his overview of the development of the homiletical field to show how homileticians over the years have tried to grapple with the deconstruction of authority. His own solution, which draws on Emmanuel Levinas's idea of "the human other as a site for the revelation of the Holy other," argues for a conversational approach.[38]

Authority is also at the center of discussion in Casey Thornburgh Sigmon's thesis "Engaging the Gadfly: A Process Homilecclesiology for a Digital Age"), one of the few longer, in-depth contributions to the homiletical field that specifically engages with preaching in digital culture. According to Sigmon, digital media sheds light on how preaching has been caught in a "pulpit-pew binary," where the pulpit represents the locus of authority and the pew the attentive, silent audience. Sigmon points out that the pulpit and pew easily fall into the dualistic framework in the Western Christian tradition, which justifies one part's dominance over the other. Furthermore, the binary hinges on static, substance-oriented categories often regarded as unchangeable truth.[39]

According to Sigmon, homileticians have tried to solve the problem of the pulpit-pew binary since the 1960s, and she describes a movement toward more relationality and mutuality. However, since the homileticians have not had a clear understanding of the problem, they have not completely

---

37. Craddock, *As One Without Authority*, 2.
38. McClure, *Other-Wise Preaching*, 47–59.
39. Sigmon, "Engaging the Gadfly," 5–6.

solved the problem. In an overview of different approaches to the problem of authority and asymmetric power relations, Sigmon discusses both the new homiletic movement and other-wise homiletics, as well as feminist, postcolonial, and postmodern perspectives, and while she acknowledges the different tactics to handle the pulpit-pew binary problem, she claims that none of them have actually solved the problem.

She hopes that digital culture will prompt homileticians and preachers to create a preaching event that takes an "exit from the house of the sanctuary," and thus will avoid being delimited by liturgy, architecture, and strictly oral-aural relations. Sigmon underlines that this change does not come about by itself, since digital culture is an algorithmic, capitalist system that can be every bit as problematic as the classic Western binary schema. To avoid the negative effects of digital culture, there need to be "theo-ethical norms" to guide its development. Sigmon draws on process theology to describe such a theology of preaching, calling it a "homilecclesiology."[40]

Especially important to Sigmon in her vision of homilecclesiology is the preaching priesthood of all believers. The contribution of unordained laypeople who lack theological training should define the work of the ordained preachers, whose task is to build up the laypeople for the task of interpreting and communicating God's words and actions. The preachers are to model the interpretation of sacred texts and traditioned dogmas in relation to culture through their own words and actions, in particular from the pulpit. Authority ought to be relational, no one should assume power over others, and there can be no imposition of truths and timeless statements.[41] Sigmon concludes:

> Rather than seeking to become the authority on everything for the church, we seek to cultivate in the laity a sense of their own authority and capacity to challenge the grasp of unidirectional authorities on their life. . . . They [preachers] cultivate the ability to affirm, embrace, and expect ever-growing complexity and beauty without losing Christianity's spiritual center and identity among different realities.[42]

---

40. Sigmon, "Engaging the Gadfly," 16–33.
41. Sigmon, "Engaging the Gadfly," 169–87.
42. Sigmon, "Engaging the Gadfly," 185.

She also offers a few suggestions of how this could be done in practice, both on digital platforms (social media) and in hybrid engagement when technology serves to disrupt the monologue from the pulpit.[43]

Though Sigmon does not discuss Bakhtinian approaches to preaching in her overview of different homiletical approaches to the "problem" of authority, I would argue that her vision of authority seems to share traits with the polyphonic preaching discussion and with Bakhtin's thoughts on a relational authority. The notion of authority described by Lorensen and Rystad seems quite similar, not only to Sigmon's vision of a homilecclesiology suited for a digital culture, but also to the notion of relational authority as described by Campbell's digital strategists and the participants in this case study. In other words, polyphonic preaching is well-suited as a tool for homiletical discussion of the results from exploration of RDCs' engagement in the preaching event.

WHEN DO THE RDCs ENGAGE IN THE PREACHING EVENT?

In order to envision when the RDCs engage in the preaching event, I will use Engemann's description of the communication and comprehensions processes involved in the preaching event. Engemann divides the preaching event into several phases of text interpretation and text production. First, there is the Phase of Tradition, in which the authors of the Bible interpreted the biblical events and produced the Bible text. Next comes the Phase of Preparation, when the preacher, as author, interprets the Bible texts and produces a sermon manuscript. Then comes the Phase of Verbalization, when the preacher, as sender, interprets his or her sermon manuscript and produces the delivery of the sermon. The final stage, according to Engemann, is the Phase of Realization, in which the listener interprets the delivery of the sermon and produces the auredit (Latin for "what is heard"). All these phases take place in a specific context that contributes to the processes of interpretation and communication. Below is visualization of that process.[44]

---

43. Sigmon, "Engaging the Gadfly," 200–215.
44. Engemann, *Homiletics*, 1–13. The figure is a version of Engemann's diagram.

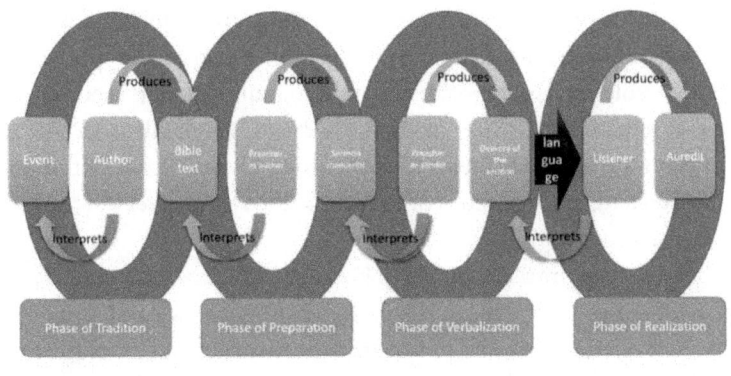

Figure 1. Engemann's diagram of the preaching event

When the RDCs come into the interpretation and production process of the digitally mediated preaching event, the process is affected in several ways. One important factor that decides how the preaching event is affected is which kind of digital technology—the mediational means—is involved. In this study, the sermons were prerecorded on Tuesdays, edited during the following days, and published at a certain time later in the week (1 p.m. on Fridays in Järfälla and 10 a.m. on Sundays in Täby). Both communities published the sermons on the congregation's website and on Facebook, YouTube, and Instagram. When this study's RDCs, with their particular use of digital technology, are inserted into Engemann's diagram (Figure 2), the processes of interpretation and production changes.

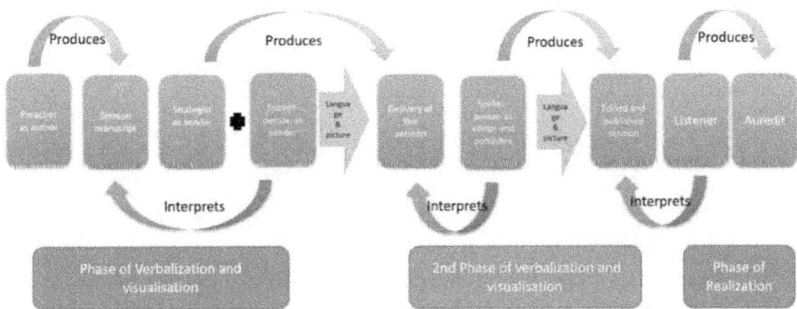

Figure 2. The Religious Digital Creatives (RDCs) involvement in the digitally mediated preaching event

While the phases of tradition, preparation, and realization remain the same in many ways, the phase of verbalization changes. The strategist is no longer the sole interpreter of the sermon manuscript. She is accompanied by the spokespersons who record the sermon. As mentioned above, the technicians are intensely involved in the worship service where the sermon is delivered and, as I will show, directly influence the delivery of the sermon as well as its content.

This change draws attention to how the verbalization phase is not just a phase of the spoken word. It is a phase of verbalization *and* visualization. While it in one sense always has been,[45] the visual character of the preaching event is emphasized.

This is in line with an increased emphasis on the visual in contemporary culture. In their overview of visual culture studies, Promey and Brisman show that the notion of contemporary culture as "hypervisual" has grown in importance. They refer to the work by Nicholas Mirzoeff, who argues that contemporary culture has a tendency to picture or visualize experience and create meaning through pictures rather than written words, a tendency linked to the development of digital technology.[46]

Furthermore, in these two cases, a second phase of verbalization and visualization is introduced through the churches' particular use of digital technology. The listeners no longer interpret the delivery of the sermon; instead, they interpret the *edited* version of the sermon. If the listeners access the sermon from a social media platform, they get yet another additional layer of interpretation: the spokespeople's description of the sermon that accompanies and frames the recording. In the following section, how the strategists and spokespeople engage through each phase will be described in detail.

---

45. Here we may notice that Engemann's model is an example of the phenomenon I discussed in the introduction. While he does acknowledge that materiality plays a role in the interpretation as part of the particular context, it tends to tread into the background as part of the overall context. The main foci in his homiletical discussion are the Bible text, the preacher, and the listener, and consequently the phase is conceived as centered on words.

46. Promey and Brisman, "Sensory Cultures," 188–91.

HOW DO THE RDCs ENGAGE IN THE PREACHING EVENT?

Engagement in the First Phase of Verbalization and Visualization

The two categories of RDCs considered here engaged in several ways during the first phase of verbalization: through visualization and mediational means, through direction, and through changes to the sermon's content.

As mentioned earlier, during the recording sessions the spokespersons were in charge. They arrived early to the recording location to set up cameras, microphones, lights, and other technical equipment. If the recording took place inside a church, they would adapt the space in different ways to suit their needs. The spokespersons in Järfälla stated that "everything visual is our responsibility." When asked if they ever discuss the visual with the strategists, they said:

> Some preachers have very clear ideas and thoughts and wishes, and we try to incorporate that if it is possible, suitable, and looks good. But most, in particular pastors, just want to get up and do their thing and do not think about how they stand and how it looks.[47]

They continued to explain how they strive to include the atmosphere from the location, and not just from the preacher's perspective. This was confirmed in the observations. The setting of the recording space varied every time in relation to what the spokesperson thought would catch the atmosphere of, for example, the liturgical year, the theme of the Sunday, or the theme of the sermon (if they had been told what it was in advance). They could also choose a location inside the church that showcased something they thought the participants/viewers would appreciate and meditate on, like a painting or an artifact. Sometimes they chose locations or artifacts that the worshippers would not normally see were they listening from the pew. In other words, the spokespeople were deeply engaged in choosing mediational means intended to interact with the strategists' words.

The spokespersons in Järfälla could also choose a location outside of the church, for example a garden, a square, the cemetery, the children's

---

47. This is briefly discussed also in the Evangelical Lutheran Danish Church (ELDC) research report on worship services during the COVID-19 pandemic. The choice of location in the local church space has theological significance. It also enables perspectives that would not normally be possible for the participant, like being face-to-face with a preacher who stands in the pulpit, or a bird's-eye view from the church ceiling. (*Når Folkekirken Skal Spille efter Reglerne*, 177–85.

corner in the parish hall. In those cases, the choice often made in consultation with the strategist. This kind of collaboration with strategists was much appreciated by the spokespersons, since it allowed for creative work and mutual exchange. The spokespersons got inspiration for how the sermon could be visualized, and they were also able to inspire the strategists. It is worth noting that the authority emerging here, both in words and action, is relational authority.

The spokesperson—the communications director—in Täby, who also doubled as technician during the recording sessions, worked in the same way. He came early to prepare and choose the location, camera angles, and mediational means and to set the scene for what he called "the right atmosphere." During one of the observations, there was a slight dissonance between the spokesperson's choice of location and visualization, and the words of the strategist's sermon. The worship service was to be published on All Saint's Day, and the strategist—who had assumed the recording would take place in the old thirteenth-century church—had chosen to talk about the life of one of the saints depicted in the medieval paintings in the roof of the church. When the team met on the morning of the recording session, she found out that the spokesperson had chosen a modern church that possessed a very large, beautiful globe for lighting candles. During All Saint's weekend, it is very common for people in Sweden to light candles on graves and in churches, and the spokesperson wanted to feature that in the video. He also wanted to include something about the possibility for people to light a digital candle at the CofS's website. After some negotiation, they agreed that the recording session would take place in the modern church after all, but the picture in question would be added during the editing of the recording. The preacher added a paragraph to the sermon about lighting candles.

Just like his counterparts in Järfälla, the spokesperson in Täby reported that most of the strategists let him take full responsibility for the visualization, but a few strategists wanted to partake in planning how the sermon and worship service should be envisioned. Likewise, he preferred collaboration since it enabled a creative working environment. He mentioned an example that he was particularly pleased with: a worship service with a pilgrimage theme in which they walked during the recording session. This had required a lot of discussion and negotiation on how he could envision the strategist's words along the path, and how his choice of imagery could be verbalized by the strategist.

The spokespersons also engaged through directions. In both churches, they directed the delivery of the sermon in detail. They told the strategists where to stand, look, how to talk, how to interact with the technology, and even what to wear (for example avoid liturgical clothing in certain situations). When asked about this, the spokesperson in Täby commented that he, in addition to the directions we had observed, often also had to instruct the strategist on style, tone of voice, facial expressions, and so on.

When the strategist (pastor) in Täby was asked about her thoughts on these directions (in particular, being told not to wear liturgical clothes), she commented:

> If we are a team and we need to make decisions as a team, and then no one's opinion can be superior. And [the communications director] obviously has a reason for it. Even if I do not understand exactly what it is, I have to let this process grow and see if it turns out well. Perhaps he will say: it turned out the way I wanted, and then I will understand.

Both here and in the example of the negotiation about sermon location, the authority that emerges in words and actions is relational. That authority is negotiated through communicative interaction in an interdependent relationship.

This strategist was not the only one who appreciated directions. On the contrary, according to the spokespeople in both Järfälla and Täby, the strategists often asked for them, especially in the beginning of the transition to digital worship services during the pandemic. The Järfälla spokespeople were sometimes even asked to review the sermon manuscript beforehand. Here, there is a slight difference between the two congregations. As earlier mentioned, the spokesperson in Täby suggested changes to the sermon manuscript that the strategist accepted, an example of relational authority. In Järfälla, the spokespeople stated that they tried to be careful not to control the content of the sermon manuscripts and that they thought it was "very strange to poke around in someone's sermon." They would only weigh in when they were asked to do so.

In other words, the spokespersons' starting point was a role-based authority, one that they were accustomed to from their lengthy service as wardens in the local worship services. However, in the digitally mediated service, they were invited to wield relational authority and consequently did. The Järfälla spokespersons stated that the invitations had been more common in the beginning of the pandemic. They thought the preachers had listened to their feedback and had improved the content of their sermons over time. The spokespersons felt that the strategists had learned to compress their sermons, keeping them short and to the point and delivering them with a personal and casual style.

In sum, the digital spokespersons engaged in the preaching event through visualization of the sermon manuscript, the choice of mediational means, the giving of direction, and the occasional advising on the content of the sermon. In this engagement, there are traces of role-based authority emerging in the spokespeople's narratives, but a relational authority is prominent and emerges in practices and narratives, as enabled and encouraged by the digital mediation.

RDC Engagement in the Second Phase of Verbalization and Visualization: Editing

The engagement of the RDCs in the preaching event created a second phase of verbalization and visualization: editing. In the editing process, it was mainly the spokespersons who were engaged in adding B-roll imagery, texts, and sound.[48] In all cases, the goal of these additions was to enhance or contextualize the message of the delivered sermon.

An example of how the use of B-roll imagery could enhance the delivered sermon can be found in the previously mentioned All Saint's sermon. The spokesperson and the strategist negotiated that the sermon was to be recorded in the modern church, and the painting from the medieval church would be added during editing. When asked about this, the spokesperson thought the editing facilitated the visibility of the painting. On-site, in the church, the picture was difficult to spot since it was located near the roof at the entrance of the church, and was thus impossible to see if you were seated in the pews. Online, the picture was easier for the viewer to see since the editing included a close-up where the picture's colors and outlines were enhanced. The effect enhancing the painting was that the preacher's words also were enhanced. As the preacher named and explained the saint's particular attributes, the relevant details were highlighted.

The team in Järfälla also frequently added pictures and clips of artifacts, art, surroundings, and other meditational means in the editing process. The spokespersons (technicians) in charge of editing reported that

---

48. "B-roll" is a term used in film production that designates supplemental or alternative footage that is intercut with the main shot.

they had an extra hard drive with such material. When asked about how they selected what to include and where to place it, the spokespersons said that they would usually get inspiration after listening to the sermon. They were extremely positive about being able to contribute in this way: "Wow, here we can help and contribute to what they are trying to say through imagery." They gave an example of a pastor who, during Advent, preached on the theme "make way for the Lord," and brought his son's tiny toy car as a prop. The strategist's sermon related to the movie *Cars*, and how the main character, the racing car Lightning McQueen, was sentenced to repair the road he had accidentally destroyed. At first, he tried to do it quickly and sloppily, but then he learned that it was better to do it diligently and slowly. Taking it slow also allowed for detours where Lightning McQueen got to know others, including the judge in the town (whom the strategist interpreted as a God figure). The preacher concluded by asking what would be the best way of preparing our hearts for Christmas: fast and expensive, or to take small, slow steps and allow for detours?

To the spokespersons, it had been natural to add a stop-motion animation in the end with the toy car, showing how it drove by slowly, taking a couple of turns. In this way, they wanted to enhance and comment on an element of the sermon that they thought was important.

The spokespersons in Järfälla also stated that they tended to work more with imagery when the preacher had structured their sermon in relation to a metaphor or prop of some kind. In addition, according to them, this practice of bringing in mediational means had increased dramatically among the preachers in the digitally mediated preaching events. In the subsequent focus group conversation, the spokespersons and strategists discussed the reasons for this and concluded that the digital format encouraged the use of mediational means. Interestingly, the reason for this was not just because it was easier to preach from an artifact or art when you were sure that the listeners would actually see it (for example, a tiny toy car would be very difficult to spot from the pews). The strategists also testified that it made them feel that they were less "lonely" in the delivery of the sermon. They saw it as another "body" with which to share the camera's attention.

The spokesperson in Täby worked in similar ways when editing. He added pictures from a variety of shots including imagery that he thought would suit the delivered sermon. Interestingly, in the conversation about this practice, the musician mentioned that she worked in similar ways with her choice of music, for example during funerals. According to her, it happened quite often that she had planned to play certain music during the funeral service, but after hearing the funeral sermon, she changed to something that she thought would enhance or even comment on the message. Both the musician and the pastor in the team commented that they appreciated the communications director's work on imagery, and that they thought it enhanced or even brought new dimensions to the message of the sermon. The pastor, especially, thought it was very interesting "to hear how he thinks in pictures, and how he thinks they [words and pictures] are theologically connected."

Of course, more than pictures could be added during editing. Sound or text could also be added. For instance, in Täby, the music from the hymns could be added to the opening and/or closure of the sermon, which functioned in similar ways as the musician's choice of music during the funeral service: as a contextualization of or enhancement of what the communications director thought was an important message in the sermon. In Järfälla, the communications director captioned the sermons, interpreting the spoken language of the preacher into textual language.

In sum, the digital spokespersons engaged by adding visual, aural, and textual enhancement or contextualization of what they thought were important parts of the digital strategists' sermon message. The strategists engaged by adapting to the increased visual dimension of the sermon and the spokespersons' directions. Notably, the collaboration between these particular strategists and the spokespersons was characterized by negotiation and trust. While there were no instances when, for example, the choice of B-roll imagery obscured or contradicted the strategists' words, it could potentially have occurred since the strategists did not review the spokespersons' choice of additions before publication in digital media. The spokespersons' interpretation and idea about what messages are important to enhance or convey is even clearer in the publication part of the second phase of verbalization and visualization.

RDC Engagement in the Second Phase of the Verbalization and Visualization Process: Publishing

When publishing the delivered, edited sermon, the spokespersons (communications directors) followed the rules of engagement in social media: they chose a thumbnail, a small image representation of the content of the recording of the worship service. They also wrote a short accompanying text—often a summary of the theme or content of the sermon—to encourage those who encountered the sermon on the church's website or social media channels to watch the video. In this way, yet another layer of interpretation and production was added to the process. Notably, the core messages presented in social media were not always the same as the preachers' core message in the sermon itself. Take, for instance, the All Saint's sermon that was previously mentioned.

As discussed, the spokesperson wanted to pay attention to the practice of lighting candles on graves and in churches during the All Saint's feast. The strategist adapted her sermon to accommodate that wish, and the sermon was recorded with the preacher standing next to the candleholder in the back of the church. This was mirrored in the publication phase. The main part of the sermon was the strategist's original sermon where she spoke about the saint as an example of how having Jesus as a light in your life, and how living your life with a firm hope of paradise, can affect your whole life. However, the sermon's framing in social media did not mention that at all. Instead, it included a thumbnail picture of the preacher next to the globe of light, with a text that read: "During the All Saint's weekend we remember those who have passed away. On [link to website] you can light a digital candle for someone you miss and watch it burn alongside candles lighted by other people. You are not alone in your grief."

A second example can be found in the Järfälla church. In this case, the sermon was on John 4. The strategist started by asking if the listener had heard about "the woman at the well who met Jesus," and painted a picture of a woman who was cast out and living in shame. However, when she met Jesus she became a "living advertisement poster" for Jesus. It was not an advertisement as in trying to sell a product, but:

> She advertises because she is deeply touched by what he has said. He tells her about her life and it is true. She responds in honesty, bares herself. She dares to stand there with her shame and meets the man who will totally change her life. She receives the living water and wants to pass it on to others. The story is about us. We get to be living advertisement posters, here and now, with a message about love. A message that goes beyond what we can think and imagine, where there is no room for shame and self-loathing, and we are surrounded by love, grace, and mercy, where we can live in love, here and now, and pass it on to the people we meet, just like that woman went to others and told them about the meeting with the man who had told her everything.

In social media, the communications director wrote: "Maybe shame can't get a hold on someone who has been seen for who they truly are? Reflect together with [pastor] who tells the story about the woman at the well in the first digital worship service of the year. From St. Luke's church."

The message about passing love on and our calling to preach a message of love in our everyday life was omitted. Instead, the spokesperson chose to emphasize the part about shame and being seen. In this case, there is a shift in content. Instead of the strategist's message about how Jesus changed the woman's life and wiped away her shame (sin) with grace and mercy, the spokesperson's message was that it is difficult for shame to even get a hold of someone who is seen for who they really are. A smaller but important difference: the description of the woman had changed from "the woman at the well who met Jesus," as the pastor wrote, to "the story about the woman at the well."

When asked about this practice in the first interview, the communications director in Järfälla smiled and said, "Oh, you caught on to me!" She continued to acknowledge that in a way she was doing the short summary as a translation to nontheologians in relation to her own experience of being interested in spirituality and theology, but "would probably not qualify as Christian, believing Christian, like pastors and people like that." Yet, she thought that Christian faith had been important to her, and that it could be important to others, if they are not excluded or turned away by a "churchy" language. In the final interview, she stated:

> What is my goal? It is to do a short summary, make accessible what [the sermon] is about, if possible in an unchurchy way . . . and I just try to formulate it without thinking too long or too deeply. In the beginning it just made me come into biblical formulations, and I thought that this will sound nice to the pastors, and to the people who do not read the Bible it is going to sound like gibberish. [laughs] And I thought about it: what am I trying to do? . . . If we are trying to meet as wide target audience as possible, then it is worth trying to not exclude the people who do not read the Bible.

Here we may note several interesting things. First, the spokesperson talks about her authority as role-based. According to her, she merely "packs" or "translates" the message. This is in line with the digital spokespersons described by Campbell, who emphasized that their work was not about theological interpretation but about making the message of the church accessible. However, as shown in the example above, the reality is that the adaptation to a format and style that suits her understanding of contemporary secular culture and digital platforms is a theological interpretation in its own right. Furthermore, since this interpretation contextualizes the sermon to the listener, it contributes to the listener's own "auredit."

It is also important to note that her colleagues do not view her framing as mere translation but as collaboration and interpretation. When the rest of the team was asked about the digital spokesperson's work, they were very appreciative. For example, the other spokespersons (technicians) in Järfälla thought that "she writes amazing texts about the content of the worship service that really encourage people to watch."

In sum, the spokespersons engaged in the preaching event through the framing of the delivered and edited sermon in social media. As shown above, they engage in many other ways including through editing, directing, altering of the sermon manuscript, enhancing, and contextualizing. The strategists' engagement is characterized by relational authority—authority as created and negotiated between different parties through communicative interaction in an interdependent relationship. The spokespersons' engagement is often characterized by relational authority. While their way of expressing themselves points to their being accustomed to wielding role-based authority, in practice they are often wielding a relational authority. How, then, might this engagement be understood?

HOW CAN THESE EFFECTS OF RDC ENGAGEMENT IN THE PREACHING EVENT BE UNDERSTOOD?

It Can Be Understood as Co-preaching

In relation to the homiletical discourse on polyphonic preaching, in which preaching is seen as a "dialogical, polyphonic coauthorship" that is created through various voices that supplement each other, I propose that the engagement of RDCs in the preaching event can be understood as co-preaching.

The engagement of the RDCs in the preaching event differs from the engagement in the roundtable conversations described by John McClure,[49] for example, where the preacher listens to others but ultimately serves as a curator of what should go into the sermon or not. In the conversational approach, the preacher is still very much in control.

---

49. McClure, *Roundtable Pulpit*.

In these two cases, however, the preacher/strategist no longer serves as a curator. The digital spokespersons have agency and authority in their own right, and it would be very difficult for the preacher/strategist to silence their voices if she wanted. This could explain why the strategists frequently mention the experience of loss of control. Notably, the loss of control is only mentioned as a problem in relation to the listeners who might misunderstand or scrutinize, not in relation to the spokespersons. On the contrary, they are regarded as gatekeepers who through their engagement described here will decrease the risk of misunderstandings.[50] The relational authority they practice and describe in their interviews also points toward something more than a regular conversational approach. This is mutual collaboration, a co-preachership.

Since the material for this case study was assembled within the framework of an action research project, the practitioners were introduced to the concept of RDCs and co-preaching and asked what they thought about this theory as an interpretation of their work. They all confirmed it, although one of the spokespersons, the communications director in Järfälla, was a bit reluctant at first. She again emphasized her role as translator who is only concerned with the form of the message, not the message itself. However, in the next interview two months later, she stated: "I think it was very interesting how we found out that what I'm writing—well, I feel that I have snuck into a preaching niche." The other RDCs confirmed that they indeed functioned as co-preachers; however the spokespersons' feelings about this were a bit ambiguous. They stated that it was empowering, but at the same time they recognized the stakes involved in this statement. As one of the spokespeople in the Järfälla team put it, half jokingly: the tack of co-preaching "is a great responsibility to put on three "morons [like herself and her colleagues]. Isn't that fatal?"

Though this digital form of co-preaching is new, co-preaching as practice is nothing new in the history of the Christian church. During late antiquity and the Middle Ages, it was common for distinguished preachers to engage scribes who wrote down their sermons. The scribes also interpreted and edited the sermons, thus contributing to the content. Bernard of Clairvaux and Nicholas of Montiéramey are, together, an example of such "co-preaching."[51] In some churches, it is an established practice to interrupt the preacher if the Holy Spirit encourages you to say something. The

---

50. Mannerfelt and Roitto, "Mellan rit och reklam del 2," 74–75.
51. de Gussem, "Bernard of Clairvaux," 190–225.

practice of call and response could also be called co-preaching.[52] When it comes to the practice of framing the sermon, this also occurs in some communities, for example when the preacher is introduced or when the worship leader is praying for the preacher and/or the sermon before or afterward. Sometimes the worship leader gives a summary of the sermon afterward.[53] Singing could also be seen as a practice of co-preaching, as is very evident in the revival movements.[54] As I noted above, the musician in Täby also made this parallel.

Furthermore, there might be others involved in a digitally mediated preaching event who could be considered co-preachers. As I have discussed elsewhere, people who comment on and share sermons in social media could be understood as co-preachers.[55]

No matter who the co-preachers are, a consequence of co-preachership is that it may facilitate polyphony.

It Can Be Understood as Enabling Polyphony

The polyphonic preaching approach also aids in understanding how the co-preaching in these two cases, enabled as it is through digital media, effectively makes the preaching event more polyphonic. More voices contribute, including those of persons and mediational means. In these cases, it is not as with Rystad's preachers who started out with polyphony but fell into old patterns of "one single harmonized voice." The dialogical polyphony held up all the way, for better . . . or worse.

Indeed, it is worth asking what happens when the voices in the polyphony belong to people without formal theological education and who have not been ordained—or as the practitioners in Järfälla very pejoratively put it: "morons"—have such a large influence on the preaching event. Is

---

52. Crawford, *Hum*; Richards-Greaves, "Say Hallelujah, Somebody"; Thomas, *Introduction*.

53. It is interesting to see that these kinds of introductions and summaries to elements of the services are practices that congregations tend to cut out in digital worship services. Mannerfelt, "Old and New Habits," 100.

54. Halldorf, "Mötet i frikyrklighet och väckelse," 144–53. One of the first and most well-known examples of a preacher singer collaboration where the singer acts as a sort of co-preacher is Dwight L. Moody and Ira D. Sankey. In the Swedish context there are several examples, like Nelly Hall and Ida Nihlén (Gunner, *Nelly Hall*) and Lewi Pethrus and Einar Ekberg (Halldorf, *Biskop Lewi Pethrus*, 216).

55. Mannerfelt, "Back to the Roots," 209.

there not a risk that the message of the gospel becomes contorted? As mentioned earlier, this is discussed by Sigmon, who in her homilecclesiological vision underlines the importance of preachers building up laypeople for the task of interpreting and communicating God's words and actions. The preachers' own preaching must model how the sacred texts and traditioned dogmas can be interpreted and communicated, while also helping them both to acknowledge their own authority and to discern when they are subordinated to unjust authority by others.[56] Sigmon's proposition points to the importance of a concept like co-preaching, which reveals that spokespersons (and perhaps other types of RDCs) are actively partaking in the interpretation of the message of the church.

Finally, while the digitally mediated preaching events could be said to enable polyphonic preaching through the engagement of co-preachers, there are certain limitations to the polyphony, limitations that are caused by the very same digital mediation. In a discussion on liturgy in digital spaces, art historian Johannes Stückelberger points to the fact that the choice of camera angles and visual content affects how the words of the preacher are interpreted. This means that the pictures included in a digitally mediated worship service are not just contributing to an atmosphere, they are liturgical elements that create a dialogue with the sermon. However, at the same time as digital mediation enables new constellations of visualization and verbalization that would otherwise be impossible in the on-site church, it also delimits the listener's choice of which visual element will contribute to the interpretation. The listeners cannot let their gaze wander around the church and choose something else, for the camera and editor are directing it.[57]

SUMMARY

This case study of six digitally mediated preaching events in two Church of Sweden (CofS) Stockholm-area congregations aimed to describe and discuss what happens when the use of digital technology introduces new human actors into the preaching event. These actors were identified as "religious digital creatives" (RDCs), a concept coined by Heidi Campbell in her study of religious authority and new media. The case study involved RDCs from the categories "digital strategist" (pastors and musicians) and "digital spokesperson" (technicians and communications directors).

56. Sigmon, "Engaging the Gadfly," 178–80, 185–87.
57. Stückelberger, "Liturgie in Virtuellen Räumen."

The research questions that guided the study were, "When and how do the RDCs engage in the preaching event?" and "How can these effects of RDC engagement in the preaching event be understood?" The source material consisted of observations, individual and focus group interviews, recordings of the services, and screen shots of how the recordings were presented when they were published on the congregations' websites and social media platforms. This material was analyzed with regard to their practices, how they understood those practices, and what kind of authority that emerged in those doings and sayings.

I found that the RDCs in this case study engaged in the preaching event in the verbalization phase, turning it into a phase of both verbalization and visualization. In addition, their engagement introduced a second phase of verbalization and visualization. More specifically, the RDCs engaged through editing direction, altering the sermon manuscript, enhancing, commenting, and framing. The RDCs' engagement was characterized by relational authority, that is authority created in negotiation through communicative interaction in a mutual and interdependent relationship.

The results were discussed in the light of the concept of polyphonic preaching, which draws on the communication theory of Michail Bakhtin to describe preaching as dialogical and listeners as coauthors or even the primary authors of the sermon. In line with this, the RDCs were understood as co-preachers. The perspective of polyphonic preaching also shed light on how the practice of co-preaching increased and upheld the polyphony of voices that contributes to the dialogical character of the sermon.

BIBLIOGRAPHY

Bjerg, Svend, and Sten Lynglund. "Den karnevalesque praediken: En anderledes homiletisk model." *Praesteforeningens Blad* 100 (2010) 943–46.

Boyd, Jason. *The Naked Preacher: Action Research and a Practice of Preaching*. London: SCM, 2018.

Bruce, Sarah Katherine. "The Vital Importance of the Imagination in the Contemporary Preaching Event." PhD diss., Durham University, 2010.

Brueggemann, Walter. "The Preacher, the Text, and the People." *Theology Today* 47 (1990) 237–47.

Campbell, Heidi. *Religious Creatives and the Rethinking of Religious Authority*. London: Routledge, 2021.

Campbell, Heidi, and Ruth Tsuria. "Introduction to the Study of Digital Religion." In *Digital Religion: Understanding Religion in a Digital Age*, edited by Heidi Campbell and Ruth Tsuria, 1–12. 2nd ed. London: Routledge, 2021.

Campbell, Heidi, and Sophia Osteen. *When Pastors Put on the "Tech Hat": How Churches Digitized during COVID-19*. The Network for New Media, Religion & Digital Culture Studies, 2021. https://oaktrust.library.tamu.edu/handle/1969.1/194959.

Claypool, John. *The Preaching Event*. New York: Church Publishing, 1980.

Craddock, Fred B. *As One Without Authority, Revised and with New Sermons*. St. Louis: Chalice, 2001.

Crawford, Evans E. *The Hum: Call and Response in African-American Preaching*. Nashville: Abingdon, 1995.

Davies, Andrew. "A New Teaching without Authority: Preaching the Bible in Postmodernity." *The Journal of the European Pentecostal Theological Association* 27 (2007) 161–72.

de Gussem, Jeroen. "Bernard of Clairvaux and Nicholas of Montiéramey: Tracing the Secretarial Trail with Computational Stylistics." *Speculum* 92 (2017) 190–225.

Engemann, Wilfrid. *Homiletics: Principles and Patterns of Reasoning*. Berlin: Walter de Gruyter, 2019.

Fahlgren, Sune. *Predikantskap och Församling: Sex Fallstudier av en Ecclesial Baspraktik Inom Svensk Frikyrklighet Fram Till 1960–Talet*. Örebro: ÖTH rapport, 2006.

Gaarden, Marianne, and Marlene Ringgaard Lorensen. "Listeners as Authors in Preaching: Empirical and Theoretical Perspectives." *Homiletic* 38 (2013) 28–45.

Garpe, Sara, et al. "Inledning." In *Kyrka i Digitala Rum: Ett Aktionsforskningsprojekt om Församlingsliv Online*, edited by Sara Garpe and Jonas Ideström, 5–17. Uppsala: Enheten för Forskning Och Analys, 2022.

Gunner, Gunilla. *Nelly Hall: Uppburen och Ifrågasatt*. Uppsala: Swedish Institute of Mission Research, 2003.

Halldorf, Joel. *Biskop Lewi Pethrus: Biografi Över Ett Ledarskap—Religion och Mångfald i det Svenska Folkhemmet*. Skellefteå: Artos, 2017.

———. "Mötet i frikyrklighet och väckelse." In *Kristen Gudstjänst—En Introduktion*, edited by Stina Fallberg Sundmark, 137–69. Skellefteå: Artos, 2018.

Harris, James Henry. *The Word Made Plain: The Power and Promise of Preaching*. Minneapolis: Fortress, 2004.

Holmberg, Andreas. *Kyrka i Nytt Landskap: En Studie av Levd Ecklesiologi i Svenska Kyrkan*. Skellefteå: Artos Academic, 2019.

Ideström, Jonas. "Implicit Ecclesiology and Local Church Identity: Dealing With Dilemmas of Empirical Ecclesiology." In *Ecclesiology in the Trenches: Theory and Method under Construction*, edited by Sune Fahlgren and Jonas Ideström, 121–38. Eugene, OR: Pickwick, 2015.

Karlsson, Jonny. *Predikans Samtal: En Studie av Lyssnarens Roll i Predikan hos Gustaf Wingren Utifrån Michail Bachtins Teori om Dialogicitet*. Skellefteå: Artos, 2008.

Kaufman, Tone Stangeland, and Hallvard Olavsson Mosdøl. "More than Words: A Multimodal and Socio-material Approach to Understanding the Preaching Event." In *Preaching Promises within the Paradoxes of Life*, edited by Len Hansen and Johan Cilliers, 123–32. Stellenbosch: African Sun Media, 2018.

Latour, Bruno. "Technology Is Society Made Durable." In *Sociology of Monsters: Essays on Power, Technology and Domination*, edited by John Law, 103–31. London: Routledge, 1999.

Lorensen, Marlene Ringgaard. "Carnivalized Preaching—In Dialogue with Bakhtin and Other-Wise Homiletics." *Homiletic* 36 (2011) 26–45.

———. *Dialogical Preaching: Bakhtin, Otherness and Homiletics*. Göttingen: Vandenhoeck & Ruprecht, 2014.

Lorensen, Marlene Ringgaard, and Gitte Buch-Hansen. "Listening to the Voices: Refugees as Co-authors of Practical Theology." *Practical Theology* 11 (2018) 29–41.

Maddock, Ian. "'Like One of the Old Apostles': The Acts of the Apostles and George Whitefiel's Criteria for Describing Preaching Events." *Colloquium* 49 (2017) 55–65.

Mannerfelt, Frida. "Back to the Roots or Growing New Branches: Preaching, Orality and Mission in a Digital Age." In *Missio Dei in A Digital Age*, edited by Jonas Kurlberg and Pete Phillips, 195–220. London: SCM, 2020.

———. "Old and New Habits: The Transition to Digitally-Mediated Worship in Four Swedish Free Church Denominations during COVID-19." In *Svensk frikyrklighet i pandemin: En studie av församlingen i corona och corona i församlingen*, edited by Ulrik Josefsson and Magnus Wahlström, 107–14. Örebro: Forskningsrapporter från Institutet för pentekostala studier Nr. 9, 2021.

Mannerfelt, Frida, and Rikard Roitto. "Mellan rit och reklam del 1: Berättelsen om två församlingars utveckling." In *Kyrka i digitala rum: Ett aktionsforskningsprojekt om församlingsliv online*, edited by Sara Garpe and Jonas Ideström, 47–60. Uppsala: Svenska kyrkan, 2022.

———. "Mellan rit och reklam del 2: Interaktion, synkronicitet och integritet i förinspelade digitalt förmedlade andakter." In *Kyrka i digitala rum: Ett aktionsforskningsprojekt om församlingsliv online*, edited by Sara Garpe and Jonas Ideström, 61–79. Uppsala: Svenska kyrkan, 2022.

McClure, John. *Other-Wise Preaching: A Postmodern Ethic for Homiletics*. St Louis: Chalice Press, 2001.

———. *The Roundtable Pulpit: Where Leadership and Preaching Meets*. Nashville: Abingdon, 1995.

Mervin, Dick. "Preaching with Authority." *Direction* 12 (1983) 14–22.

Når Folkekirken Skal Spille efter Reglerne—Men Uden for Banen Folkekirkens Håndtering af Coronaperioden i Foråret 2020. Folkekirkens Ud-dannelse-och videncenter. https://www.fkuv.dk/_Resources/Persistent/0/7/3/0/07305f2673d70b2b89dd4cfb23eef898654e01e7/N%C3%A5r%20folkekirken%20skal%20spille%20efter%20reglerne%20-%20men%20uden%20for%20banen.pdf.

Promey, Sally M., and Shira Brisman. "Sensory Cultures: Material and Visual Religion Reconsidered." In *The Blackwell Companion to Religion in America*, edited by Philip Goff, 177–205. Oxford: Blackwell, 2010.

Richards-Greaves, Gillian R. "'Say Hallelujah, Somebody' and 'I will Call upon the Lord': An Examination of Call-and-Response in the Black Church." *Western Journal of Black Studies* 40 (2016) 192–204.

Rystad, Linn Sæbø. "Overestimated and Underestimated: A Case Study of the Practice of Preaching for Children with an Emphasis on Children's Role as Listeners." PhD thesis, MF Norwegian School of Theology, 2020.

Schatzki, Theodore. *Social Change in a Material World*. London: Routledge, 2019.

Sigmon, Casey Thornburgh. "Engaging the Gadfly: A Process Homilecclesiology for a Digital Age." PhD thesis, Vanderbilt University, 2017.

Stückelberger, Johannes. "Liturgie in Virtuellen Räumen: Der Raum in Online-Gottesdiensten." Universität Bern, Theologische Fakultät, 2021. https://www.liturgik.unibe.ch/unibe/portal/fak_theologie/kompz_lit/content/e359272/e973272/e973422/e973425/Stuckelberger_RauminOnlinegottesdiensten_ger.pdf.

Sundberg, Carina. "Här är rymlig plats: Predikoteologier i en komplex verklighet." PhD thesis, Karlstad University, 2008.

"Sweden in the Digital Economy and Society Index." Digital Economy and Society Index (DESI), 2022. https://digital-strategy.ec.europa.eu/en/policies/desi-sweden.

Thomas, Frank A. *Introduction to the Practice of African American Preaching.* Nashville: Abingdon, 2016.

Tornfelt, John V. "Preaching with Authority When You Don't Have It." *The Journal of the Evangelical Homiletics Society* 4 (2004) 23–50.

Watkins, Clare. *Disclosing Church: An Ecclesiology Learned from Conversations in Practice.* London: Routledge, 2020.

4

Symbol Preaching in the Digital Age
From Symbol Recognition to Symbol Interpretation in Facebook Ads

PIERRE HEGY

INTRODUCTION

The thesis of this chapter is that in the digital age we are moving away from words and concepts characteristic of the print age, toward the use of images and symbols. Any word has a clear dictionary definition, but images are open to an infinite number of symbolic interpretations. The image-centered culture of the digital age does not replace the concept-centered world of the print age, but it adds a new dimension to it. In order to pass from one to the other, readers must overcome the one-dimensional world of rationality and discover the multidimensional universe of symbols. This will be accomplished by moving from mere symbol recognition characteristic of elementary education to the level of symbol interpretation in art, poetry, and religion.

This chapter will proceed in three steps. I will first define the concepts. Next, I will present my findings from religious ads posted on Facebook. Finally, from these findings I will suggest guidelines for the future.

THEORY OF SYMBOL RECOGNITION AND SYMBOL INTERPRETATION

The word symbol has two basic meanings, depending on the context. In the sciences, symbols function as signs defined by one specific meaning, as in the mathematical formulas. These are *objective symbols*. In the cultural sciences and religion, symbols have many meanings. They are *cultural symbols*. Elementary education teaches the recognition of objective symbols like the letters of the alphabet and the structural parts of a word, while higher education introduces students to the cultural symbols of Shakespeare and the arts. Objective symbols are rational creations of the written culture that must be learned. They are objectively defined and recognized universally. Cultural symbols, by contrast, are special to a given culture or field, although some are shared worldwide. Children do not begin with objective knowledge but with images that blur reality and the imagination, with words that are both objective and subjective. Education must first teach the rationality of objective symbols, that is, symbol recognition. In this chapter I take the move from symbol recognition to symbol interpretation (or from objective to culture symbols) as the passage from the rationality of the written culture to that of image interpretation which prevails today.

Let us begin with a very elementary question: what is the meaning of meaning? This was the title of the 1923 book by C. K. Ogden and I. A. Richards. They came up with twenty-three categories of answers, none of which was more important than the others.[11] Instead of trying to find a single answer, I will turn to two basic schools of thought, the American school of philosophers of language, Charles Peirce (1839–1914) and Charles Morris (1901–79), and the European tradition of semiotics initiated by Ferdinand de Saussure (1857–1913). My presentation is obviously a simplified version of the very diverse field of semiotics.

Morris and Peirce were mainly interested in the psycho-social processes relating objects and words. For them, "something is a sign only because it is interpreted as a sign of something by some interpreter."[22] This perspective emphasizes the objective dimension of communication, namely, the speaking subject, the topic of communication, and the language of the written or spoken words. This view has many consequences for preaching. When reading the Bible in this perspective, the preacher

---

1. Ogden and Richards, *Meaning of Meaning*, 186–87.
2. Noth, *Handbook of Semiotics*, 49.

will inquire about the objective meaning of the words in Greek or Hebrew. When a passage contains a story, the preacher may develop the psychology of the biblical actors. Finally in the applications, the emphasis will be on willful acts and decisions.

Quite different is the semiotic tradition, which focuses on linguistic and syntactic structures. Now words are analyzed not just within sentences as in Aristotelian rhetoric, but within a whole cultural corpus, e.g., all the writings of a given author or a literary genre. In exegesis, historical criticism will look for broad scriptural structures, e.g., the four sources of the Pentateuch or the differences between the three synoptics. In all forms of creative learning—and in preaching—the basic structure is that of an analogy between a source and a target domain. Learning involves the analogical imitation of a model, e.g., a literary masterpiece, an artwork, the heroes of history, or the examples found in the scriptures.

These two schools are complementary. Here is my outline for this section. 1) I will first turn to semiotics to define the basic structure of learning and preaching as analogical. 2) Next, I discuss the move from symbol recognition to symbol interpretation according to Ricoeur. Finally, 3) I show that symbols add an experiential dimension to reality, as in psychoanalysis and religion. After this theoretical first part, I present findings from Facebook ads, and conclude with guidelines for preaching in the digital age.

The Analogical Structure of Learning and Preaching

An analogy is created by the structural similarity between a source and a target domain. Its purpose is to transfer knowledge from one to the other. Hence there are three elements: two structures that must be similar and a subject or mind that sees the similarity between the two.[3]

A mother may expressively say "mama" or "papa" to invite the infant to imitate these sounds. Here we have the model "mama," the imitation of the model by the child, and the need for the child to understand the relationship between the two. In infancy the child may learn how to use the plural of nouns simply by adding an "s" in imitation of what adults do, but this imitation will be successful only if the child understands the implicit rules of grammar. Over the years the child learns basic rules of social behavior not just grammatical rules. Once these structures are internalized, a teenager can find solutions to new situations, e.g., the plural of a word in a

---

3. Holyoak and Thagard, "Analogical Mind," 35–44.

foreign language or the appropriate behavior at college away from home. In elementary school the child is motivated by its desire to please parents, but in high school it may lose interest in learning, and also reject religion and church attendance. Motivation is a key factor in learning.

The lack of learning motivation is a problem not only in education but also in preaching. The description of the life of Jesus as a model to emulate is not enough to motivate the audience to apply this analogy to themselves. Analogical reasoning, which is basic in all forms of learning, is not enough to change the hearts of people. It is the agency of the listeners that allows the move from symbol recognition to symbol interpretation.

Christian preaching consists of presenting paradigmatic events or biblical texts as interpretive models. Before the text of the New Testament was available, the first Christians used events and texts of the Jewish scriptures as types for understanding the message of Christ. Thus, the psalms were scrutinized for images of Jesus Christ. This typological model of exegesis has been followed ever since. But here is the catch: it did not work with Jews who did not relate Jesus to their scriptures. It did not work well with gentiles who did not know the Jewish scriptures. Today it does not work when the biblical model does not fit the listeners' expectations. The message of Jesus Christ is meaningless to those who doubt the existence of God. Cradle believers may suddenly stop believing when they can no longer make sense out of the religious symbols of their childhood.

Moving from Symbol Recognition to Symbol Interpretation

In elementary education and catechetical teaching, symbol recognition is usually sufficient. In the first grade, students learn to recognize words ending with -at (as in cat), then -an (as in man), etc. In a fifth-grade social science class, they must recognize "the most common gas on earth's atmosphere." And in tenth grade, after reading a one-page letter from Abigail Adams to her husband, they must recognize its basic ideas in a multiple-choice test.[4] In national exams, multiple-choice testing has become the norm when there is no practical alternative. There are multiple-choice exams even in college, being preferred by both students and teachers. Obviously, there is also symbol interpretation throughout the course of elementary and secondary education, not just symbol recognition.

4. Examples of questions and answers at "Reading Comprehension."

I follow Ricoeur in his *Interpretation Theory* to explain the passage from recognition to interpretation in the cultural sciences.[5] In the humanities and the social sciences (mainly in cultural anthropology, clinical psychology, and qualitative sociology), the mind must go back and forth between a text and the understanding of its meaning. For Ricoeur, interpretation is the process of multiple readings with increased understanding; interpretation may never be complete. The first reading may be naive, the second one a little more sophisticated. At the beginning, understanding is a broad guess of the general meaning. At the end, we reach appropriation. The latter is a "dynamic of interpretative reading"; it does not lead to a transfer of knowledge from the speaker or writer to the listener; it is much more. "Interpretation is completed as appropriation when reading yields something like an event, an event of discourse."[6] Interpretive reading is the creative process that produces a discursive event in the mind of the reader, says Ricoeur. It is not a thing, but a new perspective, that of a fusion of horizons. In appropriation, "the world horizon of the reader is fused with the world horizon of the writer."[7] It is not a transfer of knowledge but a sharing of perspectives.

For Ricoeur, interpretative reading is a process similar to what I call symbol interpretation. Appropriation does not mean taking possession of the message of a writer; it means accepting "a mode of being in the world that the text opens up." When the meaning of a text has been appropriated, the reader has been transformed. For Ricoeur, interpretative reading—or symbol interpretation—reveals "new modes of being [which give] to the subject a new capacity of knowing himself."[8] Ricoeur gives as an example of appropriating the letters of Paul, which are read and explained in Sunday worship. When the Bible is read interpretatively, it is transformative. Unfortunately, not many people reach this high level of understanding.

In Ricoeur's perspective, one moves from the recognition of objective symbols to their interpretation through multiple readings. It is this repeated reading that is the bridge between the two structures of an analogy, the knowledge of objective symbols on the one hand and the perception of meaning on the other. In fashion, each individual bridges the gap between the objective models of fashion and personal preference. In biblical

---

5. Ricoeur, *Interpretation Theory*, 74.
6. Ricoeur, *Interpretation Theory*, 92.
7. Ricoeur, *Interpretation Theory*, 93.
8. Ricoeur, *Interpretation Theory*, 94.

understanding, one moves from the objective understanding of a biblical text to its understanding through multiple readings in a deliberate and active pursuit. At a global level, one will move from objective symbols to their interpretation through a deliberate and active pursuit of meaning in all areas of knowledge. For this, the use of symbols as cultural creations adds a new dimension. Moving from objective symbols to symbol interpretation must also take place in preaching. How this move can be achieved will be discussed through examples from Facebook ads below.

Cultural Symbols as Experience of a New Reality

When words are used as cultural symbols, they add a new dimension of depth and experience. The phrase "a woman with a mysterious smile" is a one-dimensional discourse. Leonardo da Vinci's painting *Mona Lisa* is two-dimensional: an image and a message. No number of words can express this mysterious smile, but art and poetry can. Looking at the Alpine scenery of snow-capped mountains, cows only see grass. When one is blind to the symbolic dimension, words are only things; they describe a world without art, a scenery of grass without the beauty of snow-capped mountains. Any objective symbol can be seen symbolically, but it requires a qualitative jump.

Symbols in psychoanalysis and religion belong to two universes; one is linguistic (the story of a dream or a sacred text) and the other is nonlinguistic and nonsemantic (the hidden psychic conflicts or the "wholly other" in Rudolph Otto's description of the holy[9]). The second dimension refers to an experience that affects the self, not just the brain. But there are not two significations, one (grass) added to the other (the Alpine scenery), because an implicit dynamic must unite the two.

According to Ricoeur, discursive language (that of the written culture) belongs to the order of *logos* (reason) while symbols belong to *bios* (experience). What complicates things is that the experiences of *bios* are usually expressed according to the linguistic rules of the *logos*,[10] that is, in words rather than in images. How can we move from words to experience?

The distinction between cultural symbols and ordinary language may help our understanding of symbols as experience. I can describe a dream to a friend without understanding its psychoanalytic meaning; I just tell the facts. I can write a sincere love letter but without being able to convey my

---

9. Otto, *Idea of the Holy*.
10. Ricoeur, *Interpretation Theory*, 59.

deep feelings symbolically; I just give information. I can quote the Bible like a newspaper; it may show no faith. Ordinary language belongs to the order of the *logos*, of objective symbols that describe objective realities; the listeners may get the intellectual message but not the depth of the experience. But psychic conflicts, deep feelings, and mystical experiences are lived experiences that transcend ordinary language. Knowing the technical language of specialists is not enough. One may assemble a collection of technical terms as Freud did in *The Interpretation of Dreams* or Mircea Eliade in *Patterns in Comparative Religions*,[11] but knowing that a wolf is a psychanalytic symbol and a mountain top is a symbol of divine encounter does not make me a psychoanalyst or a religious prophet. These words become symbols only, for instance, when a wolf is experienced in a dream as a threat, and a mountain top is experienced as an encounter with the divine, e.g., in meditation.

The interpretation of texts through multiple readings belongs to the age of print. Symbols are more prominent in the digital age. Religious teaching is usually just the explanation of doctrines or sacred texts, and so is explanatory preaching. More appropriate for our age is symbolic interpretation and preaching as the sharing of experience. This is what happens in successful religious advertising.

FINDINGS FROM FACEBOOK ADS

Sixty-nine percent of Americans use Facebook. Seventy-three percent of US adults visit Facebook *every day*. Thirty-seven percent of them *get their news* from Facebook, and most Facebook users access the app on a mobile phone.[12] In the field of popular entertainment, the top ten world celebrities receive over 100 million visitors every day; Lady Gaga (the only name I recognized) ranked 128th with 55 million visitors daily. There are probably more visitors to celebrities in a single day than to all US churches in a month. Social media functions as constant social reinforcement. Americans check their cell phones every ten minutes and the 18- to 24-year-old age group checks twice as often, for an average of ninety-six times a day.[13] By contrast, they go to church—if they do—only four times a month. Hence, it seems imperative that the gospel be present in this environment.

11. Eliade, *Patterns in Comparative Religions*.
12. Carmicheal, "63 Facebook Statistics."
13. Williams, "Americans Check Their Smartphones."

Now some personal data. In 2016, I started posting weekly biblical reflections on the internet without ever checking how many people read them—actually, very few. Realizing that advertisements on Facebook were available for as little as five dollars a day, I started advertising in November 2019 for seven dollars a day in a three-day week (Friday to Sunday or $21 a week). I have not increased this amount since then.

Methodology and Research Design

In the social sciences, a research project usually involves 1) a sample; 2) several independent variables like the age, religion, education, and income of the respondents; and 3) one dependent variable, in my case the number of people who see my ads, and their approval or engagement rate. Such a research design is not possible on Facebook.

One cannot select a sample, only the amount of USD one wants to spend, and the country where one wants to advertise. The number of people who will see the ads is decided by the Facebook algorithm. For each ad, the computer evaluates its desirability for the viewers. Thus, my ad of November 5, 2022, was seen by 118.8 thousand viewers in the English-speaking audience of about 8.5 million people, and by 328.8 thousand viewers in the French speaking audience of only 2.5 million. The difference in the number of viewers is mainly decided by the computer and I cannot make sense out of it. Moreover, if the same ad were advertised every week for six months, the results would be different because each week the selected viewers would be different; they are not selected randomly as in academic research.

The age, religion, education, and income of the respondents are not known. I do not know the country of the respondents. Thus, on January 15, 2023, I posted an ad to be seen in all the countries of the world and in all possible languages. It was seen by 169 thousand people, but I do not know their country or language; actually, I know nothing about them.

The independent variable cannot be clearly defined. Is it the number of viewers (which is said to be an estimate)? Or is it the number of people who click "like" or "love?" Or those who write a comment? To make things worse, for these measurements Facebook gives two sets of statistics, and I cannot make sense of their differences; in any case, no one gets to see the computer language that measures these variables.

This system works to the satisfaction of all advertisers because it increases sales, often considerably. I also found the results trustworthy and reliable because I always used the same method and selected the same statistics, while also introducing limited changes. This is what I have done for the data presented below. In short, this endeavor was not a conventional research project typically conducted on Facebook; rather, it was an experiment meticulously outlined and documented through its various phases.

My advertising has gone through many phases. First, I experimented with many audiences to increase the number of viewers. Then I somewhat changed the content. Here is my outline for this section: 1) How audiences are selected on Facebook; 2) my attempts to improve my audiences; 3) presentation of basic findings; 4.) moving from religious information to faith experiences; and 5) getting involved through comments.

The Problem of Audience Selection

There is a Facebook tool to help the selection of an audience according to people's preferences; but this option has not been available since mid-2022. Thus, in 2019 one could ask how many people are interested, e.g., in tennis, a car model, or Protestantism. This tool indicated the number of interested people, their gender, and their ten basic preferences, namely their preferred retail company, their preferred public speaker, political candidate, news media, etc. When in December 2021 I selected "Protestantism" as my US audience, the computer indicated that this audience was 74 percent female; Walmart was the preferred retailer for 28 percent of them, Donald Trump was the preferred political candidate for 21 percent, and Fox News the preferred source of information for 18 percent. When I selected "Catholicism," the audience was 78 percent female; Franklin Graham was their public figure (29 percent), although he was not a Catholic; and Donald Trump was their preferred political candidate. It is important to note that people interested in Protestantism or Catholicism are not necessarily Protestant or Catholic, as we do not know their religious identity, only their religious preferences.

Sample selection is a major concern in advertising. On Facebook (henceforth FB) one cannot select a sample of a given size consisting of people of specific social backgrounds. Instead, one can only select people with specific interests. The FB mega-computer codes the interests of all FB members expressed in their posts. As a consequence, the FB algorithm can find appropriate viewers for nearly any kind of ad.

In 2019 I wanted an audience interested in biblical reflections about the Sunday readings of the Catholic lectionary. I wanted an audience that would be ideologically neutral, neither predominantly conservative nor progressive. I selected three available interests: Catholic devotions (conservative), charismatic renewal (progressive), and Pope Francis (progressive in most parts of the world but not for conservative Americans). These criteria yielded a US audience of 7–8 million viewers that was 76 percent female and mainly conservative. With this audience the response rate to my ads was low. I tried similar audiences in Canada, Ireland, and the United Kingdom with similar modest results.

In July 2020 I expanded by including India and the Philippines. Then the results increased ten- to twenty-fold. When the audience included the five English speaking countries of India, the Philippines, Nigeria, Tanzania, and Ruanda, the number of responses from America became insignificant. Consequently, I limited my audience to the five foreign countries just mentioned. While the American audience was 76 percent female and old, the audience of these five foreign countries was about 70 percent male and young, and their response rate was about ten to twenty times higher.

The FB algorithm first evaluates a submitted ad and then sends it to appropriate recipients. The viewers can react to a post by clicking "like," or "love," or "share," or writing a comment. The number of people who react is the engagement rate. This is the most important statistic: it indicates the importance of an ad to the viewers.

The number of viewers of an ad is decided by the FB algorithm. My top three ads in 2021 were seen by a weekly average of 58.9 thousand viewers while the three least popular ones were seen by 16.9 thousand people. The advertisers do not have any input about the number of viewers, but they can change or increase their target audiences.

Selecting a Better Audience

My main goal in advertising biblical reflections was at first to increase the number of viewers. It is only later that I paid attention to the quality of the responses. There are no techniques for audience improvement. It is by accident that I discovered that by changing my audience, I reached more viewers. When at the beginning I got 1,000 or more viewers in my American sample, I had good reasons to be satisfied. Adding Canada, Ireland, and the UK made no difference, but adding the Philippines increased the number of viewers substantially. This prompted me to add India. Later I added English-speaking countries in Africa. Finally, I created a French audience (France and eleven African countries) using the English ads in a translation. Here are the various steps of my audience development.

- An audience of 60 million in the US. About 1,000 to 3,000 viewers. From September 2019 to May 2020.
- Audience of 50 million in the US, Canada, Ireland, and Philippines. About 10 to 20 thousand viewers. From June 2020 to October 2020.
- Audience of 650 million of all the FB viewers in US, Canada, Ireland, Philippines, India, Nigeria, and Tanzania. About 30 to 40 thousand viewers. From October 2020 to May 2021.
- Audience of 500 million from Philippines, India, Nigeria, and Tanzania (without the US). About 40 to 60 thousand viewers. From September 2021 to June 2022.
- Lookalike audience of 8.5 million from Canada, US, India, Philippines, Nigeria, Tanzania, and Rwanda. About 80 to over 100 thousand viewers. From June 2022 to September 2022.
- French version of the English ads. Audience of 2.5 million with about 80 to over 100 thousand viewers from May 2022 to September 2022.

There are no recipes for increasing one's audience; it is mainly a question of trial and error. I do not know why my recent audience of 8.5 million got better results than the previous ones of 650 million. I used a FB tool to create "lookalike" audiences, that is, new audiences with the characteristics of previous successful ads, that is, national audiences that had the characteristics of people who liked my ads. What these special characteristics are, and how lookalike audiences are created, is the secret of the computer algorithm. In trial-and-error learning, what counts are the results. The French audience of 2.5 million is much smaller than all the English ones. At first, its performance was worse, but progressively it improved and at times surpassed the English results. Audience selection may be unpredictable, but in the long run, trying new methods is likely to produce positive results; innovation is the key. The same is likely to be the case in preaching.

THE DIGITAL PULPIT

Presentation of the Basic Findings

A FB ad consists of a picture and three to five lines of text. The viewers can react by clicking "like," "love," "share," or writing a comment. The number of reactions per ad is called the engagement rate. Here are the ads from 2020 and the first half of 2021 that received the lowest approval rates. These rates are high in comparison to the average for all ads on FB, which is supposedly .3 percent. The ads below are about fifteen times higher than this average of .3 percent. Here are the titles:

9.8%	"Golden-rule Christians are kind and helpful."
10%	"Three options for after-pandemic church life."
10.2%	"Most addictions are pleasant."
14%	"Nature is the image of God."
14.3%	"Mary's Assumption is also called her Dormition."
16%	"Jesus's position was inclusive: 'Who is not against us is for us.'"
16.8%	"All things come from God and return to him."
17.7%	"No need to shout: God is not deaf."
18.7%	"The first Christians shared meals and possessions."
19.3%	"When life is like jumping from a cliff, we need faith."
20.6%	"The 2021 readings are from Mark."
21.2%	"Pentecost: Unity in diversity."

Here are a few more titles of the same type as those above:

"Simon was a fisherman living next to the lake. His house has been excavated."

"We are pilgrims: all flesh is like grass."

"The opposition between flesh and spirit is basic in our spiritual struggles."

"We live in eschatological times."

"Conflicts between liberals and conservatives have existed since the beginning of the church."

"Worldwide migration is likely to increase due to climate change."

"There are checks and balances in the Catholic Church."

"We are in a coronavirus winter. We must become self-reliant."

The content of these ads is informational, cognitive, and moralistic. They present information for symbol recognition, not symbol interpretation. Some are only informational: the Assumption is also called the Dormition, or the 2021 readings will be taken from the Gospel of Mark. Many are general: nature is an image of God, all things return to God, the first Christians shared possessions, Jesus's position was inclusive, and Pentecost was unity in diversity. Many ads are moralistic: addictions are pleasant, God is not deaf, we need faith, prepare for Lent. The lowest rating went to "The Golden Rule Christians." This title refers to a sociological paper by Nancy Ammerman[14] showing that the lived religion of Americans is centered on morality not doctrine.

Like any Sunday preacher, I tried my best. The above topics, in my view, are like what can be heard in many churches. For months I was satisfied. It is only when reviewing my results for a paper that I was struck by the following results, which I had not noticed. Here are the ads with the highest engagement rates from 2021.

57%	"Christ is risen."	
56%	"Christ is risen" (another week).	
53%	"God is beyond our images."	
52%	"God reveals himself in people's lives."	
49%	"A common false belief: God punishes you for your sins."	
48%	"Both awe and joy at the Transfiguration."	
48%	"Proclaim the good news to the end of the world."	
47%	"Christ is really present at Mass."	
47%	"What is salvation?"	
47%	"What is the origin of evil?"	
46%	"Yes, God still heals today."	
45%	"The Passion of Jesus Christ."	
43%	"The Passion of Jesus Christ" (another week).	
44%	"The Easter joy will last forever in the eternal banquet."	

---

14. Ammerman, "Golden Rule Christianity," 196–216.

The above examples suggest that people wanted to learn about the mysteries of faith and the core insights of Christianity. This is also what people in the pews probably expect from preachers.

What can explain the change from low engagement in 2020 to high engagement in 2021? How can viewers (and the people in the pews) reach the level of symbol interpretation when the writer or preacher communicates at the level of symbol recognition, that is, the level of information and morality? It seems that there must be first a transformation in the writer or preacher, rather than in the viewers or auditors.

Moving from Religious Information to Faith Experiences

Starting in the middle of 2021, I changed my writing procedure. In the ads with low engagement rate, I first reflected on the text, and it is only after writing my reflections that I sought a picture to illustrate it. In my new procedure I would first search for a picture to illustrate a main idea of the Sunday reading, and next add the title *within the picture* (e.g., Jesus is coming soon). The writing of a reflection came third. Now the title and the writing were *inspired by the picture* selected for its expression of the reading. Previously the process was a dichotomy, my biblical reflections on the one hand and a picture to illustrate my reflections on the other. Now the process was reciprocal, the image giving depth to the understanding of the text and vice versa. Previously I started with a concept from the biblical text, that is, symbols of information; now I start with images as symbols of interpretation.

Moreover, while previously I limited the size of my pictures to about 30 percent of the width of the page, in 2022 I extended the size to 90 percent of the width, which gave pictures a prominent place. What affected the viewers, the text or the image? The answer is probably both, through a single image-text production. The unity of picture and text is likely to foster active interpretation rather than passive recognition. As explained above, psychoanalytic or mystagogical symbols belong to two orders of things, one is linguistic or iconic, and the other transcendent and experiential. But when the two dimensions are interrelated, the viewer can easily pass from one to the other. In my first series of ads, I juxtaposed a text and an image. I was only communicating at the cognitive and informational level. Now I was personally engaged in the experience of image-text. More generally, while previously I endeavored to give information and moral conclusions, now I tried to explain the mysteries of faith, that is, write about mystagogy.

The Comments of Viewers

Viewers can click "like" and "love," but they can also write a comment, which is a more demanding engagement. Every week up to several hundred viewers leave a comment. Their number is an indication of the importance of the ad to them. Here are the ads ranked by the number of comments:

579	Sermon on the Mount. "Blessed are the poor."
502	The Transfiguration is a pre-figuration of the resurrection of Jesus and ours.
477	"Peace be with you!" God's peace is more than the absence of conflict.
426	"Simon, do you love me?"
397	The return of the lost son. More joy for 1 conversion than for 99 righteous.
375	Blessed are the poor. Blessed are the poor because God cares for them.
372	The four temptations of Christ. "I will give you power and glory if . . ."
369	Christ King. "Be this sign [the cross] you shall conquer!"
339	"I am with you to the end of time." "I will send you an advocate."
321	Martha & Mary. "Martha, you worry about details!"
316	The abundance of wine in Cana was a symbol of the eternal feast.
283	"Remember me in your kingdom." For the sake of your sorrowful passion, have mercy on us.
275	Our Father in Heaven. "Ask and you will be given."
261	"He is alive!" "John saw and believed."
256	"Where is your faith?" Faith gives peace in the middle of the storm.
243	No one can serve two masters. Who is your master: God or money?

237	The friends of Jesus: the outcasts. The prayer of the Pharisee: "God, I do not need you. I am fine."
224	Jesus is rejected from Nazareth. God is often ignored because people are too busy.
224	Baptism: a passage to a new life.
206	The Good Shepherd. Where is the good shepherd today?

This list gives priority to core beliefs rather than peripheral ones, as in the ranking by engagement rates, but here there is a more personal dimension. People responded more to ads that involved them personally, as in: Peace be with you; Simon, do you love me? The return of the lost son; blessed are the poor; "I am with you to the end of time"; "Martha, you worry about details"; "remember me in your kingdom"; and "ask and you will be given."

The content of these comments suggests that the viewers value faith more than doctrine. At the end of a Sunday service, one may say to the preacher something like, "Well done!" or "I liked this . . . or that. . . ." Not here. There was never a complimentary comment, but all were affirmations of faith. For instance: Amen; praise the Lord; praise you Jesus; amen in Jesus's name; Jesus Christ is the Lord God; I love you, Lord Jesus; amen, joy, Jesus. Most comments simply repeated "amen" or "alleluia" or both with exclamation points. These simple words were the expression of faith of viewers with low literary skills from the emerging economies of Asia and Africa.

CONCLUSION: GUIDELINES FOR PREACHING IN THE DIGITAL AGE

I use the word "mystagogy" as the process of leading people to the mysteries of faith, although at the time of Augustine this word referred to the sacred mysteries themselves (and it does so today in the Catholic preparation of adults for baptism). Teaching doctrine is not enough today; preachers must lead listeners to some spiritual awakening. Teaching and lecturing are used to impart knowledge through symbol recognition; this is useful at all levels, especially at the level of beginners. Mystagogical preaching has higher goals; it endeavors to transform the listeners through the symbolic interpretation of the mysteries of faith. Teaching belongs to the order of the *logos* (rationality), but mystagogical preaching to that of *bios* (experience) in Ricoeur, or to the orders of *pathos* and *ethos* in Aristotle. Both types, *logos* and *bios*, are needed but they have different effects, one is more informational, the other more transformative.

My FB ads consisted of over 400 weekly campaigns involving over 5 million people. The bulk of this information leads me to three basic guidelines. Effective preaching in the digital age implies 1) paid advertisement, 2) sermon evaluation, and 3) mystagogy (symbol interpretation) rather than basic religious information (symbol recognition). Here are more detailed guidelines.

Advertising

Streaming Sunday services and sermons on YouTube is quite common. Unless these events are advertised, few people will know about them. Advertising on FB is inexpensive: a one-day ad is available for as little as five dollars per day. All churches can afford this. Advertising is not enough; it is necessary to check the results. FB, Google, and other platforms offer statistics about the number of people who visited a given web page. These programs are free of charge.

The need to advertise has been advocated and practiced by successful media preachers of the past. Robert H. Schuller was known to millions of Americans for his *Hour of Power*. He started modestly by preaching in an open-air movie theater. "Immediately after our first Sunday in the drive-in theater [in March 1955], I sent out a postcard to everybody on the mailing list."[15] It increased his success. Six months later, he invested $4,000 in advertising, and collected over $8,000 in donations, which he reinvested in more ads. In Schuller's opinion, the senior pastor should be personally in charge of advertising. "By being personally responsible for the publicity, I was forced to create, produce, and generate sermons and programs that were newsworthy."[16] This was also my experience: writing, posting, and reviewing my weekly reflections forced me to make numerous improvements.

Rick Warren started Saddleback Church by going door to door to listen to people's complaints, and sending a letter to 15,000 homes inviting them to attend his first Sunday service.[17] For him, money and evangelism

---

15. Schuller, *Your Church*, 145.
16. Schuller, *Your Church*, 146
17. Warren, *Purpose Driven Church*, 139.

go together. "Money spent on evangelism is never an expense, it's always an investment." But this money is often the first to be slashed. "When finances get tight in a church, often the first thing cut is the evangelism and the advertising budget. That is the *last thing* you should cut." He saw both as "the source of new blood and new life for your church."[18] Advertising is as important as evangelization; usually one goes with the other.

Sermon evaluation and adaptation to audiences

The performances of teachers, salespersons, and most public agents are evaluated regularly, but sermons are not. FB ads give reactions and comments. Digital technology can provide unique tools of evaluation. For instance, at church during the sermon people in the pews could interact with the preacher by sending text messages on their cell phones. Such an initiative would require overcoming the view of the pastor as the main or sole source of theological learning. Zoom conferences already offer such instantaneous interactions; while the screen shows the speaker, the audience can react by writing messages off screen in the chat room. The speaker can later review these messages and respond if appropriate. Without sermon evaluation, there will be little improvement in preaching.

Any church involves multiple audiences but usually the same sermon is given to each of them (e.g., the Anglos and the Latinos in a given church). Bill Hybels popularized seeker-friendly services that cater to an average customer called Harry. Every aspect of the service (music, topic, language, stories, exhortations) was geared to Harry.[19] Rick Warren developed his own style of seeker-sensitive services by adopting pop music, a church campus built like a shopping mall, and nondenominational sermons preached in street clothes. But what worked for Hybels and Warren in the 1970s and 1980s may not be appropriate in the digital age of today.

The two basic audiences identified by Apostle Paul were those living in the spirit and those in the flesh. He catered to both. He was angered by the Corinthians whom he saw as fleshly (1 Cor 3:1–3); he also addressed the spiritually mature in most of his letters (e.g., 1 Cor 2:6). We all need to improve, whether at the level of the beginners or the advanced. At Saddleback, there is a Sunday service for the Harrys and a mid-week service for the advanced. In small churches where there is only one service, the

18. Warren, *Purpose Driven Church*, 202.
19. Pritchard, *Willow Creek Seeker Services*, chapter 9.

preacher should address both publics, the Harrys and the advanced, but at different Sundays.

Traditionally the members of the two publics were identified as the regular Sunday attendees and the devout of pious societies. Today spiritual growth is often expressed in terms of discipleship and a personal relationship with God.[20] Without at least occasional preaching at this advanced level, the spiritual quality of sermons and of the preacher's life is likely to remain average.

Preaching as the Interactive Sharing of Spiritual Experiences

"What we have seen and heard, we now proclaim to you, so that our joy may be complete" (1 John 1:3). John did not write to give information about what he saw and heard but to give a testimony of the power of God that he experienced. This is what makes preaching effective: the faith experience of the preacher speaking to the faith experiences of the listeners. Then preaching is at the level of *bios* (experience) rather than that of *logos* (rationality and information), although one does not exclude the other.

My FB experience suggests how to move from symbol recognition to symbol interaction. In information preaching, the sermon presents the preacher's knowledge and wants the audience to accept it. In symbol appreciation, the preacher selects images that evoke faith experiences in him or her, and shares these visual faith experiences with the public; most of the time it works very effectively. Preaching becomes the sharing of faith rather than the sharing of information. In other words, instead of giving objective information about the sightseeing in town, the preacher indicates the ones he/she found most attractive. This is required by the very nature of images as cultural symbols. For the merchant, the value of art is in its objective price; for the artist, art is in the eye of the beholder. In the digital age, preachers must be the artists of the word of God.

BIBLIOGRAPHY

Ammerman, Nancy T. "Golden Rule Christianity: Lived Religion in the American Mainstream." In *Lived Religion in America: Toward a History of Practice*, edited by David D. Hall, 196–216. Princeton: Princeton University Press, 1997.

---

20. Hawkins and Parkinson, *Move*, chapter 4.

Carmicheal, Kayla. "63 Facebook Statistics to Know for 2022." HubSpot (blog), December 14, 2021. https://blog.hubspot.com/blog/tabid/6307/bid/6128/the-ultimate-list-100-facebook-statistics-infographics.aspx/.

Eliade, Mircea. *Patterns in Comparative Religions*. New York: Meridian, 1995.

Hawkins, Greg, and Cally Parkinson. *Move: What 1,000 Churches Reveal About Spiritual Growth*. Grand Rapids: Zondervan, 2011.

Holyoak, Keith J., and Paul Thagard. "The Analogical Mind." *American Psychologist* 52.1 (January 1997) 35–44.

Noth, Winfried. *Handbook of Semiotics*. Bloomington: Indiana University Press, 1990.

Ogden, C. K., and I. A. Richards. *The Meaning of Meaning: A Study of the Influence of Language Upon Thought and of the Science of Symbolism*. New York: Harcourt, Brace, 1938.

Otto, Rudolf. *The Idea of the Holy*. Oxford: Oxford University Press, 1970.

Pritchard, G. A. *Willow Creek Seeker Services: Evaluating a New Way of Doing Church*. Grand Rapids: Baker, 1996.

"Reading Comprehension Worksheets Grades 1–10." K12 Reader, n.d. https://www.k12reader.com/subject/reading-skills/reading-comprehension/.

Ricoeur, Paul. *Interpretation Theory: Discourse and the Surplus of Meaning*. Fort Worth: The Texas Christian University Press, 1976.

Schuller, Robert H. *Your Church Has Real Possibilities!* Greendale, CA: G/L Publications, 1975.

Warren, Rick. *The Purpose Driven Church: Growth Without Compromising Your Message and Mission*. Grand Rapids: Zondervan, 1995.

Williams, Chris. "Americans Check Their Smartphones 96 Times a Day, Survey Says." *Fox 13 Seattle*, September 28, 2021. https://www.q13fox.com/news/americans-check-their-smartphones-96-times-a-day-survey-says/.

5

Metaverse Preaching

JEAWOONG JUNG

INTRODUCTION

The COVID-19 pandemic amid the Fourth Industrial Revolution fueled the emergence and popularization of digital preaching by using various new digital media platforms. Metaverse preaching is one of the new homiletical practices that such a new normal brought about. Although the concept of the metaverse was introduced decades ago, it didn't draw much attention from the public until then. The situation was changed as physical meetings in public became prohibited in prevention of mass contamination of coronavirus. As with other public meetings, churches began to use online platforms for gatherings and the metaverse was one of them. However, it is hard to find homiletical discussions about metaverse preaching, though research on digital preaching has been done by a couple of scholars.[1] A few mention metaverse preaching only as a form of online preaching but lack a serious homiletical discussion about what metaverse preaching does.[2]

Despite this, since the metaverse has distinctive media characteristics that distinguish it from the existing online media, it is necessary to study the characteristics of the metaverse and its impact on preaching more specifically. Unlike other online platforms, the metaverse provides users with a 3D-based hyperrealistic experience that implements a decentralized

---

1. For the recent research on digital preaching, see Yang, "Word Digitalized," 75–90; Mannerfelt, "Listening to Listeners," 16–31; O'Lynn, "Te Digital Media Sermon," 736.

2. Harris and Reed, *Sharing Jesus Online*, 18–19, 38–41.

and collaborative communication method rather than a unified message delivery concentrated on content creators. Therefore, it is necessary to have a more specific discussion on metaverse preaching, which is differentiated from online preaching based on other kinds of online platforms, focusing on users' experiences and communication styles. Recognizing the current situation and the need for further study, this chapter aims to discover the characteristics of metaverse preaching in reflection of actual practices and to discuss the possibilities and limitations of metaverse preaching. The chapter will first analyze the cases of metaverse preaching based on understanding the characteristics of the metaverse, and then make a homiletical evaluation of metaverse preaching, analyzing the homiletical experience and relationship between preacher and listener that it constitutes.

UNDERSTANDING OF METAVERSE AND ITS FEATURES

Definition and Features of Metaverse

Simply put, metaverse preaching is a practice of preaching performed and experienced through a metaverse platform. The problem is that it is hard to grasp "what metaverse is" due to its fluid concepts and various understandings of it. Thus, before discussing metaverse preaching, it is required to define metaverse and understand its characteristics.

The word "metaverse" is a combination of the prefix *meta* (meaning beyond or transcend) and *verse* (shortened for universe). Since the term metaverse was first used in Neil Stevenson's science fiction novel *Snow Crash* in 1992, which describes metaverse as the three-dimensional "virtual world" where the characters act through avatars, it refers usually to a virtual world in which people interact with each other using an avatar. However, in recent years, the term has expanded beyond this consultative concept to include any interface or platform that enables the merging of the real and virtual worlds. For example, the US Acceleration Studies Foundation (ASF) defined metaverse as "the convergence of virtually enhanced physical reality and physically persistent virtual worlds" in a 2007 report called "Metaverse Roadmap." In this line, some categorize four types of metaverses according to the implementation space and the form of information: virtual reality (VR), augmented reality (AR), mirror worlds, and life-logging.[3] In application of this broad sense, metaverse preaching includes almost all kinds of

---

3. Smart, Cascio, and Paffendorf, "Metaverse Roadmap Overview."

online preaching performed through online platforms that connect reality and virtual reality. Thus, preaching through YouTube, Facebook, or Zoom can be considered metaverse preaching. However, this categorization is too broad to make sense of the characteristics of the metaverse precisely. Therefore, a more concise definition is required.

Probably, the most recognizable definition of metaverse is given by Matthew Ball, the renowned expert on metaverse who popularized the current concept of metaverse. He offers a concise definition of metaverse in his international bestseller, *The Metaverse*, as follows:

> Metaverse is "a massively scaled and interoperable network of real-time rendered 3D virtual worlds that can be experienced synchronously and persistently by an effectively unlimited number of users with an individual sense of presence, and with continuity of data, such as identity, history, entitlements, objects, communications, and payments."[4]

This definition reveals several features of the metaverse. First, the metaverse offers a real-life-like experience through 3D virtual reality. Second, it enables the users to act in the metaverse on their will so that it can create a personalized experience of the event. Third, the metaverse provides a networked interaction in which users communicate with others freely. That is, the metaverse offers a real-life-like experience, in which one can meet and communicate with others, conduct economic activities with virtual currency, participate in performances and events, and enjoy play. Thus, one says that people live in the metaverse rather than use it.[5] According to this narrower definition, metaverse preaching is the preaching that involves the participation and execution of a preacher and audience in the form of avatars in a virtual world realized through a virtual reality metaverse platform.

To figure out the features of metaverse preaching, it is necessary to delve into the characteristics of the metaverse as a new media platform more specifically. First, it should be noticed that the metaverse provides the behavioral experience of the actor in a three-dimensional space, while the former online platforms provide the experience of the observer in a two-dimensional screen. For example, the traditional Internet is limited to watching and observing prerecorded or live performances on a screen. In the metaverse, however, users are allowed to participate in the event by approaching the stage, raising their hands, dancing, and doing other actions

---

4. Ball, *Metaverse*, 29.
5. Lee, *What Is Metaverse?*, 85.

in their avatars, similar to being physically present in the theater. If a user utilizes an HMD (Head Mounted Display) equipped with a positioning sensor such as a gyroscope sensor, this behavioral experience is still limited, but it can provide an embodied experience that combines the experience of moving the user's actual body with the behavior of the avatar. Therefore, if the existing Internet experience is called an observation experience, the metaverse experience can be called an activity experience or behavioral experience.[6]

In other words, the feature of behavioral experience in and through metaverse, which differentiates it from observation experience, is that it enables users to experience the event in a context so that they can construct a real-life-like experience. As the metaverse users act in virtual space, they can experience an event that happens there as well as take account of information in the context of the event. It enables the communication of emotion as well as information with other actors. In this sense, metaverse users are no longer audiences or consumers who listen passively to content creators telling stories or watching videos showing stories, but active participants, prosumers, and cocreators who become characters in the story, experiencing the story firsthand and living the story.[7]

Second, the metaverse constructs user-created experiences rather than provider-controlled experiences. For example, when one broadcasts an online performance to YouTube, it's up to the provider to decide what to show and how to show it. A YouTuber can adjust the distance from the stage, close-ups, camera angles, etc. in the performance to show what they want to show, and the watchers see it as it is shown. The difference between online streaming and television or video is that the watcher of online video can adjust the playback speed and navigate to the scene they want to see by adjusting the progress bar.

However, in the metaverse, various experiences can be created depending on the action of individual participants.[8] Through their avatars, participants can view the stage from up close or far away and move from side to side of the stage. This allows them to focus on a particular performer among the many performers. Thus, recording a performance in the metaverse can result in many different videos of the same performance, depending on the experience of the participants, rather than just one. Furthermore,

6. Lee, *Metaverse Begins*, 48–74.
7. Lee, *Metaverse Begins*, 68–69.
8. Lee, *Metaverse Begins*, 166–68.

users can customize their avatars and create their own metaverse spaces. In the metaverse, users can create not only mirror-world spaces similar to the real world, but also imaginary spaces that cannot be experienced in the real world due to the limitations of space and time, or alternative spaces that cannot be created due to political and social constraints, as far as the platform allows. In this way, users can spontaneously and proactively create their own experiences in the metaverse.

Finally, the metaverse can provide a more interactive experience. In Web 2.0 environments, users are more interactive than in earlier internet environments, but their interaction is still limited. If you're watching a YouTube video, you can give feedback on the content by clicking the "like" button or commenting on it. If you're on a live YouTube air, you can express your feelings and thoughts in real-time with emojis and comments, but it's up to the other person to decide whether to give you real-time feedback. In some cases, you can control the interaction with users by closing the comment box.

However, the metaverse allows for a more enhanced interaction experience that more closely resembles a real conversation. People attending a performance in a metaverse platform, like iFland, Zepeto, AltSpace VR, or Roblox, can express their emotions in real time through emoticons and other gestures as the show progresses. In Gather Town, when you move around the map and come across another user's avatar, a video conference window automatically opens, and you can video chat in real time. In iFland, users can communicate through emoticons and chat. This interactivity of the metaverse allows users to collaborate with other users and make fellowship with them.[9]

To sum up, the metaverse provides an experience of activity rather than observation, allowing users to create their own experiences, and being interactive in a way that approximates real-world conversation. These media features of the metaverse create a unique form of communication in the metaverse called User-Oriented Digital Storytelling, by which metaverse preaching creates a distinctive experience of the Word.[10]

---

9. Lee, *Metaverse Begins*, 92–94.
10. Lee, *What Is Metaverse?*, 143–50.

Digital Storytelling in Metaverse

Digital storytelling is "storytelling that uses digital media technologies as a media environment or means of expression."[11] Digital storytelling is characterized by the fact that it does not only tell stories through language and text but also combines digital information, such as images and videos, with oral language and text to create a story. This characteristic constitutes the complexity of the narrative information in digital storytelling. In addition, while on-site oral storytelling often restricts audience questions and feedback during the story to prevent interruptions in the flow of the story, digital storytelling allows the audience to react to the story and the speaker in real-time with comments, emoticons, and more. This constitutes the other characteristics of digital storytelling: interactivity, nonlinearity of story construction, and networkedness.[12]

The general characteristics of digital storytelling, such as interactivity, nonlinearity of narrative structure, networkedness, and complexity of narrative information, are also present in digital storytelling through metaverses. However, as we have seen, the metaverse is unique in that the user's freedom is much greater than in previous media, and the user experiences events or stories through the user's real-time actions, resulting in a more powerful user-centered storytelling experience than in previous media. So how do users experience digital storytelling in the metaverse?

First, the metaverse allows users to create stories through planning and collaboration, much like a drama or movie. In the metaverse, the users' avatars are the characters, the metaverse is the narrative space, and their interactions make a story. From the moment they log in to the metaverse to the moment they log out, users interact with other users in the metaverse space, creating events over time, stories, and experiencing stories. Because the user is the author of the story, the story experienced by each user is unique. As mentioned earlier, a metaverse is not a passive consumption of digital content precreated by content creators through observation or appreciation, but rather, by interacting and engaging with avatars in the metaverse, users can gain personalized story experiences in these metaverses. That is, depending on how users interact and engage in the metaverse, they can have completely different experiences, even if they are on the same metaverse platform and map at the same time, making the story experience

---

11. Jeon, "Using Digital Storytelling," 145.
12. Jeon, "Using Digital Storytelling," 147–50.

unique to each user. In short, the metaverse can provide a user-centered digital storytelling experience.

However, if users are active on the same metaverse platform and map, they will inevitably have some common experiences. In other words, the user experience of the metaverse's platforms and maps functions as the material from which individual users construct stories. In this sense, the metaverse is the medium that holds the materials of the story and the structured structure within which the user experiences the story. Therefore, in a metaverse, content creators can create fields that organize the experiences of individual users, but they cannot create the experiences of individual users.

In this respect, the digital storytelling experience in the metaverse is distinct from the storytelling experience in other digital media. While visual media such as TV dramas, movies, and YouTube videos tell stories created by creators, stories in the metaverse are created by user interaction. In a metaverse, there is no scenario or plot. The story is driven by the impromptu reactions and choices of the users in the metaverse. Even if there is a narrative theme, the stories experienced by individual users within it can be very different. Just like the lived world, where people live every day, life in the metaverse can be an unscripted narrative where chance and improvisation come into play.[13]

In summary, metaverse storytelling reflects the intentions of the creators, but it is the participants of the metaverse who shape the story and complete the ending.[14] There is an outline storyline, but the details are not set in stone, and the ending is open-ended. The question for this study is how those characteristics of the metaverse's user-oriented digital storytelling experiences create an effect on the experience of metaverse preaching. Thus, it spawns the following questions: How are metaverse sermons currently being practiced? What are the homiletical implications of digital storytelling experiences through the metaverse? What new understandings between the audience and preacher do metaverse sermons bring? In the following part, I seek to answer these questions.

13. Lee, *What Is Metaverse?*, 145.
14. Lee, *What Is Metaverse?*, 147–50.

THE DIGITAL PULPIT

EXAMPLES AND HOMILETICAL ANALYSIS OF METAVERSE PREACHING

Examples of Metaverse Preaching

Metaverse Sermons at the Church of Fools

The Church of Fools in the UK, founded in 2004 using Second Life, was technically the first metaverse church. It was the first church to have a 3D representation of the church space and worship through avatars. On YouTube, one can watch a Church of Fools sermon called "On Holy Folly" from July 2004.[15] The short one-minute, seven-second clip features a preacher in the guise of an avatar named Steve Tomkins. The preacher preaches from a pulpit in a chapel, a 3D representation of a traditional church found in England, with no voice. The theme of the sermon was biblical literalism. He tells the story of a couple in Tewsbury in 1650 who crucified themselves in their garden to literally follow Jesus's words. "If anyone would come after me, let them deny themselves and take up their cross and follow me" (Matt 16:24). The preacher must respect their commitment, but the video ends by asking whether it is "wholly folly" or "holy wolly."

In this preaching event, the preacher and congregation communicate via text as the platform doesn't support an audio system, and most congregants are seated and listening, but some move around during the sermon. Because of technological limitations, the earliest metaverse preaching couldn't realize realistic communication but the participants communicated with each other only through text and movements by avatars. While the preacher gives a sermon through texting without voice, the avatar cannot express facial expressions or movements. Thus, preaching at the Church of Fools was a written sermon.

Picture 1: Preaching at Church of Fools (video screenshot via YouTube)[16]

---

15. Ship of Fools, "Sermon at Church of Fools."
16. Ship of Fools, "Sermon at Church of Fools."

Life.Church's Metaverse Sermon

Life.Church, a megachurch well-known for its active online ministries, offers another model of metaverse preaching. Life.Church launched its metaverse worship service on Second Life in April 2007, but the service was not well-received. On December 13, 2021, during the coronavirus pandemic, the church resumed it by using AltSpace VR. In the Life.Church metaverse, sermons are streamed in the form of a sermon video by Craig Groeschel projected on a screen inside a three-dimensional virtual reality church where avatars of congregants are seated. Since the sermon video is streamed, not delivered by an avatar of the pastor, congregants watch the sermon as they used to do at the real-world chapel. The audience remained passive during the sermon and reacted to the sermon by giving emojis. Thus, the interactivity works partially because the listeners can react to the sermon of their own free will, but it can be said that they do not have a high degree of freedom in that most of the time they are passively listening to the preacher's sermon.[17]

Picture 2: Preaching at Life.Church[18]

Metaverse Sermon at Cornerstone Church

Cornerstone Church in Yuba City is notable for operating a metaverse church in the form of a phygital church, which is a combination of a digital and physical church. Cornerstone Church was a traditional church founded in 1955 but it began to offer metaverse worship service as the senior pastor Jason Poling planted the first metaverse campus using AltSpace VR on April 2020, and a second metaverse campus using VR Chat in April 2021. He reports 16,000 visitors in twenty-one months for the metaverse

---

17. Einselen, "Life Church Adds One More Site."
18. Einselen, "Life Church Adds One More Site."

campus powered by AltSpace VR, and 7,300 visitors in nine months for the metaverse powered by VR Chat.[19]

Picture 3: Preaching at Cornerstone Church of Yuba City (video screenshot via YouTube)[20]

Yuba City Church's metaverse service is a combination of video and VR experiences. In the video of the metaverse service on August 14, 2022, the service begins with avatars entering a church built in a virtual reality space, and the entire screen switches to a streaming video of praise performed in a real church.[21] At the end of the song, the preacher's avatar appears superimposed on the song video, and the song video stops and proceeds with the next sequence of prayers and advertisements. And then the camera moves to an outdoor chapel, where a preacher's avatar named JayPo is standing on a large screen in the center of the chapel, delivering a sermon titled, "King Jesus Is Coming Soon."

The sermon is primarily delivered by the preacher's voice, accompanied by images of sermon materials, the primary text (Rev 1:1–20), and secondary texts on the screen. The preacher and audience do not move during the sermon, providing an experience similar to listening and watching a sermon in a real church. After the sermon, the audience is invited to take an active role in the service. First, attendees are guided by the worship leader to a small altar on the side of the open-air chapel to partake of the sacrament, followed by testimonies from attendees and a Q&A with the

19. Reed, *VR and Metaverse Church*, 28–30; Reed, "Jason Poling."
20. Cornerstone Church of Yuba City, "King Jesus Is Coming Soon!"
21. Cornerstone Church of Yuba City, "King Jesus Is Coming Soon!"

preacher about the content of the sermon. While the audience participates in the service under the control of the pastor, there is a moderate amount of freedom for the audience to make their voices heard.

Metaverse Sermons in VR Church

VR Church is distinguished from the other churches listed above since it offers a metaverse sermon that is fully operated by a VR platform without video streaming. VR Church was founded in 2016 by DJ Soto as a purely virtual reality church using AltSpace VR. The first year of the church's existence saw little attendance outside of atheists and those who wanted to debate religion, but the church slowly began to grow. It gained popularity during the coronavirus pandemic and now has about two hundred people attending weekly services. Soto launched a Metaverse Campus via VR Chat and, more recently, a VR MMO (Massive Multiplayer Online) church utilizing the 3D game space of Final Fantasy XIV.[22]

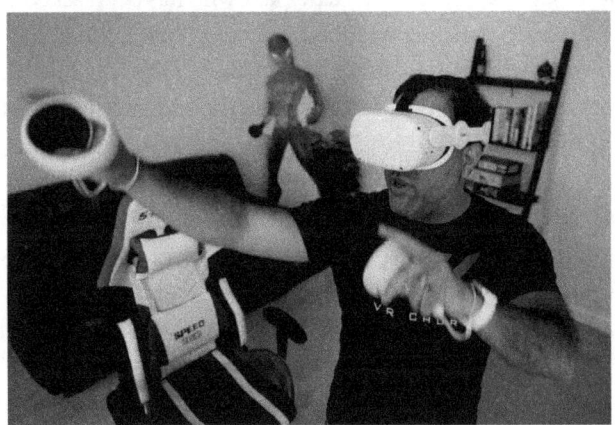

Picture 4: DJ Soto's Preaching with HMD[23]

VR Church's Easter sermon delivered on April 10, 2021, shows its characteristics well.[24] The environment in which the sermon takes place is a 3D VR church that looks like a gym where avatars participate. There is a large screen in the center of the room, and there are no rows of pews

22. Karnadi, "Future of Religion."
23. Henao, "Faith in the Metaverse."
24. VR MMO Church, "Easter at VR Church."

in front of it, but rather free-standing pews. Pastor Soto freely interacts with attendees through his avatar, giving high fives to them, while a video introducing VR Church is played on the screen. A moderator appears in front of the screen to say hello, and the congregation responds with emoticons such as hearts. Prayer and announcements follow, followed by a video introducing the topic of the sermon. Pastor Soto then steps to the front of the screen and begins his Easter sermon.

The preacher begins to preach by briefly explaining the background of the text and then reads the text (John 18–19) on the screen in a relatively dramatic manner, controlling the pitch and pace of his voice. The preacher then dynamically moves the avatar's body, including hands and arms, to illustrate the text. The preacher then leads the audience out of the church and into a space that looks like the hill of Golgotha. Three crosses are set up there, and the text of John 3:16–17 floats in the air. The preacher describes the robbers and Jesus on the cross, while the congregation, gathered in front of the crosses, moves their heads to explore the space. The preacher explains John 3:16–17, read by a participant who has been asked to read the text, and then leads the congregation to the next space, the tomb. The walls inside and outside the tomb show the words of John 20. After explaining the text outside the tomb, the preacher takes the audience into the tomb and asks one of the attendees to read the text as before. The preacher then explains the text again and continues to explain the text as he moves to where Jesus's body was laid. He then goes outside the tomb to a house, which is where the disciples are hiding. The preacher then reads John 20:19–22 and expounds on the text, before entering the house and continuing in the same way to read and expound on the text of the conversation between Jesus and Thomas. He then exits the house and reads and explains the final verses of John 20 written on the wall, challenges the audience to apply the message, and concludes the sermon with prayer. The sermon is followed by a Q&A between the preacher and participants.

For the audience, this approach to preaching is similar to experiencing an Easter-themed exhibition or museum. The audience's experience of the sermon is not given to them by the preacher but completed by their participation. Instead of sitting in a pew and watching a video of the sermon, the audience explores the text with the preacher. This experience of the Word is more aptly described as living and experiencing the story of the resurrection rather than hearing and understanding it. Compared to the metaverse sermons we've seen before, you can see that there is much more freedom for the audience and a more horizontal relationship between the preacher and the audience. In addition, unlike Robloxian Christians, which is created by teens and run by teens, where the audience is jumping up and down and expressing their emotions, the preacher is somewhat guaranteed a stable message delivery environment and the audience is provided with an environment where they can have an empathetic and complex digital storytelling experience of the Word, which reflects the way adults are expected to communicate digitally.

Picture 5: Easter Sermon at VR Church (video screenshot via YouTube)[25]

From the examples of metaverse sermons we've seen so far, we can recognize two main types of sermons. One is a video-streaming sermon by a preacher in a virtual world, and the other is a virtual reality sermon by an avatar of a preacher in a virtual world. The former type of sermon usually takes the form of a topical sermon or homily, while the latter type takes the form of a topical sermon and homily, but also attempts a digital storytelling sermon. DJ Soto's Easter sermon is a prime example of a digital storytelling metaverse sermon. Therefore, this chapter focuses on Soto's Easter sermon, which is a metaverse sermon in the strictest sense, and attempts to make a homiletical assessment of metaverse sermons in terms of the preaching experience and the relationship between preacher and audience.

25. VR Church, "Easter at VR Church."

Homiletical Evaluation of Metaverse Sermons

Homiletical Evaluation of the Preaching Experience

The examples of metaverse preaching provide important implications for homiletical discussions. The first is that metaverse preaching constructs a digital storytelling experience in which participants explore the world as well as the word. In the case of Soto's preaching, the preacher enters the space of the story with the audience to explore and travel through what happened. It is similar to the experience in preaching events that Fred Craddock and Eugene Lowry describe as a trip in and through the biblical world.[26] They describe preaching as a journey in which one experiences biblical events in time. The problem is that there is an experiential gap between the actual event and the verbalized sermon. In oral preaching, which is the most commonly practiced form, the preacher can only provide an aural experience for the audience, but when one experiences the actual event, s/he experiences it through our five senses: sight, touch, taste, and smell, in addition to hearing. To fill this gap, homileticians have called for preaching in figurative and evocative language that allows the audience to use their imagination to reconstruct the event. Although multimedia has made it possible to preach with visual images and videos since the 1990s, the sermon experience has been more of an audiovisual understanding of the information the preacher conveys than a journey through time. However, Soto's metaverse sermon, which moves through the world of a biblical story embodied in a three-dimensional metaverse space, can be seen as a realization of the sermon as a journey advocated by contemporary homiletics scholars. In a digital storytelling metaverse sermon, the audience not only hears and understands the word, but can also see, hear, travel, and explore the word.

It is no coincidence, then, that the movement of metaverse digital storytelling preaching is very similar to the sermonic forms proposed by contemporary homileticians. For example, Eugene Lowry's narrative sermon and David Buttrick's phenomenological sermon both embody the stream-of-consciousness or narrative experience structure of the audience as they listen to the sermon as a way of organizing the sermon.[27] The way and structure of an audience's narrative experience as envisioned by contemporary homiletics is very similar to the way users experience stories in

---

26. Craddock, *As One Without Authority*, 115; Lowry, *The Sermon*, 11.
27. Lowry, *The Homiletical Plot*, 11; Buttrick, *Homiletic*, xii.

the metaverse. What a user experiences in metaverse from the time they log in until they log out can be described as a sequence of scenes, the sum of successive scenes that have occurred. If we were to film user A's experience in the metaverse, taking a screenshot every ten seconds, saving it, and stitching it together, we would have a story with a single flow. Or, more simply, if you picked a few scenes and stitched them together around a shift, you'd have no trouble understanding the story.

Buttrick's phenomenological sermon reflects this lived experience of human beings, structuring the moves and shifts of a story or thought according to the preacher's rhetorical strategy.[28] Lowry's narrative preaching is also a way of organizing this experience, following a plot to organize scenes from the Bible and scenes from the world. Where the metaverse experience differs from the narrative experience envisioned by Lowry and Buttrick is that the metaverse is not only about language and text, but also about the three-dimensional virtual space that is represented by images, videos, and computer graphics. In other words, while traditional narrative sermons and phenomenological expository sermons are primarily based on a written text, the Bible, and provide a storytelling experience through the spoken language of the preacher, the metaverse combines text and spoken language with images, videos, and three-dimensional virtual space to create an empathic digital storytelling experience. This leads to the expectation that metaverse preaching will give the audience a vivid experience of the Word.

However, Soto's VR sermon exposes several problems. First, the experience of a metaverse sermon lacks physicality. The metaverse is essentially a virtual space embodied in digital information. Therefore, experiences in the metaverse are limited in that they are essentially digitally remediated experiences. Humans essentially perceive through their bodies. The experience gained through the avatar in the virtual space of the metaverse can only be a secondary experience through digital media, not a primary experience through the body. Therefore, it is impossible to experience the physicality of on-site preaching in a metaverse sermon. It is even harder to imagine a cartoonish avatar preacher and the interaction between the preacher and the audience as in a live sermon. This is why it is necessary to utilize the characteristics of the metaverse well, but it is not a good substitute for real-life preaching.

It should also be noted that the issue of manipulation of the sermon experience can arise. If the preacher predetermines how the audience will

---

28. Buttrick, *Homiletic*, 23, 32–34.

experience the sermon and embodies it in the metaverse, there is room for the audience's experience to be manipulated in ways that the preacher desires. A manipulated experience threatens the authenticity of the experience and its message. In this regard, I'm glad that Soto only constructed the biblical story space and didn't show the characters in the story. Technically, it would have been possible for one of the members of the VR Church to take on the role of a character in the story and relive the biblical narrative through their avatar, and it would have been possible for the preacher to engage the audience more deeply. However, in this case, the distance between the story being told by the preacher and the participants in the story would collapse, undermining the authenticity of the story they were experiencing. People trust a story when they feel it is a truthful story, and this requires that an appropriate aesthetic distance be maintained between the participants and the story. If this aesthetic distance is disrupted, and there is a strong sense that the preacher is trying to persuade with a fictionalized story, immersion in the story can be disrupted and the authenticity of the story undermined.[29] In this respect, Soto's Easter sermon, which did not feature the characters of the story, but traveled through the key spaces that make up the story and was guided by biblical text that appealed to the authenticity of the story, served to maintain an appropriate distance between the audience and the story they were experiencing.

The Relationship between Preacher and Audience

The next homiletical issue to consider is the relationship between the preacher and the audience. As we have seen, the metaverse is characterized by its use of various devices to facilitate interactivity between users, providing a user-oriented digital storytelling experience. These features intersect with the listener-oriented preaching advocated by contemporary homiletics. Fred Craddock argued for a turn to the listener, proposing an inductive sermon as a form of a listener-oriented sermon. Craddock's argument stemmed from the realities of the American church in the 1960s when democracy and postmodern culture were on the rise, and the perceived conflict between traditional homiletics' understanding of preaching as heralding, in which the preacher speaks on behalf of God, and the corresponding authoritarian image of the preacher as a divine agent. In Craddock's view, the way forward for the renewal of preaching in the American

---

29. Jung, "Distance in Preaching," 274–75.

church was to embrace the audience as partners in preaching and to move toward preaching that considers their hermeneutical experience. Craddock argued that the role of the listener is not to be a passive recipient of the message prepared by the preacher but to be a cocreator of the sermon, and it is based on this understanding that he proposed inductive preaching that reflects the hermeneutical experience of the audience.[30]

Craddock's arguments broke new ground in homiletics, and he received both praise and criticism from many pastors and homiletics scholars.[31] Craddock was criticized for deconstructing preaching by those who held to the traditional homiletical understanding of preaching and praised for providing a new paradigm for preaching by those who advocated for the innovation of preaching to meet the needs of the times and contemporary culture. A group of scholars radicalized Craddock's ideas, seeking more practically to engage the audience in the preaching event and create a more horizontal relationship between preacher and audience. The representative scholars are John McClure, who advocated for collaborative preaching, and Lucy Rose, who pursued conversational preaching.[32] McClure and Rose pointed out that Craddock's inductive preaching was still preacher-centered and limited the experience of the audience. While their point is valid, there are practical limitations: the congregation's actual participation in the sermon in a weekly church service is limited, so even if the congregation is involved in the preparation of the sermon through brainstorming or the preacher is conversational with the audience, a strictly egalitarian preacher/audience relationship is difficult to achieve.

However, metaverse preaching has the potential to eliminate this problem. As we've seen, a key feature that distinguishes the metaverse from previous digital media is that users are much more interactive than in previous media environments. While previous digital media, unlike print and analog broadcast media, left open but somehow limited avenues for content users to interact with creators, metaverse platforms have a variety of devices that allow users to interact with content creators in real-time. Also, unlike previous media, users are not just passively consuming content prepared by creators but can travel and explore the metaverse space and create their own metaverse experiences or stories. Finally, while acting through avatars

---

30. Craddock, *As One Without Authority*, 53–55.
31. Ottoni-Wilhelm, "= Turn to the Listener," 110–19.
32. McClure, *Roundtable Pulpit*, 7–8, 48–58; Rose, *Sharing the Word*, 89–131.

participants remain anonymous, allowing them to communicate freely regardless of real-world power relations.

Applying these media features of the metaverse to preaching may undermine the authoritarianism in preaching. While the authority of the preacher is still too much elevated in some traditions, preachers in metaverse preaching may no longer be able to claim a privileged authority as God's herald and can respect the congregation as a partner or cocreator of the preaching event. One can see that Soto tries to connect with his audience as members of his congregation rather than assert his authority as a pastor during his sermons. Soto constantly invites the audience to participate in the sermon, and his sermons are followed by Q&A sessions about the sermon. He played the role of guide for the homiletical journey rather than the role of authoritative expositor or a spiritual father.

This potential disempowerment of preachers might be considered a factor that makes metaverse preaching risky for some traditions that cherish clerical authority. However, I think it is required to construct a more egalitarian relationship between preachers and congregation, considering postmodern ethos. As it is increasingly evident that young generations avoid authoritarianism and seek mutual respect and egalitarian relationships, metaverse preaching that facilitates such a deauthoritarian ethos due to its tendency of decentralization would be more desirable for contemporary hearers.

CONCLUSION

During the pandemic, the world has experienced a rapid digital transformation in which human life has become more dependent on new digital media. Metaverse preaching is a phenomenon that emerged amid such a new technological innovation during the time. Investigating its characteristics as a new media platform, I showed that metaverse can construct a user-oriented digital storytelling experience in which users can create their own experiences of story, less bound to the content creator's designed experience. Owing to such a feature, metaverse preaching enables the participants to experience the homiletical trip in which they can explore the biblical worlds by themselves, and it can facilitate a deauthoritarian relationship between preacher and listener by conferring listeners a hermeneutical autonomy. Doubtlessly it could cause backlash and negative effects, as it does have drawbacks. Also, as it is still under construction, it is too hasty to convince what it would do. Thus, it would be unwise to take it as an ideal for a desirable preaching for the new era. However, as a compass is needed for a traveler who walks through the unknown path, I wish this chapter help those who are looking for a path as it is.

BIBLIOGRAPHY

Ball, Matthew. *The Metaverse: And How It Will Revolutionize Everything*. New York: Liveright, 2022.

Buttrick, David. *Homiletic: Moves and Structures*. Philadelphia: Fortress, 1987.

Cornerstone Church of Yuba City. "King Jesus Is Coming Soon! Revelation 1." Cornerstone Church of Yuba City, August 14, 2022, 1:28:12. https://www.youtube.com/watch?v=yTM4om3cHNY.

Craddock, Fred B. *As One Without Authority, Revised and with New Sermons*. St. Louis: Chalice, 2001.

Einselen, Sarah. "Life Church Adds One More Site—In Virtual Reality." *The Roys Report*, December 21, 2021. https://julieroys.com/life-church-multi-site-megachurch-virtual-reality/.

Harris, John, and Jeff Reed. *Sharing Jesus Online: Helping Everyday Believers Become Digital and Metaverse Missionaries*. Coppell, TX: Exponential, 2023.

Henao, Luis Andres. "Faith in the Metaverse: A VR Quest for Community, Fellowship." *Winnipeg Free Press*, January 31, 2022. https://www.winnipegfreepress.com/arts-and-life/life/faith/2022/01/31/faith-in-the-metaverse-a-vr-quest-for-community-fellowship.

Jeon, Young Mi. "Using Digital Storytelling in Religious Education." *Journal of Christian Education & Information Technology* [in Korean: 기독교교육정보] 28 (2011) 143–66.

Jung, Jaewoong. "Distance in Preaching: From the Perspective of Aesthetic Distance." *Theological Forum* [in Korean: 신학논단] 104 (2021) 267–303.

———. "Homiletical Assessment on Metaverse Preaching, Focusing on Characteristics of the Media and Contemporary Homiletical Discussions." *Theology and Praxis* [in Korean: 신학과 실천] 81 (2022) 173–208.

Karnadi, Chris. "The Future of Religion in the Metaverse." *Religion and Politics*, August 9, 2022. https://religionandpolitics.org/2022/08/09/the-future-of-religion-in-the-metaverse.

Lee, In Hwa. *What Is Metaverse?* [in Korean: 메타버스란 무엇인가]. Seoul: Story Friends, 2021.

Lee, Seung-Hwan. *Metaverse Begins: Revolution of Human Space and Time* [in Korean: 메타버스 비긴즈: 인간 공간 시간의 혁명]. Seoul: Good Morning Media, 2021.

Lowry, Eugene L. *The Sermon: Dancing the Edge of Mystery*. Nashville: Abingdon, 1997.

———. *The Homiletical Plot: The Sermon as Narrative Art Form*. Expanded ed. Louisville: Westminster John Knox, 2001.

Mannerfelt, Frida. "Listening to Listeners in a Digital Culture: The Practice of Listening to Digitally-Mediated Sermons." *Homiletic* 48.1 (2023) 16–31.

McClure, John. *The Roundtable Pulpit: Where Leadership and Preaching Meet*. Nashville: Abingdon, 1995.

O'Lynn, Rob. "The Digital Media Sermon: Definitions, Evaluations, Considerations," *Religions* 14 (2023) 736. https://doi.org/10.3390/rel14060736.

Ottoni-Wilhelm, Dawn. "The Turn to the Listener: Developing an Ear for Listening and Preaching." In *What's Right with Preaching Today*, edited by Mike Graves and Andre Resner, 110–32. Eugene, OR: Cascade, 2021.

Reed, Jeff. "Jason Poling and the Math of the Metaverse Mission Field." *Leadership Network*, February 20, 2022. https://leadnet.org/jason-poling-the-math-of-the-metaverse-mission-field.

———. *VR and Metaverse Church: How God Is Moving in This Virtual, Yet Quite Real, Reality*. Coppell, TX: Leadership Network, 2022.

Rose, Lucy A. *Sharing the Word: Preaching in the Roundtable Church*. Louisville: Westminster John Knox, 1997.

Ship of Fools. "Sermon at Church of Fools." YouTube, September 29, 2011, 1:08. https://www.youtube.com/watch?v=LotPrI3rzOY.

Smart, J. M., J. Cascio, and J. Paffendorf. "Metaverse Roadmap Overview." Metaverse Roadmap, 2007. https://www.metaverseroadmap.org/overview/.

VR MMO Church. "Easter at VR Church." YouTube, April 15, 2020, 1:18:54. https://www.youtube.com/watch?v=tpAcWhU-6Vg.

Yang, Sunggu. "The Word Digitalized: A Techno-Theological Reflection on Online Preaching and Its Types." *Homiletic* 46.1 (2021) 75–90.

6

Being There Even When You Are Not

Presence in Distance Preaching

TIM SENSING

INTRODUCTION

I first began asynchronous distance teaching in 1999. During that time, I have used four different learning management systems (LMS) to assist my teaching at a distance. While being the associate dean at a seminary for nine years, I reflected on all our teacher evaluations that students complete at the end of the term. While our faculty conveys a high level of pedagogical diversity, effective online faculty possessed a convergence around one theme in the student evaluations. Effective faculty, by various means, are successful because they establish "presence" even though they are absent.

What does asynchronous pedagogy have to teach preachers about preaching online?[1] More specifically, whether the event is a live stream or digital recording, "Can the preacher still be present when distant?"

---

1. In asking the question, I am not attempting to answer the questions of "how" to use technology or "how" to digitally produce the product. Those questions are better answered by others who have experience in digital media. Additionally, I am not addressing the theological question of the "real presence" of Christ in preaching often summarized by the phrase "the preached word of God is the Word of God" found in "Second Helvetic Confession." I am addressing the rhetorical side of the argument, not the theological side. Yet, method is a theological choice, and my theological convictions are evident as I make the following constructive theological proposal. See Knowles, "E-Word?" for a theological counter to my rhetorical argument.

Specifically, "How does the preacher engender ethos?" And "how does identification engender ethos?"[2]

I define "presence" as referring to both "presence in a place" and "presence at a time." When two people are present together in space and time, they can interact; make connections; and exchange ideas, feelings, and objects. Things present in space and time act directly on our sensibility, awareness, and receptivity. Furthermore, Veling notes, "The French philosopher Jacques Derrida is well known for his ability to ground his work in the fertile phenomenality of human life. He offers the following reflection on his approach to contextuality: 'This is my starting-point: no meaning can be determined out of context, but no context permits saturation.'"[3] Being absent, or not being present, is being "out of context." Derrida names this situation as "the metaphysics of presence." When Derrida includes temporal and spatial differentiation when describing *différence*, he includes both the notions of "differing" in space and "deferring" or "delaying" in time. Knowledge itself is contextual and changes over space and time. Writers, by definition, would not need to write if they were not absent from readers in both time and geographical separation. Derrida qualifies "presence" by saying there is no "saturation" even when in context.[4] So, it is not just the question, "Can the preacher still be present when distant?" but also, "Can the preacher be present when present?" A person is always "other" to another.

If Derrida is right, then, "presence" must also be qualified by noting that even in face-to-face (f2f) contexts, "otherness" exists. Veling suggests, "Every face we encounter is a face of otherness. Every face says: 'Don't kill me; don't absorb me into your world; don't obliterate me by making me the

---

2. "Ethos" according to Perelman and Olbrechts-Tyteca, *New Rhetoric*, 60–74, and "Identification" according to Burke, *Rhetoric of Motives*, 55, are acts by the speaker that are designed to persuade. But these are not the only two strategies available to the speaker. Various rhetorical devices are suggested in the literature for the overcoming of distance. According to *"Rhetorica ad Herennium,"* Book IV. LXVIII, *Hypotyposis* or *demonstratio*, for example, are figures "which sets things out in such a way that the matter seems to unfold, and the thing to happen, before our very eyes." Perelman and Olbrechts-Tyteca, *New Rhetoric*, 42, also suggest several other figures of speech such as repetition, anaphora, amplification, etc. to increase presence.

3. Veling, *Practical Theology*, 163, citing Derrida, "Living On," 81. See also Derrida *Writing and Difference* and *Positions*.

4. Derrida, *Positions*, 38–39.

same as you. I am other. I am different. I am not you."[5] Preachers are often absent and not present even when preaching in the same room.

The space between people is not a new phenomenon. Online preaching simply introduces some obvious time and space obstacles that limit how I traditionally preach in a f2f sanctuary. The disorientation of online preaching, especially heightened during the pandemic, makes an old problem visible. The "distance" in digital environments delimits my homiletical options. What was taken for granted and, therefore, unattended, in a f2f space, now becomes vital. Overcoming "distance" becomes a primary objective.[6]

ENGENDERING PRESENCE

The problem of being there even when you are not is not new. Ancient epistolary theorists regarded the letter as a substitute for one's actual conversation and presence. As written communications between two or more parties who are separated spatially, the letter functions as a substitute for being personally present. Letters provided personal information, make requests and recommendations, and promote goodwill between the sender

---

5. Veling, *Practical Theology*, 123, citing Levinas, *Totality and Infinity*, 185–219. See also McClure, *Other-Wise Preaching*, 31, 63–64.

6. The term "distance" is sometimes used differently from my use in the homiletical literature. Brothers (*Distance in Preaching*) advocates that some level of performative "distance" in preaching is necessary for hearing the sermon. He briefly surveys the literature (142–45) that promotes distance in preaching. I am not making that argument. I am saying that presence can be achieved or maintained even through distance. Brothers (*Distance in Preaching*, 47–87) discusses Craddock's (*Overhearing the Gospel*) recognition of the distance between the preacher and hearer. Craddock, therefore, speaks of "over-hearing" or indirection. Brothers, speaking of Craddock, states, "Distance preserves the integrity of the biblical text, is theologically and morally warranted as a function of sermon style, is beneficial to the hearer, and thus should be used 'intentionally' as part of the sermon style and delivery" (47). Brothers (140–41) acknowledges that critics of Craddock's use of "distance" belongs to a cultural setting that addresses people who "already know." Craddock is addressing a context that no longer exists in post-Christian America. We live in an age where biblical illiteracy abounds. The distance that familiarity fosters is not the issue. One might argue that narrative, through indirection, is still current and needed in a digital age. Yes, story works to create identification. However, I would advocate narrative, plotted toward a concrete dénouement, is needed. As one of my teachers would say, "Do not play hide and seek with the text." The distance of "not knowing" is overcome by direct speech.

and recipient. Classifications include letters of friendship, apologetic, paraenetic, protreptic, and others.

Cicero writes, "That there are many kinds of letters you are well aware; there is one kind, however, about which there can be no mistake, for indeed letter writing was invented just in order that we might inform those at a distance if there were anything which it was important for them or for ourselves that they should know."[7] A letter writer by definition is not there, and letter writing is subject to misinterpretation. The recipient cannot ask for immediate clarification. Therefore, a letter needed to be more intentional and precise than actual conversation. Clarity is essential; however, so too is the formation of ethos by establishing presence.[8]

Let me illustrate with Paul.[9] Although shaped by the form of letters in his day, Pauline letters also adapted and evolved the forms. Paul's letters are oral speech acts or recorded homilies. Paul's letters are neither epideictic, deliberative, nor forensic; however, they often contain elements and mixtures of all three in style and purpose. Paul made alterations to the basic form of the letter to suit purposes that tell us the most about his self-understanding, intentions, and theology. True letters are personal, dialogical, and the closest literary form to oral conversation that was available until recent years. When you read a letter, you can hear the writer talking and feel the writer's presence. Personality is revealed. Something of the situation is revealed. But, there is still distance. Letter writing gives the sense of being there and not being there at the same time. There is the blending of personal presence with the reality of absence.

First Thessalonians exemplifies the absence motif with the words προσώπῳ οὐ καρδίᾳ; essentially, "in person, not in spirit/heart" (1 Thess 2:17). The larger context reads, "As for us, brothers and sisters, when, for a short time, we were made orphans by being separated from you—in person, not in heart—we longed with great eagerness to see you face to face." This is how Paul described his absence from the Thessalonian believers. Paul felt that although he might not share in the presence of his sisters and brothers f2f, he nevertheless shared a deep and abiding fellowship on a heart level with them that transcended the distance between them. Did the Thessalonians feel the same way? The thought Paul expresses has tremendous power, but were the feelings mutual? Did the Thessalonians feel as strongly

---

7. Cicero, *Cicero*, 100–101.
8. White, "Ancient Greek Letters," 86.
9. Note my "Bibliography on Paul."

about their connection to their teacher as Paul seems to feel about his bond with them? Theologically, the answer is "yes," although there is no proof.

I believe that what Paul is saying back then is also in the present tense for a twenty-first century congregation. Today, Paul's letters are even more asynchronous distance proclamations separated by even a wider gap in time, space, culture, and language. When the travel distance is greater, therefore, the attention to traversing the distance is more needful. It is the recipients' responses that most interest me here, whether the Thessalonians or us.

Funk identifies the travelogue as the primary place Paul communicates personal presence. He identifies five elements: (1) mention of Paul's letter writing activity, (2) mention of his relationship with the recipients, (3) statement of plans for paying a visit (desire to visit, delays in coming, sending an emissary, announcement of a visit), (4) invocation of divine approval and support for the visit (connected to a request for prayer, their prayer, or his own prayer), and (5) benefits of the impending visit of Paul to the recipients.[10] Funk goes on to describe how Paul's presence in a letter is considered the same as if he were personally present among his recipients.[11]

Owing to Paul's understanding of the significance of his apostolic presence to his congregation (and, of course, the significance of their presence to him, e.g., 2 Cor 7:6–7, 13b–16; 1 Thess 3:6–8 [cf., 2:19–18]; Phil 4:14–18), Paul gathers the items that may be scattered about in the common letter or appended as additional information, into one more or less discrete section, in which he: (a) implies that the letter is an anticipatory surrogate for his presence; (b) commends the emissary who is to represent him in the meantime; and (c) speaks of an impending visit or a visit for which he prays. Through these media, his apostolic authority and power are made effective.[12]

Friendship is dependent upon the presence of the parties to each other.[13] Friendship letters, especially, are key to establishing the author's presence. Funk describes how the motif "absent in body, but present through letter," can be traced from the beginning of the Christian era well into the

---

10. Funk, "Apocalyptic 'Parousia,'" 252–53.
11. Funk, "Apocalyptic 'Parousia,'" 264.
12. Funk, "Apocalyptic 'Parousia,'" 266.
13. Aristotle, *On Rhetoric*, 1, 2.16; 2, 4:1–28.

Middle Ages and represents well-known formulae of Greek epistolography (e.g., 1 Cor 5:3; Col 2:5; Phil 1:27; 2:12).[14]

Being a written record, a letter transcends time and space. For example, a company receives a note from a satisfied customer who details reasons why the employees deserve commendation. The manager of the company posts the letter on the breakroom's bulletin board. Employees, over the next several months, read the letter that praises their good service. The customer's praise is copied to a newsletter and posted on the website. Finally, the letter is placed in a folder for archival purposes. There is a lasting quality due to its preservation. You can read it again. And each time it is read, even through multiple mediums, the customer's presence is felt. The customer's intent to praise impacts the employees' feelings of goodwill and prompts them to continue to act hospitably on the behalf of future customers. You see this same dynamic when students or alumni write to their professors, evaluate courses through qualitative questionnaires, or post comments on websites. And if you personally know the customer, student, or alumnus, you also experience their presence even though they may live in another region, province, or country.

Two scenes from the film version of Alice Walker's novel The *Color Purple* illustrate these points.[15] The first scene is set in a world controlled by abuse. Celie's abuse comes from three sources: her father, her husband, and society at large. There is seemingly no escape. The climax of Celie's initial response is seen in her desire to slit her husband's throat. She is on the front porch of the ramshackle house that imprisons her. As she shaves her abuser with a straight razor, she hesitates as she draws the blade near his jugular vein.

In the second scene, Celie discovers a set of long-hidden letters from her missionary sister in Africa.[16] Through reading the letters, she imagines a different life, she experiences the immediate presence of her sister. She imagines what life could have been. She imagines an alternative way of being in the world. Reading these texts, so to speak, from a situation so far removed from her own as to be nearly untranslatable, Celie encounters "a world in front of the letters," a world where black women can write, travel, think, mature, and be free. And when she encounters this world, a world

---

14. Funk, "Apocalyptic '*Parousia*,'" 264.

15. The example of *The Color Purple* is borrowed from Greenhaw, "Changing the World."

16. Zam Zhinga, "Color Purple."

emerging in front of these texts, her own world is enlarged. In the film, it is only after she imagines this new world and its new possibilities that she has the courage and capacity to get off the porch, leave her abuser, and change her world. As the story of Celie moves to resolution, Celie finds redemption. Celie begins to heal and live in a new way of being. The letters Celie reads were written asynchronously, from a different time and place, yet communicated a life-changing presence.

ENGENDERING PRESENCE THROUGH ETHOS

Persuasion through the character of the speaker or ethos corresponds with one of the most recognizable definitions of preaching in the modern era. Brooks stated preaching is "the communication of truth through man to men" or, as it is more often said, "preaching is truth communicated through personality."[17]

The concept of "voice" is often connected to ethos. Reid describes voice as the "assumptions" of the preachers' stances, personas, and "implied identities" that shape their "effects" and reveal their cultural consciousness.[18] Aristotle argues that a person's character as communicated in the speech is the single most important ingredient to persuasion.[19] Aristotle elaborated, "There are three reasons why speakers themselves are persuasive; for these are three things we trust other than logical demonstrations. These are practical wisdom (*phronesis*) and virtue (*arête*) and goodwill (*eunoia*)."[20] Reid summarizes the three canons of persuasion as follows, "Congregants come to trust wise counsel (*logos*) from the preacher who seems to possess good character (*ethos*), who becomes appropriately passionate (*pathos*) about matters that the community views as central to their corporate shared

---

17. Brooks, *Lectures on Preaching*, 5, 8. Sometimes, though technically different, similar discussions about the preacher, author, or writer's "presence" occur when looking at the rhetorical categories of voice, stance, or tone. Voice often connects to the "authenticity" of the rhetor. Authenticity is interrelated to the speaker's character and ethos. In rhetorical studies, the connection between voice and presence is debated (see for example "authorial presence" or "authorial intention")

18. Reid, *Four Voices of Preaching*, 12. Reid's use of "voice" differs from Cicero's classical canons of rhetoric where voice is discussed under "delivery."

19. Aristotle, *On Rhetoric*, 1.2.4.

20. Aristotle, *On Rhetoric*, 2.1.5.

identity."[21] Although all three—*logos*, *ethos*, and *pathos*—contribute to the preacher's credibility and authenticity, *ethos* is primary.

Historically, ethos is defined in three ways. First, as a mode of persuasion that relies upon the virtue of the speaker. For example, Plato's essentialist view relied on the speaker's character. Plato defined the role of rhetoric as instruction in ideal truth. In *Gorgias*, the object of persuasion is the cultivation of the moral good. For example, "Socrates: Well then Polus, if you prefer to hear it from me, that it is better when these things are done justly."[22] Only an orator with intrinsic virtue could instruct others in moral values and bring about order. Or, as seen in Isocrates, *Antidosis*, who talks about the same words carry greater conviction when spoken by one with good repute than spoken by a person who lives under a cloud.[23] A person's life carries greater weight than his or her words. Likewise, Quintilian, when discussing the importance of moral education for young pupils, argues that "no one can be an orator who is not a good [person].["24] Ethos is the embodiment of a preexisting state of virtue in the speaker. More recently, this neoplatonic view might be best seen in Booth's *Modern Dogma and the Rhetoric of Assent*.

Secondly, ethos is defined as a mode of persuasion that relies upon the speaker creating a credible character for a particular rhetorical occasion in a single speech act. For example, Aristotle's relativistic attitude relied on the occasion of the rhetorical event. Aristotle's concern focused on rhetoric as a means of bringing about decisions in matters affecting civil life. Ethos conveys credibility. Effective ethos inspires the audience's confidence in the speaker's good sense, moral character, and goodwill. Not to be confused with the speaker's reputation or social authority, ethos must be created at the moment by the speech itself. The speaker might even adapt the speech in order to meet the expectations of different audiences. The speaker tries to anticipate the response of the audience and adjust the speech accordingly. Speakers will be persuasive, according to Aristotle, when speakers have characteristics we trust, namely wisdom, virtue, and goodwill.[25]

Cicero sounds like Aristotle but relies more on the speaker creating sympathy in the audience. Cicero states that ethos depends on securing

21. Reid, *Four Voices of Preaching*, 17.
22. Plato, "Georgias," 75.
23. Isocrates, "Antidosis," 52.
24. Quintilion, "Institutes of Oratory," Book II XV, 33.
25. Aristotle, *On Rhetoric*, 1.2, 2.1, 7–17.

the audience's goodwill and depends upon the speaker's ability to present a favorable character and moral conduct.[26] Also, for Cicero, ethos or *dignitas* develops over time, and emerges from (1) natural talent for eloquence; (2) prudent character (the ability to adapt a discourse to any situation by conveying to the audience the moral issues at stake and the need to adhere to the cause he is championing); and (3) passion and commitment. Cicero did not talk about ethos under the category of invention, but under the categories of style and delivery—a trend seen often among the later stoics who downplayed ethos (as part of the exordium) and pathos (as part of the epilogue).

So, the discussion of ethos in rhetoric has either been a division between instructions for the moral good or the facilitation of decisions and actions. Sometimes this division is artificially drawn between the Greek democratic society and the Roman more autocratic society. The artificial nature of the argument is seen in Plato's *Phaedrus*, where he states that the orator should possess a good character and be knowledgeable, alert, and able to adapt an argument to the audience.[27]

Christians relied on a more platonic approach as seen in Augustine's *On Christian Doctrine*.[28] Augustine emphasized the piety of the preacher. Without piety, the preacher cannot interpret the Scriptures; without being able to understand God's word, the preacher cannot explain it to others. However, throughout the Middle Ages, when the emphasis was on the instruction of skills for professional and civil use, the public was taught the Aristotelian–Ciceronian approach to ethos; namely, the importance of adjusting the presentation of character to the audience's context and subject at hand.

Augustine's high view of ethos persisted in homiletics as seen in George Campbell's *Philosophy of Rhetoric* and Hugh Blair's *Lectures on Rhetoric and the Belles Lettres*. They also argued that every speaker must be perceived as a wise and good person in order to appeal to the audience's intelligence and emotions. Adjusting the presentation of the self to the expectations of those addressed involved convincing the audience. Campbell and Blair, not using the word ethos, but sympathy, argued the speaker must establish sympathy with the audience to engage the emotions that move the will.

26. Cicero, "Of Oratory," 1:31; 2:42.
27. Plato, "Phaedrus," 131.
28. Augustine, *On Christian Doctrine*, IV: 59–63.

Much of this argument about ethos anticipates Perelman, where the speaker must inspire confidence and appear to be credible. Perelman discusses ethos in the context of self-praise and attacks upon the opponent. In my reading of Perelman, while he acknowledges that the individual speech act should inspire confidence, the character of the speaker is paramount. "A worldly or irreligious cleric who goes up into the pulpit is just a phrasemonger. On the other hand, there are saintly [persons] whose character, alone, carries the power of persuasion. They appear moved and, as it were, persuaded by their presence. The sermon they are about to preach will do the rest."[29] That sounds like Quintilian who says, "The same language is often natural when used by one speaker, foolish in the mouth of another, and arrogant in that of a third."[30]

It reminds me of the white college student MLK Day speaker, who said the same words and even imitated the style of King, yet appeared foolish, at least with the folks sitting in my aisle. His presence created distance. The MLK speaker's failure to bridge the distance leads me to speak of the final way ethos is established, i.e., through identification.[31]

ENGENDERING ETHOS THROUGH IDENTIFICATION

Burke defines "identification" by saying, "You persuade [people] only insofar as you talk [their] language by speech, gesture, tonality, order, image,

29. Perelman and Olbrechts-Tyteca, *New Rhetoric,* 318–19, citing La Bruyère, *Euvres Complètes,* 464.

30. Perelman and Olbrechts-Tyteca, *New Rhetoric,* citing Quintilian, *Institutio Oratoria of Quintilian,* XI, i, 37.

31. The term "identification" possesses a wide semantic field ranging from everyday language to philosophy to psychoanalysis. Burke, *Rhetoric of Motives,* provides an in-depth look at "identification" in rhetoric. See such categories as "identification and consubstantiality," "identifying the nature of property," and "identification and the autonomous," to name a few categories that push beyond rhetoric. Yet, Burke also cites the usual suspects in rhetorical studies, e.g., persuasion and the use of symbols. Loscalzo, *Preaching Sermons that Connect,* is one of the few authors who incorporate Burke's work into the preaching field. Identification overcomes dissociation and alienation between the speaker and the audience. Is that not what the mystery of the incarnation is all about? To identify with the congregation, the preacher must know the people (be one with the people). The preacher will need to be aware of the real concerns, dreams, hurts, and weaknesses of the people who come expecting to hear a word from the Lord. Only then is change possible. Therefore, Loscalzo offers strategies that both enable the preacher to analyze the congregation and build sermons that will bring about identification. Loscalzo concludes with a chapter on how delivery contributes to identification.

attitude, idea, identifying your ways with [theirs]."[32] Identification crosses boundaries to share experiences and perspectives of another. Some would argue that instead of persuasion, Burke's identification redefines rhetoric itself.[33] Identification is portrayed in the literature as more hospitable and collaborative than persuasion. Identification is established on the common experience that is shared.

Reid, Fleer, and Bullock argue that the new homiletic is built around the experience the speech act generates. Through an examination of the Sophists, experience and ethos closely resemble Burke's identification.[34] During the pandemic, the congregation was not in the same room.[35] Most of us experienced the alienating effects of the screen on our TVs or laptops. Reciting the Lord's Prayer in digital space felt lonely. You could say, "The church has left the building." Can I get a nod of recognition? The rhetorical idea of "identification," the nod of recognition, overcomes distance. The memetic experience creates identification. Identification establishes affinities between two parties, so the other can experience the unfamiliar.

Identification is a way a speaker generates ethos to overcome the distance that exists between the speaker and the listener even if the two are in the same room, and even more so if separated by time and space. I speak of digging postholes and stretching barbed wire when speaking to cattle farmers in Oplin, Texas. But the farmers in Trent, Texas, raise cotton. I do not have a hook in my experience with cotton farmers. I need a different identifier for them. Identification is a way to overcome such division, estrangement, separation, alienation, and distance. Identification creates belonging to overcome isolation and joins people together. When people identify with one another, like sharing the experience of listening to sermons during the pandemic, they share a common experience that generates an affinity between them. Not even time or space can divide people

---

32. Burke, *Rhetoric of Motives*, 55.
33. As the quote above indicates, Burke himself would not make this claim.
34. Reid et al., "Preaching as the Creation."
35. A review of how churches responded to the pandemic in significant ways is found in Campbell's two articles "Distanced Church" and "What Religious Groups Need to Consider." Additionally, worship leaders exasperated these uncharted digital waters by practicing "ministry transliteration by simply changing to digital platforms and presuming that the methodology that was somewhat effective in face-to-face context would be equally or even more effective digitally" (Ashlin-Mayo, *Digital Mission*, 5). See also research on digital preaching and the problem of presence in Bishop, "Sensing the Presence."

when they share common sympathies, interests, backgrounds, or other consubstantial elements. If people share a common ground, an experience, then a rapport develops. A person might develop a rapport with a character in a book, a politician on the radio, or a subject in a newsfeed. And if the sermon creates affiliation through sharing a common experience, the speaker's ethos grows, and distance is overcome.[36] And even though sharing the same "essence" or a strict consubstantiation is not always possible, there is a sense of recognition that is possible.[37]

One way to move toward an identification through resonance is by using narratives. Auerbach's *Mimesis* contrasts two literary worlds of ancient Greece and biblical scriptures, hence his subtitle, *The Representation of Reality in Western Literature*.[38] He describes how a telling of a story becomes a "representation" for the transformation of the reader/hearer because of their mimetic participation. Accordingly, I too define *mimesis* as more than mirrored imitation, but a poetic/performative/representative act. Mimetic acts are representations of reality. If the story represents the lived experience of the hearer, identification increases. Has a chill overtaken you when the storyteller describes her blue lips, numb toes, and frozen breath as the sun sets in northern Alaska? Do you recall the joy you felt after the birth of your own child when the movie gives you a close-up of a childless couple walking into the maternity wing to meet their adopted newborn daughter? Did you catch Celie's excitement when you watched a clip of the scene from *The Color Purple* on YouTube? The closer the story imitates life, the more you are drawn into the experience yourself. Identification occurs.

36. Similarly, bonding might also occur when people share a common opposition to an idea or group. An "us" versus "them," identifying a common enemy, often bonds people who might otherwise not connect.

37. Burke, *Rhetoric of Motives*, 20, 65. The literature on identification develops Burke's notions by exploring in-depth how narrative functions to fill the gaps between two parties. The use of identification in narrative is also seen as early as Aristotle. Identification happens when the audience connects with the "familiar" concrete situations of life and persons more than some anonymous or distant event or person according to Aristotle, *Poetics*, XIV.4. And in those particulars, the hearer will glimpse something common to all (the universals). Swinton and Mowat (*Practical Theology*, 45) recognize a degree of shared experiences that are common to humans and suggest the category of "resonance." I see "resonance" as a way to mediate between mere recognition and consubstantiation. Research from a particular context is not directly transferred in a one-to-one fashion to another, but a degree of resonance can invoke a sense of identification and fittingness. While no context is identical to another, there are enough similar experiences and phenomena between two settings for someone else to utilize.

38. Auerbach, *Mimesis*.

The word *poetics* (ποιητικός) means "things that are created, crafted, or made." The poetic arts are not copies, but are creative acts of representing realities into other mediums. When using words as the medium, by an act of imagination, the maker of the art is rendering realities or actions into language. Aristotle's *Poetics* primarily talks about how the Greek tragedy represents the dramatic field at its height. While Aristotle talks about other dramatic works such as comedies and epics, his work is fragmentary and only supplements what he says about tragedy. Additionally, he explicitly connects what he says about tragedy to include other artists, such as painters, musicians, sculptors, and dancers.[39] The potential intersection of drama and preaching is intriguing. Aristotle notes that the arts are essential for public education.[40] Art education is analogous to religious arts, practices, and rituals in their symbolic enactments, initiation processes, and socialization functions. The arts these poets make, by definition, represent an object by imitating the life and action of an object. The arts are representations of the countless forms the world and human life may take. If preaching is an art form, then it has the potential to create mimetic affect in order to increase identification with the audience.[41]

When a sermon is preached online, for some listeners, the preacher will only have a delimited opportunity to establish presence through ethos via identification within the single-speech act. These stratagems might work in the context of a single oration, e.g., an attorney presenting the case to a jury that has no previous experience with the lawyer. Although professionally produced in ways that preaching fifty-two times each year cannot imitate, TED Talks exhibit a similar effect. This is sometimes the case for a preacher too. In an online environment, the necessity of this being the case increases. How does this happen? While the ancient rhetors describe rhetorical techniques that enhance the speaker's ability to establish ethos in a single-speech act, the ecclesial demands of pastoral relationships call for something else. Presence must involve *koinonia*—participation in a communal relationship.

On the one hand, while some television evangelists use rhetorical tactics for nonvirtuous ends, the issue is for them, "as long as it works, it is acceptable." Hendahl warns, "A devaluation of the role of ethos is actually at work in television preaching. Religious programming often stresses

39. Aristotle, *Poetics*, I.4–5, II.3.
40. Aristotle, *Politics*, VIII.
41. Sensing, "Aristotle's *Poetics*."

overall context, thus diverting any critical assessment of character through emphasis on beautiful music, attire, setting, and a reassuring mix of secular and religious symbols and cliched speech."[42]

On the other hand, when virtuous motives fund practice the question remains, "How can the preacher establish ethos in a single speech act?" Perhaps the answer lies in asking 1,000 home viewers why they never miss watching a popular preacher on live stream on Sunday. Is it because the preacher engenders presence through mechanics/lighting/story/gesture, etc., because they trust the preacher's reputation, because of the preacher's charisma (being an Enneagram 3), because they know the preacher in person; so, is it about the relationship, or simply due to convenience? While the option of watching the Sunday morning worship hour is not new, the phenomenon is happening, with increasing frequency, as Christians choose to watch sermons on the internet.

Conversely, when the single-speech act does not engender the ethos desired, the number of views anticipated, or the "likes" are few, the questions about competency, calling, and significance begin to whittle down the preacher's confidence. Questions emerge as to the theological significance of a single-speech act. For presence to exist, time is necessary. Maybe the value of the single speech act is merely to open the door for more meaningful encounters. The ecclesial problem of distance is not delimited to the sermon, but the distance in relationships and community that the online environment inhabits. Online services exasperated the lack of community that already existed within the four walls of many ecclesial structures. The church is called to be a communal body, where people engage, support, and care for each other. Campbell notes how the concept of "social distancing is highly problematic because . . . physical separation at times of increased isolation will lead to increased fear, anxiety, and depression."[43] She calls this situation a "disembodied" church.[44]

The preacher's ethos and presence develop over time. It does not emerge in a single-speech act, but listeners will tune in week after week, download multiple sermons over time, and maybe view the same sermon or podcast multiple times. My mother, for example, faithfully tunes in every Sunday to the same Facebook live feed week after week. The listeners in these cases, like my mother, have a previous orientation to the preacher

---

42. Hendal, "Character," 67.
43. Campbell, *Distanced Church*, 4.
44. Campbell, *Distanced Church*, 4.

and already trust the preacher's reputation, and demonstrate their affinity by coming back every Sunday. The listeners already have a predisposition that the preacher functions as father/pastor/one with authority before they press play. And like my mother, they deem the preacher as a "good and virtuous" human.

I am persuaded by Cicero's *dignitas* argument that ethos develops over time and involves multiple factors. Much of the preacher's ethos emerges from the previous pastoral relationship with the audience or that which happened prior to the sermon. Paul knew the Thessalonians well before he wrote to them. Campbell lists six "communication traits" that online worshippers most value about their communities that represent a dialogue about what *dignitas* might mean online. These six traits enhance the re-embodiment of the online community: (1) a sense of relationship; (2) looking for care—a "space where they can give and receive support and encouragement"; (3) looking for value—they want to be seen and appreciated as significant persons; (4) they long for connection with others; (5) looking for "intimate communication—a safe place where they are themselves and communicate openly with others"; and (6) they want to associate with others who share their faith commitments.[45]

My convictions may lie in the fact that I am cynical about the power of one isolated speech act being able to establish *dignitas*, presence, and ethos; and I am convinced that the normative power of a sermon derives its impact over time and is built through relationships. For example, I know a minister whose ministry in the community and in the foyer is what makes him a good preacher. Although his preaching ministry is less than five years old, through the lost art of "visitation," he has established an ethos in the pulpit. His ethos is more dependent upon his character and reputation than any particular speech act's ability to create sympathy.

One concrete implication of these musings on presence is that the preacher must leverage the opportunity to establish presence—sacramental priestly presence. The preacher attends to the "give and take" dynamic of personal communication, empathy, and care. Answering, responding, listening, exploring, and the other aspects of f2f presence gives an opportunity to thrive in the online environment. The technological advancements available through various digital media options enable the preacher to make these priestly connections intentionally. Often, listeners who might not speak in a f2f environment will become quite prolific online. In a f2f

---

45. Campbell, "What Religious Groups Need," 50.

context, a listener might sit in the back, never interact, and leave quickly. The online environment, for these listeners, creates a safe space. They may email, make comments in the chat, or engage in other social media mediums. The more the online listener encounters your presence, your self, your pathos for the Gospel, your pathos for them, and your commitment to engagement, the opportunity for hearing increases dramatically (see appendix A for other applications).

CONCLUSIONS

The speaker's need to overcome absence and engender presence is not new. Practicing the art of establishing ethos and identification existed long before technology's arrival. Distance by time, space, and otherness has long been traversed by multiple mediums for thousands of years. Digital platforms and social media give churches and ministers opportunities to hold space for developing a relationship and witnessing the Gospel.

APPENDIX A. OTHER CONCRETE POSSIBILITIES

While there are rhetorical techniques for online preachers that would enhance their ability to create presence in a single-speech act, for my purposes, the philosophical musings on the topic of presence by John Hadley, *On Presence*, prove helpful. I will conclude with these musings as suggestive of concrete possibilities for online preaching that cohere with ancient letter writing.

Philosophical Musings:

1. Here is a list of characteristics needed to establish a personal presence within the act of communication—an offering of the self. While Hadley is not addressing a religious context, I have taken the liberty to frame his ideas for preaching:

    a. Presence must include significant content. Attending to the logos of the act of communication is vital, although over-attention to content delivery and content coverage can also limit presence. Too much of a good thing is not so good in this instance because not all content is significant.

    b. The preacher must be open to self-disclosure.

SENSING ♦ BEING THERE EVEN WHEN YOU ARE NOT

    c. The preacher must anticipate a response from the other. Providing some feedback mechanism is vital, e.g., a chat room.

    d. The preacher is hospitable to the opportunity to form a personal relationship, e.g., invitations to one-on-one communications.

    e. And, similarly, provide an opportunity for the development of a network of relationships.

    f. Establish an environment of trustworthiness/genuineness.

    g. Provide an opportunity for the other to also offer their presence.

    h. Presence moves towards love and hope.

    i. Presence cannot be possessed, but only experienced in giving.

    j. Presence must move beyond content and emotion for it to be holistic. A whole person must move toward being fully present with another whole person.

2. Yet, there are also limits to the act of communication that exists when one is distant in either time or space:

    a. It is not just the physical distance, but also the psychological, emotional, and spiritual distance that requires attention.

    b. We can only be present to others to the extent that we have become present to ourselves.

    c. The lack of trust or ethos limits presence. We do not disclose ourselves fully or with genuineness.

    d. Recipient's lack of presence-to-self.

    e. The other is still other (Derrida). You can never know another fully.

BIBLIOGRAPHY

Aristotle. *Poetics*. Translated by Francis Ferguson. New York: Hill and Wang, 1961.

———. *Politics*. 2nd ed. Translated by Carnes Lord. Chicago: University of Chicago Press, 1984.

———. *On Rhetoric: A Theory of Civic Discourse*. Translated by George A. Kennedy. New York: Oxford University Press, 1991.

Ashlin-Mayo, Bryce. *Digital Mission: A Practical Guide for Ministry Online*. Toronto: Tyndale, 2020.

Auerbach, Erich. *Mimesis: The Representation of Reality in the Western World*. Princeton Classic Edition. Princeton: Princeton University Press, 2013.

Augustine. *On Christian Doctrine*. Translated by D. W. Robertson, Jr. The Library of the Liberal Arts. New York: Macmillan, 1958.

Bishop, Justin Dwight. "Sensing the Presence of God through Online Worship at Heritage Fellowship, Canton, Georgia." DMin thesis, McAfee School of Theology, Mercer University, 2022.

Blair, Hugh. "Lectures on Rhetoric and the Belles Lettres." In *The Rhetorical Tradition: Readings from Classical Times to the Present*, edited by Patricia Bizzell and Bruce Herzberg, 796–827. Boston: Bedford, 1990.

Booth, Wayne. *Modern Dogma and the Rhetoric of Assent*. South Bend: University of Notre Dame Press, 1974.

Brooks, Phillips. *Lectures on Preaching: Delivered Before the Divinity School of Yale College in January and February 1877*. New York: E. P. Dutton, 1877.

Brothers, Michael. *Distance in Preaching: Room to Speak, Space to Listen*. Grand Rapids: Eerdmans, 2014.

Burke, Kenneth. *Rhetoric of Motives*. Berkeley: University of California Press, 1969.

Campbell, George. "Philosophy of Rhetoric." In *The Rhetorical Tradition: Readings from Classical Times to the Present*, edited by Patricia Bizzell and Bruce Herzberg, 746–95. Boston: Bedford, 1990.

Campbell, Heidi A., ed. *The Distanced Church: Reflections on Doing Church Online*. Network for New Media, Religion & Digital Culture Studies. College Station, TX: TAMU Digital Religion Publications, 2020. https://hdl.handle.net/1969.1/187891.

———. "What Religious Groups Need to Consider When Trying to Do Church Online." In *The Distanced Church: Reflections on Doing Church Online*, edited by Heidi A. Campbell, 49–52. Network for New Media, Religion & Digital Culture Studies. College Station, TX: TAMU Digital Religion Publications, 2020. https://hdl.handle.net/1969.1/187891.

———. *Revisiting the Distanced Church*. Network for New Media, Religion & Digital Culture Studies. College Station, TX: TAMU Digital Religion Publications, 2021. https://hdl.handle.net/1969.1/193368.

Cicero, Marcus Tullius. *Cicero. The Letters to His Friends I (Books I–VI)*. Loeb Classical Library 205. Translated by W. Glynn Williams. Cambridge: Harvard University Press, 1965.

———. "Of Oratory." In *The Rhetorical Tradition: Readings from Classical Times to the Present*, edited by Patricia Bizzell and Bruce Herzberg, 200–250. Boston: Bedford, 1990.

Craddock, Fred. *Overhearing the Gospel: Preaching and Teaching the Faith to Persons Who Have Heard It All Before*. Nashville: Abingdon, 1986.

Derrida, Jacque. *Writing and Difference*. Translated by Alan Bass. Chicago: Chicago University Press, 1975.

———. *Positions*. Translated by Alan Bass. Chicago: Chicago University Press, 1981.

———. "Living On." In *Deconstruction and Criticism*, edited by Harold Bloom et al., 75–176. Translated by Harold Hulbert. New York: Continuum, 1986.

Funk, Robert W. "The Apostolic 'Parousia': Form and Function." In *Christian History and Interpretation*, edited by W. R. Farmer et al., 249–68. Cambridge: Cambridge University Press, 1967.

Greenhaw, David M. "Changing the World in Front of the Preacher: Ricoeur's Theory of the Text as a Model for Preaching for Social Change." *Academy of Homiletics Working Papers* 18 (2012) 15–20.

Hadley, John. "On Presence." *The New Blackfriars* 86 (2005) 505–17.

Hendahl, Susan K. "Character." In *Concise Encyclopedia of Preaching*, edited by William H. Willimon and Richard Lischer, 66–67. Louisville: Westminster John Knox, 1995.
Isocrates. "Antidosis." In *The Rhetorical Tradition: Readings from Classical Times to the Present*, edited by Patricia Bizzell and Bruce Herzberg, 50–54. Boston: Bedford Books, 1990.
Knowles, Michael P. "E-Word? McLuhan, Baudrillard, and Verisimilitude in Preaching." *Religions* 13 (2022) 1131. https://doi.org/10.3390/rel13121131.
La Bruyère, Jean de. *Œuvres Complètes*. Established and Annotated by Julien Benda and Bibliothèque de la Pléiade. Paris: Gallimard, 1941.
Levinas, Emmanuel. *Totality and Infinity: An Essay on Exteriority*. Translated by Alphonso Lingis. Pittsburgh: Duquesne University Press, 1969.
Loscalzo, Craig A. *Preaching Sermons that Connect: Effective Communication through Identification*. Downers Grove, IL: InterVarsity, 1992.
McClure, John S. *Other-Wise Preaching: A Postmodern Ethic for Homiletics*. St. Louis: Chalice, 2001.
Perelman, Chaim, and Lucie Olbrechts-Tyteca. *The New Rhetoric*. Translated by John Wilkenson and Purcell Weaver. South Bend: University of Notre Dame Press, 1971.
Plato. "Gorgias." In *The Rhetorical Tradition: Readings from Classical Times to the Present*, edited by Patricia Bizzell and Bruce Herzberg, 61–112. Boston: Bedford, 1990.
———. "Phaedrus." In *The Rhetorical Tradition: Readings from Classical Times to the Present*, edited by Patricia Bizzell and Bruce Herzberg, 113–43. Boston: Bedford, 1990.
Quintilian. *The Institutio Oratoria of Quintilian*. Translated by H. E. Butler. Loeb Classical Library. New York: G. P. Putnam's Sons, 1921–33.
———. "The Institutes of Oratory." In *The Rhetorical Tradition: Readings from Classical Times to the Present*, edited by Patricia Bizzell and Bruce Herzberg, 297–363. Boston: Bedford, 1990.
Reid, Robert, et al. "Preaching as the Creation of an Experience: The Not-So-Rational Revolution of the New Homiletic." *Journal of Communication and Religion* 18 (1995) 1–9.
Reid, Robert. *Four Voices of Preaching*. Grand Rapids: Brazos, 2006.
"Rhetorica ad Herennium." In *The Rhetorical Tradition: Readings from Classical Times to the Present*, edited by Patricia Bizzell and Bruce Herzberg, 252–92. Boston: Bedford, 1990.
Sensing, Tim. "Aristotle's *Poetics*: Comparative Offerings to Homiletical Theory and Practice." *Homiletic* 42 (2017) 9–17. http://www.homiletic.net/index.php/homiletic/issue/view/208.
———. "Bibliography on Paul 2024." HomileticalSensings (blog), 2024. https://blogs.acu.edu/sensingt/resources/.
Swinton, John, and Harriet Mowat. *Practical Theology*. London: SCM, 2006.
The Second Helvetic Confession. *The Book of Confessions, The Constitution of the Presbyterian Church (USA), Part I*. Louisville: The Office of the General Assembly, 1969.
Veling, Terry A. *Practical Theology: "On Earth as It Is in Heaven."* Maryknoll, NY: Orbis, 2005.
White, John L. "Ancient Greek Letters." In *Greco-Roman Literature and the New Testament*, edited by David E. Aune, 85–106. Atlanta: Scholars Press, 1988.
Zam Zhinga. "The Color Purple." YouTube, July 20, 2014, 2:48. https://www.youtube.com/watch?v=RvTXbN7fqz4.

7

E-Word?

McLuhan, Baudrillard, and Verisimilitude in Preaching

MICHAEL P. KNOWLES

"We live in a world where there is more and more information, and less and less meaning."

—JEAN BAUDRILLARD, *SIMULACRA AND SIMULATION*, 79

INTRODUCTION

The fact that, in recent years, pastors on the technology-rich side of the digital divide have had to adapt their preaching to online modes of presentation calls for renewed consideration of the specifically theological implications of virtual proclamation. The critical issue is whether or not the content of the Christian message mandates a distinct form of communication or, conversely, whether online proclamation conforms to the theological constraints of Christian faith. In one sense, the problem is hardly new: if the preacher is nothing more than magnetic or optical coding on a tape or disc, rebroadcast at a suitably convenient hour, has the gospel truly been proclaimed? To what are viewers responding? Need they respond at all? The same questions apply to earlier forms of technology: can a sound recording, or the combination of sound recording with a series of silver halide images creating the illusion of movement convey a true representation of gospel truth?

Not all situations involving electronic representation are equivalent. There are differences between a sermon prerecorded in an empty church or studio for later playback, live preaching rebroadcast for a subsequent audience, and virtual participation on the part of viewers via live streaming. The categories themselves overlap: live streamed sermons containing prerecorded video segments may be rebroadcast on YouTube or Facebook. But while these three situations entail different degrees of separation between preacher and audience, the challenge they represent remains the same: does preaching normally require personal, and not merely virtual, presence?

A simple answer might be that the Christian gospel is in essence a verbal message: its content is conceptual, its challenge volitional and existential, no matter what the medium. So long as the intellectual content is coherent, perhaps God can be trusted to do the rest. Martin Luther, for example, avers that "God the creator of heaven and earth speaks to you through his preachers. . . . These are the words of God, not of Plato or Aristotle. It is God Himself who speaks."[1] Likewise John Calvin: "Among the many excellent gifts with which God has adorned the human race, it is a singular privilege that he deigns to consecrate to himself the mouths and tongues of men in order that His voice may resound in them" (*Institutes* 4.1.5).[2] Yet quoting Reformers on this point is not ultimately instructive, if for no other reason than that they could not have envisaged the nuances of our current technological dilemma. Granted, the Reformers' affirmation of verbal proclamation could be interpreted as a rejection of technological innovation, privileging the spoken word over popular reading of Scripture, with the latter having recently been facilitated by the invention of the printing press.[3] Yet despite its initial promise to make the problem disappear, an emphasis on verbal verisimilitude is theologically inadequate because it ignores significant dimensions both of the divine-human dynamic and

---

1. "Deus, Creator coeli et terrae, tecum loquitur per praedicatores suos . . . Illa Dei verba non sunt Platonis, Aristotelis, sed Deus ipse loquitur" (WA TR 4.531 §4812), cited in Wood, *Captive to the Word*, 93.

2. "Inter tot praeclaras dotes quibus ornavit Deus humanum genus, haec praerogativa singularis est, quod dignatur ora et linguas hominum sibi consecrare, ut in illis sua vox personet" (*Institutionis Christianae Religionis* IV:9; ET Calvin, *Institutes*, 1018).

3. So Aichele, "Electronic Culture," 12; further, O'Leary, "Cyberspace as Sacred Space," 41–44.

of electronic media as distinctive means of communication. The conceptual content of the Christian message is not separable from the manner in which it is conveyed.

The key issue is that of discerning an appropriate theological framework by which to understand the communication of Christian faith. This is not the same as, for example, making an *a priori* claim regarding the uniqueness of Christian truth; it is to ask whether the nature and content of Christian doctrine implies (even requires) a particular communicative form. Exploring this question involves (at a minimum) three critical issues: the character of divine-human communication (hence, Christology); the rôle of the Holy Spirit in that process (pneumatology); and the nature of electronic media, in principle. Beginning with the last of these categories, Canadian media theorist Marshall McLuhan (1911–80) and French philosopher Jean Baudrillard (1929–2007)—one an ardent Catholic and the other an avowed nihilist—offer particularly trenchant assessments of what is at stake for human and divine identity in the realm of virtual communication.[4]

MARSHALL MCLUHAN: MEDIA AND MEDIATION

Best known today for his slogan, "The Medium is the Message," McLuhan has been deemed "the founder and figurehead of modern media theory."[5] As a theorist, however, McLuhan tends to be experimental and diffuse rather than systematic or even linear. Since this is not the place for a comprehensive account of his wide-ranging oeuvre, the following summary focuses on McLuhan's assessment of virtual—which is to say, electronic—representation, in particular the nature of electronically mediated communication.

Foundational to his thinking is McLuhan's observation that different forms of technology create significantly different forms of perception, such that a printed text, for instance, conveys meaning differently than do the same letters on a phosphorescent screen. Physical texts are, to all appearances, fixed and final, even should we attempt to smudge the ink. From

---

4. On the influence of Catholic intellectual and devotional tradition on McLuhan's thought, see Marchessault, *Marshall McLuhan*, 35–42 ("While McLuhan's religious devotion was never a part of his public persona and was never revealed in his cultural theories, it was deeply present in his thinking" [35]).

5. Margreiter, *Medienphilosophie*, 135, cited (in translation) by Friesen, "Marshaling McLuhan," 6.

this characteristic derives their authority: particularly in an age of limited literacy, the nonliterate have no means by which to refute the assertion that "it is written" (Matt 4:4–10; Rom 1:17; etc.). By contrast, electronic images (even more so in the case of computer screens than the early televisions that McLuhan had in view) are not images at all, but rather representations of images, "discontinuous and nonlinear patterns captured and *transformed into images* in the eye of the beholder."[6] Subtly but importantly, this process accords the viewer epistemological autocracy: meaning is in the eye of the beholder because it is the beholder who must construct the images from which meaning itself may be derived.[7] At a more basic level, the viewer also maintains control simply by virtue of the ability to turn off the screen: in either case, the principle of hermeneutical command remains the same. Texts themselves—even historically "sacred" texts—are thus rendered fluid, easily overwritten, and therefore implicitly impermanent.[8] It is no longer possible to claim "it is written" when the very letters die at the flick of a switch.

The principle of an implicit (usually invisible) link between technologies and their users is the essential insight of McLuhan's familiar aphorism, "The medium is the message." He is not proposing that content is unimportant, but simply alerting us to the clandestine effects of communicative media, since "any technology gradually creates a totally new human environment" (*UM* 12). Focusing on content alone, he contends, blinds users to the effects of the medium by which it is conveyed, a point he makes in characteristically provocative fashion:

> Our conventional response to all media, namely that it is how they are used that counts, is the numb stance of the technological idiot. For the "content" of a medium is like the juicy piece of meat carried by the burglar to distract the watchdog of the mind. (*UM* 31)

More precisely, according to McLuhan, technology (like language itself) serves as an extension of human identity by mandating the manner in which

---

6. Gordon, *McLuhan*, 8 (emphasis original): "The TV image offers some three million dots per second to the receiver . . . the viewer of the TV mosaic, with technical control of the image, unconsciously reconfigures the dots into an abstract work of art on the pattern of a Seurat or Rouault" (McLuhan, *Understanding Media*, 418, subsequently cited as *UM* [emphasis original]); further, Levinson, *Digital McLuhan*, 101–3.

7. The hermeneutical labor required of the viewer is key to McLuhan's complex distinction between "hot" and "cool" media, on which see *UM* 39–50; 425; cf. Levinson, *Digital McLuhan*, 105–18.

8. Aichele, "Electronic Culture," 19–21.

we express ourselves and interact with others: "technologies function both as physical extensions of human bodies and as invisible environments."[9]

On the one hand, McLuhan is optimistic that electronic media serve to reduce distance between interlocutors, creating (at a minimum) the potential for universal community. Instantaneous and mutual awareness, made possible by electronic means, creates a new global (even "cosmic") consciousness, effectively transcending our sense of individual identity.[10] Yet the cost of this transformation is, paradoxically, our human identity: "While electric media link us to each other in depth, practically eliminating space and time from our lives, these same media strip away what we had considered for centuries as our individuality and private identity."[11] A screen image, after all, is "a voice with a face and a body but no substance."[12] For McLuhan, the electronic virtualization of human identity is a specifically theological problem:

> When you are on the air you are, in a way, everywhere at once. Electric man is a "super angel." When you are on the telephone you have no body. And, while your voice is there, you and the people you speak to are here, at the same time. Electric man has no bodily being. He is literally *dis*-carnate. But a discarnate world, like the one we now live in, is a tremendous menace to an incarnate Church, and its theologians haven't even deemed it worthwhile to examine the fact.[13]

Of course, the user is still physically seated in front of (for McLuhan) the television or (today) the computer screen. The problem is not simply a dissipated sense of identity and self but, more precisely, an unwitting distanciation whereby representation replaces true human interaction. In place of the tangible engagement implied by personal presence, we become spectators and "virtual tourists," objectifying (even commodifying) the subjects—people, places, situations—that we contemplate on our screens.[14] His point is well illustrated by a group of family members sitting together in the same room yet each fixated on a separate electronic device, having all

---

9. Marchessault, *Marshall McLuhan*, 202–3.
10. Marchessault, *Marshall McLuhan*, 122–23; further, 218–21.
11. McLuhan, "Liturgy and Media," in *Medium and the Light*, 147.
12. Levinson, *Digital McLuhan*, 39.
13. McLuhan, "Keys to the Electronic Revolution," in *Medium and the Light*, 50 (emphasis original).
14. So Marchessault, *Marshall McLuhan*, 211–12.

discovered that "screen time" is a good deal less messy and demanding than dealing with one another face to face. While promising to bridge geographical and temporal divides, electronic (including archival) representation has the opposite effect, reinforcing disconnection by internalizing it. Personal interaction—interpersonal community—is replaced by its representation: "Thus, it is with some irony that McLuhan will write in the opening pages of *The Gutenberg Galaxy*: 'The new electronic interdependence recreates the world in the image of the global village.'"[15] As Marchessault observes—and other commentators tend to overlook—McLuhan's point is that the "global village" of electronic media is simply an image, nothing more.

McLuhan presses his argument further with a series of reflections, so to speak, on the myth of Narcissus, the Greek youth who, enamored of his own beauty, fell into the pool of water that reflected it back to him, and drowned (*UM* 63–70). In McLuhan's view, Narcissus's chief error was not an eponymous narcissism, or self-preoccupation *per se*, but rather that the image on which he gazed was only a representation of himself. In effect, he dotes on his projection of an idealized self, seeing himself only as he wishes to be seen and thereby losing touch with his actual self. McLuhan is at pains to point out that "Narcissus" derives "from the Greek word *narcosis*, or numbness" (*UM* 63). As Terrence Gordon explains, "In fact, it was his inability to recognize his image that brought him to grief. He succumbed to the same numbing effect that all technologies produce, if the user does not scrutinize their operation. Technologies create new environments, the new environments create pain, and the body's nervous system shuts down to block the pain."[16] The epistemological problem McLuhan addresses is directly analogous to that of pornography, which is not that sexual desire is intrinsically disordered, but rather that the images involved are unreal: they are only as thick as the paper they are printed on, only as alive as the phosphorescent pixels on a video screen. Their apparent vivacity is simply an act of imagination, itself no more than a projection of desire. The irony is that Narcissus *fails* to love himself in all his dimensions, all his depth. Instead, he worships a one-dimensional aspiration that he does not in fact embody, because doing so relieves him of the pain of self-awareness, self-realization. As with all forms of idolatry, representation (electronic or otherwise) thus

---

15. Marchessault, *Marshall McLuhan*, 213, citing McLuhan, *Gutenberg Galaxy*, 31.

16. Gordon, *McLuhans*, 109. "All technological extensions of ourselves must be numb and subliminal, else we could not endure the leverage exerted upon us by such extension" (*UM* 404).

supplants reality; indeed, McLuhan insists, "Self-amputation forbids self-recognition" (*UM* 64).[17] Or, more ominously still, "All media exist to invest our lives with artificial perception and arbitrary values" (*UM* 269). But it is a project doomed to failure. In the words of Jean Baudrillard (to whom we will turn momentarily), "You bend over the hologram like God over his creature: [yet] only God has this power of passing through walls, through people, and finding himself immaterially in the beyond."[18]

This assessment leads McLuhan to a radical, almost unthinkable conclusion: that by successively rescripting society in its image and according to its demands, each new technology (however ostensibly benign) deprives us of our collective human identity, enticing us to surrender our freedom via an apparent exercise of it: "Once we have surrendered our senses and nervous systems to the private manipulation of those who would try to benefit from taking a lease on our eyes and ears and nerves, we don't really have any rights left" (*UM* 99). We become enslaved to the latest technological advances (and the corporations that market them) because we cannot imagine life without their configuration of it. While such a conclusion may initially seem shocking, McLuhan's point is as obvious as our addiction to constantly upgrading our hardware and updating our software.

Whereas McLuhan investigates the relationship between specific communicative media and those who employ them, Jean Baudrillard—building directly on McLuhan—focuses on the nature of signs and signification. In contrast, that is, to McLuhan's interest in *means* of communication, Baudrillard addresses questions of *meaning*. More particularly, where McLuhan is concerned for the impact of electronic media on human identity, Baudrillard warns that over-reliance on signs (and the technologies that produce them) entails the erasure of divine identity.

JEAN BAUDRILLARD: SIGNS IN PLACE OF SUBSTANCE

To explain his concern, Baudrillard recalls the image from a paragraph by Jorge Luis Borges ("Del rigor en la ciencia [On Exactitude in Science]")[19] of a map so precise that its proportions and details are identical to those of the

17. McLuhan explicitly compares the myth of Narcissus with the idolatry described in Hebrew Scripture: "They that make them shall be like unto them" (Ps 115:8 ASV, identified, however, as "the 113th Psalm"; *UM* 67).

18. Baudrillard, *Simulacra and Simulation*, 105 (subsequently cited in the text as *SS*).

19. Borges, *El hacedor*, 103; Borges, *Dreamtigers*, 90.

landscape it depicts. In Baudrillard's vision, the map comes eventually not simply to represent, but to replace the terrain itself. This, he argues, is how signs ultimately function in an "age of simulation." His complaint is not against artifice or signification *per se*, but rather, he insists, that in the subtle and inconspicuous process whereby a sign gradually substitutes for its epistemological referent, "all of metaphysics . . . is lost":

> By crossing into a space whose curvature is no longer that of the real, nor that of truth, the era of simulation is inaugurated by a liquidation of all referentials—worse: with their artificial resurrection in the systems of signs, a material more malleable than meaning, in that it lends itself to all systems of equivalences. . . . It is a question of substituting the signs of the real for the real. (SS 2)

Expressing a particular interest in "religion and the simulacrum of divinity" (unusual, perhaps, for a nihilist), Baudrillard affirms the Judaeo-Christian rejection of idolatry because of "the faculty simulacra have of effacing God . . . [thereby implying] that deep down God never existed, that only the simulacrum ever existed, even that God himself was never anything but his own image" (SS 4).[20] Although with a primary focus on visual and sacramental rather than verbal representation (as in preaching), Baudrillard asks,

> What if God himself can be simulated, that is to say can be reduced to the signs that constitute faith? Then the whole system becomes weightless, it is no longer itself anything but a gigantic simulacrum—not unreal, but a simulacrum, that is to say never exchanged for the real, but exchanged for itself, in an uninterrupted circuit without reference or circumference. (SS 5–6)

Once replaced by a sign, he concludes, "God is not dead, he has become hyper-real" (SS 159).

---

20. Acknowledgment of the surreptitious power of images, he avers, is what motivated the Byzantine Iconoclasts: "their metaphysical despair came from the idea that the image didn't conceal anything at all, and that these images were in essence not images, as an original model would have made them, but perfect simulacra, forever radiant with their own fascination" (SS 5).

Baudrillard does not reject the use of signs in principle, but insists on their epistemological subordination to that which they are intended to signify, thus making a critical distinction between "representation" and "simulation." His assessment, while doubtless provocative and extreme, is nonetheless disturbingly prescient of a culture fascinated by electronic imagery, in which one's personal "image," online presence, or persona comes to predominate over the more complex and flawed characters that we are in real life. Baudrillard is even more pessimistic in his disparagement of television (along with, by extension, electronic imagery in principle) than is McLuhan, whose influence he acknowledges throughout. As Andreas Huyssen explains, television for Baudrillard "ultimately drains the real out of commodities and out of events, reducing them to so many images on the screen that refer only to other images."[21] Such is the artificiality of the televised image "that *it is no longer an image*," not even an attempt at authentic representation or true signification:

> Nothing of any of this in the "TV" image, which suggests nothing, which mesmerizes, which itself is nothing but a screen, not even that: a miniaturized terminal that, in fact is immediately located in your head—you are the screen, and the TV watches you—it transistorizes all the neurons and passes like a magnetic tape—a tape, not an image. (SS 51)

This is McLuhan's insight into the epistemic hegemony of the viewer carried to its logical extreme. Indeed, for Baudrillard, McLuhan's formula, "The medium is the message," presages the ultimate collapse (or "implosion") not only of the message itself, but of communicative media as well.[22] By virtue of the fact that they are intrinsically linked, the demise of one necessitates the eventual dissolution of the other:

> *The medium is the message* not only signifies the end of the message, but also the end of the medium. There are no more media in the literal sense of the word (I'm speaking particularly of electronic mass media)—that is, of a mediating power between one reality and another, between one state of the real and another. Neither

---

21. Huyssen, "In the Shadow of McLuhan," 13.

22. On Baudrillard's critique of television/telecommunication and the concept of "implosion" (both aspects building on McLuhan), see Genosko, *McLuhan and Baudrillard*, 92–95.

in content, nor in form . . . the medium and the real are now in a single nebula whose truth is indecipherable. (SS 82–83)[23]

Baudrillard's assessment of electronic media is thus even more radical than that of McLuhan: at its ultimate extreme, to borrow the language of Baudrillard's compatriot Jacques Ellul, representation collapses into propaganda, which is the manufacture of "fake news"—knowing falsehood—as an intentional replacement for more uncomfortable truth.[24]

To be sure, this is an extreme assessment, one that far exceeds any potential for harm in merely posting last Sunday's sermon online. Nonetheless, McLuhan and Baudrillard alike raise an appropriate caution as to the effects of technology both on human identity (as least in terms of self-perception/self-construction) and on the relationship between mediated communication and the content of the Christian gospel. Each consideration must be weighed against the character of divine communication implied by or contained within the gospel itself.

PREACHING AND ELECTRONIC MEDIA: ASSESSING THE CHALLENGES

Although not all of its elements will prove equally serviceable, Baudrillard's account of the successive stages of mediated (mis-)representation can serve as a general framework for assessing the operational implications of—in this case—electronic rendition in Christian preaching. First, and least insidious, is what Baudrillard terms a "sacramental" order of representation, which serves as "the reflection of a profound reality." Second, the order of "evil appearance . . . masks and denatures a profound reality." In other words, the signifier begins—however subtly—to replace the signified: "Transcendent, symbolic reference is gradually evacuated as the sign becomes pure commodity."[25] At a further remove, representation of a sort

---

23. Similarly, from an earlier discussion, "there comes into being a manifold universe of media that are homogeneous in their capacity as media and which mutually signify each other and refer back to each other. Each one is reciprocally the content of another; indeed, this ultimately is their message—the totalitarian message of a consumer society" (Baudrillard, "Compte Rendu," 230, cited in Huyssen, "In the Shadow of McLuhan," 13).

24. On Ellul's concept of "propaganda," see Greenman, Schuchardt, and Toly, *Understanding Jacques Ellul*, 40–46; for Baudrillard's discussion of propaganda (exemplified by the advertizing industry), see SS 87–94 (esp. 87–88).

25. Walters, *Baudrillard and Theology*, 29.

that Baudrillard designates the "order of sorcery . . . masks the *absence* of a profound reality." Finally, the sign by itself becomes self-referential, since it is "no longer the order of appearances, but of simulation . . . it has no relation to any reality whatsoever: it is its own pure simulacrum" (*SS* 6). At this ultimate stage (which Baudrillard coins the "hyperreal"), "representation is entirely replaced by simulation. Signs have become simulacra because they no longer have any reference to reality but generate their meaning . . . through their relation to one another."[26] Much as McLuhan contends that users are typically unaware of how technology transforms their worldview—even their sense of self—so Baudrillard implies that electronic representation is intrinsically deceptive, beguiling the user by means of its visual appeal and essential malleability until all that remains is the image alone. In Baudrillard's telling phrase, the attempt at representation devolves into a "nullité spectaculaire."[27] In the hyperreal, that is, where signification does not truly signify, "illusion is the fundamental rule."[28]

How might such an assessment (however stark) apply in the present case? Perhaps unexpectedly, the critique of unwarranted epistemological substitution applies as much to preaching generally as to electronic forms of proclamation in particular. The danger of substituting verbal or sacramental instruments, or even knowledge *about* God, for actual knowledge *of* God applies to preaching of all sorts; allowing, that is, theology or "Bible knowledge" to take the place of direct submission to God. Intellect or emotion or ritual participation alone cannot serve in place of existential encounter, since each is rightly no more than an adjunct to or expression of a more foundational spiritual posture. In the context of the sermon, hearing and knowing "the word of God" may and should invite us into God's presence, but the invitation is not to be confused with its acceptance. The verbal sign cannot be substituted for its intended substance.

As a second general proviso (although without necessarily yielding to their more alarmist proposals), McLuhan and Baudrillard both alert us to the possibility that electronic media are neither neutral nor innocent. Fascination with the latest technological innovation (or impatience for the latest upgrade) is characteristic of a wired society. Yet the church is always called, in principle, to stand at least adjacent to cultural norms, even while

---

26. Walters, *Baudrillard and Theology*, 29.

27. Baudrillard, *L'Échange symbolique*, 103.

28. Baudrillard, *Impossible Exchange*, 6, cited in Walters, *Baudrillard and Theology*, 57. As Walters notes (57–58), Baudrillard turns this critique against Christianity itself.

unavoidably embedded within them. At the very least, subservience to theological priorities invites rigorous interrogation of every cultural mandate, all the more so those that seem congenial or convenient. In this case, we will want to investigate the possible impact or implications of electronically mediated communication as they apply to the content of the Christian message in principle, the nature of Christian community in particular, and the formation of Christian identity more specifically.

Incarnation and Divine Communication

The foundational paradigm for the presentation of Christian truth is the Incarnation of Jesus of Nazareth. This, after all, is the claim of John 1:1: "In the beginning was the Word . . . and the Word was God."[29] As Raymond Brown observes, "The very title 'Word' implies a revelation—not so much a divine idea, but a divine communication."[30] More precisely, the term *logos* (for all its conceptual overtones and philosophical implications) is in this instance not a concept at all but a living human being: "the *logos* became flesh and dwelt among us" (John 1:14). As the prologue to the letter to the Hebrews insists, "In many and various ways God spoke of old to our fathers by the prophets; but in these last days He has spoken to us by a Son" (Heb 1:1–2 RSV). Thus, according to Augustine of Hippo (354–430), God does not communicate primarily by means of auditions or dreams or apparitions, but rather "by means of truth itself [*loquitur ipsa veritate*]." Expanding further, he highlights the paradox of Incarnation: "Truth itself, God the son of God, put on manhood . . . so that man might find a path to the God of man through the god-man [*ipsa veritas, Deus Dei filius, homine adsumpto . . . ut ad hominis Deum iter esset homini per hominem Deum*]."[31] As a species of communication (and the epitome of divine communication in particular), the Incarnation is thus holistic, internally coherent, and unitive. As McLuhan observes, "In Jesus Christ, there is no distance or separation between the medium and the message: it is the one case where we can say that the medium and the message are fully one and the same."[32] That is to say, the self-revelation of the eternal Father, creator of heaven and earth, does not come in the form of abstract concepts, moral truisms, incentives to political

---

29. Unless otherwise indicated, biblical quotations are cited from the NRSV.
30. Brown, *Gospel According to John I–XII*, 24.
31. Augustine, *City of God* xi.2 (430–31).
32. McLuhan, "Religion and Youth," in *Medium and the Light*, 103.

action, or pixilated images, but concretely embodied in a single and singular human life. Notwithstanding the fact that the historical specificity of this formulation—the "scandal of particularity"—in one sense precludes access to the originally enfleshed Jesus for all subsequent audiences, the fact of *inhomination* implies in principle that the mode of access to divine truth is not simply intuitive or intellectual, but essentially relational. Jesus the Christ is encountered most authentically not as an idea or moral ideal, a verbal message or visual panorama, but as a flesh-and-blood individual whose reception or rejection is intrinsically interpersonal.[33]

While this conviction does not set a direct ontological precedent for the life of the later Christian community (the Incarnation of Jesus being *sui generis*), it does suggest itself as an epistemological paradigm: subsequent to Jesus's earthly presence, in the eschatological interim, the Word of God is encountered and abides "wherever two or three are gathered together" (Matt 18:20). However little recognized, this assertion has radical implications for preaching. It is one of three parallel statements in Matthew's gospel that define the nature of Jesus's past and future presence in the life of the church. First, and most familiar, is the designation of Mary's child as "Emmanuel (which means, God with us)" (Matt 1:23). More than a simple fulfillment citation (paraphrasing Isa 8:8 and 8:10), this quotation invokes the long history of God's presence with Israel as that which sets it apart from other nations.[34] Jesus himself, says Matthew, is the full and final manifestation of the divine commitment to self-manifestation in the midst of humanity. No less momentous are the final words of Matthew's gospel, with Jesus promising, "Remember, I am with you always, to the end of the age" (Matt 28:20). Absent a fully developed Matthean pneumatology, Jesus here assures his disciples that in future he will remain as vitally present and active in their midst as has been the case throughout his ministry to this point—even if less visibly so.

Jesus has already explained the precise mechanism of this ongoing accompaniment in what is (in its present context) his discourse for the gathered church from Matthew 18: "For where two or three are gathered in my name, I am there among them" (Matt 18:20). This, the third affirmation

---

33. McLuhan describes this distinction as "the great contrast between perceptual and conceptual confrontation." As he explains, "The revelation is of *thing*, not theory. And where revelation reveals actual thing-ness you are not dealing with concept. The thing-ness revealed in Christianity has always been a scandal to the conceptualist: it has always been incredible" (McLuhan, "Electric Consciousness," in *Medium and the Light*, 81).

34. See further Kupp, *Matthew's Emmanuel*, 109–55.

of his presence, is in some ways the most practical, because it alerts the church both to the preconditions for a continued encounter with the risen Lord and to its exact nature. More to the point for our purposes, it explains the proper relationship between human action—in this case, preaching—and divine favor. Whatever our notional theological convictions, we often act as though God graciously acquiesces to be present (for example, in the course of corporate worship) largely in response to our bidding, that God shows mercy if and when we pray for it, and, most pertinently, that divine revelation takes place primarily as a result of faithful proclamation. On such a view, grace is manifest in response to pious human initiative. But the history of God's people indicates the opposite. God deigns to be present in Jerusalem not because Solomon and his successors build temples for that purpose, but because God has promised to be present if they do build, and indeed has already been present in the ark of the covenant, in the pillar of cloud and fire, in the acts of deliverance from Egypt, and earlier still. Divine presence is without exception the consequence of divine promise, not of human piety, pleading, or preaching.

Matthew 18:20 offers a more precise exegetical ground for this enduring theological principle, in Jesus's stipulation that he will accompany the gathering of "two or three" disciples. As with so much of his teaching, his choice of wording (at least as the evangelist presents it) invokes a specific Scriptural precedent, in this case the provision that in order to be legally binding, "A matter must be established by the testimony of two or three witnesses" (Deut 19:15 NIV).[35] Jesus's pronouncement is less a direct quotation than an appeal to an operative theological principle: it positions disciples as witnesses rather than as direct agents, mediators, or instruments of his presence in the world. Whether, then, as worship leaders, pastoral caregivers, or preachers, our task is not somehow to "make Jesus real" to our hearers (much as we imagine this to be the case), but rather to testify to a reality immeasurably greater than ourselves and thus beyond our best-intentioned efforts at facilitating it. As Karl Barth trenchantly observes, "Under no circumstances and in no sense ought we to desire to be *creatores Creatoris*. Ours is not to give birth to God but to give testimony of him."[36]

---

35. Cf. Deut 17:6: "On the evidence of two or three witnesses the death sentence shall be executed; a person must not be put to death on the evidence of only one witness." That this legal principle remains operative in Jesus's day and beyond is evident from *m. Sotah* 6:3 and *m. Mak.* 1:7, 9 (each traditum unattributed and thus of implicitly universal application).

36. Barth, *Word of God*, 131.

This assertion offers an important qualification to Barth's oft-cited triad of the Word of God incarnate, written, and preached. The latter two, in short, derive from and bear witness to the former, not the other way around:

> Preaching must conform to revelation.... In all circumstances we must respect the fact that God has revealed himself and he will reveal himself as the one who comes again. All the action that takes place in preaching, which lies between the first advent and the second, is the action of the divine Subject.[37]

If the foregoing interpretation is correct, there is a certain irony—very nearly a contradiction—in Jesus's promise that wherever "two or three are gathered in my name, I am there among them." While Jesus establishes a requisite quorum as precondition for his presence, the minimum numerical requirement is nonetheless testimonial in nature rather than causative; as witnesses, their function is one of response and acknowledgment rather than directly causing or creating the presence of the Messiah. Joining McLuhan's basic insight that the message concerning Jesus is not separate from the person of Jesus himself, along with Barth's insistence that Jesus reveals the meaning of words about him rather than those words revealing him, to Jesus's own insistence on the communal character of testimony, constitutes an important principle for the communication of Christian truth. The substance of the Christian message, in short, does not consist of words, concepts, or convictions, much less moving pixels, but the living, active, unsubstitutable person of Jesus himself. Jesus does not simply offer words or ideas about himself (in whatever form); that is the task of those who testify to him. Rather, he offers his own person and presence as the source and unsubstitutable subject of such words. Just so, the prologue of John declares not that humanity should receive a message (*logos*) *about* the Messiah (including, therefore, the prologue itself), but that "to all who received *him*, who believed in his name, he gave power to become children of God" (John 1:12).

The Apostle Paul provides an apt illustration of this principle. Notwithstanding the obligation he is under to proclaim the Christian message (1 Cor 9:16–17), he has few illusions about his own ability to sway his hearers, much less transform them into children of God: "I came to you in weakness and in fear and in much trembling," he declares. "My speech and my proclamation were not with plausible words of wisdom, but with a

---

37. Barth, *Homiletics*, 47.

demonstration of the Spirit and of power, so that your faith might rest not on human wisdom but on the power of God" (1 Cor 2:3–5). Then in his second (canonical) letter to the church at Corinth, he clarifies the hermeneutical basis of this conviction:

> We do not proclaim ourselves; we proclaim Jesus Christ as Lord and ourselves as your slaves for Jesus's sake. For it is the God who said, "Let light shine out of darkness," who has shone in our hearts to give the light of the knowledge of the glory of God in the face of Jesus Christ. (2 Cor 4:5–6)

"New creation," in other words (so 2 Cor 5:17), is directly akin to old: both are formally dependent on divine initiative and sustained by divine illumination. But as the apostle goes on to explain, divine action is likewise integral to further transformation and growth in faith:

> Now the Lord is the Spirit, and where the Spirit of the Lord is, there is freedom. And all of us, with unveiled faces, seeing the glory of the Lord as though reflected in a mirror, are being transformed into the same image from one degree of glory to another; for this comes from the Lord, the Spirit. (2 Cor 3:17–18)

Although this passage is an exegetical minefield, its general intent is clear: the development of mature Christian identity is not simply the result of careful pedagogy, pastoral nurture, or impassioned preaching. Rather, in keeping with (at a minimum) John 1:1 and Matthew 18:20, the apostle insists that spiritual transformation is primarily the consequence of contemplation—by definition a passive submission, both epistemic and ontological, to the object of one's regard. Whether, then, with reference to content or communicative means (i.e., "media"), the Christian gospel is predicated on divine initiative (or "grace"), even when human agency is invited or allowed to play a secondary role.

Baudrillard's framework (from "sacrament" to "simulation") serves to underscore this foundational theological premise: in whatever degree, neither our words about the Messiah, nor even the Messiah's words about himself, can be thought of as substitutes for the person and presence of the Messiah himself (however intangible or ungovernable that presence may be). More finely, if neither the church nor its individual members—preachers among them—can replace the agency of Jesus via the power of the Spirit of God, much less so will this be the case for electronic sounds and images that operate at yet a further remove. This is precisely what McLuhan warns against with his observation, cited earlier, that "a discarnate world, like the one we now live in, is a tremendous menace to an incarnate Church."[38] Likewise it is Baudrillard's point about God being "reduced to the signs that constitute faith" (*SS* 5), even in the very attempt to communicate divine truth. And it is what he intends by the distinction between representation that serves as "the reflection of a profound reality" and simulation that—however unintentionally—"masks and denatures a profound reality," precisely by virtue of its attempt at an unachievable representation (*SS* 6).

Incarnation and Christian Identity

Still, such critique appears liable to a significant rejoinder: if God, as Calvin avers, "deigns to consecrate to himself the mouths and tongues of men in order that His voice may resound in them" (*Institutes* 4.1.5), why should the same not be true for electronically mediated voices and images? Barth offers a witty (if pointed) response:

> God may speak to us through Russian Communism, a flute concerto, a blossoming shrub, or a dead dog. We do well to listen to Him if He really does. But, unless we regard ourselves as the prophets and founders of a new Church, we cannot say that we are commissioned to pass on what we have heard as independent proclamation.[39]

At least when it comes to Christian truth claims, according to Barth, the medium neither validates the message nor relieves us of responsibility for careful examination of media and messaging alike. As indicated already, a more substantive response is implied both by the inescapably embodied nature of all human experience[40] and, more specifically, by the incarnational character of the Christian message. In the words of Deborah Creamer,

> Christianity's earliest and most persistent doctrines focus on embodiment. From the Incarnation (*the Word made flesh*) and Christology (*Christ was fully human*) to the Eucharist (*this is my body, this is my blood*), the resurrection of the body, and the church (*the body of Christ who is the head*), Christianity has been a religion *of*

---

38. McLuhan, *Medium and the Light*, 50.

39. Barth, *Church Dogmatics* I.1.55. This reference is indebted to Powery, "Preaching and Technology," in Brown and Powery, *Ways of the Word*, 210.

40. So Leder, *Absent Body*, 1; further, Leder, "Tale of Two Bodies," 24–27.

the body. We relate to God as corporeal bodies, and in our relations with other human bodies, we experience God.[41]

As Karen O'Donnell (who also quotes Creamer) observes,

> One cannot "do" theology without taking the embodied nature of such "doing" into account. Theology comes from bodies in material contexts. Such an exploration reveals the need for a holistic approach to theology—one in which bodies of theology, the Trinitarian Body, the Body of Christ, and human bodies, are not separated out in an atomistic fashion, but are interconnected by one another.[42]

For followers of Jesus, divine revelation and theological reflection both take place in the context of—and not apart from—fully embodied human community, as bodies within the "body of Christ." The implication of the incarnation, surely, is that the community in question should be real, substantive, and personal, rather than merely virtual. To state the matter in more ironic fashion, whereas our communion with the Savior may be to all appearances "virtual"—he is, after all, no longer visible among us—our communion with one another is normally, normatively, in the flesh. Human biology offers an illuminating parallel: although conception is possible via extraordinary technological intervention (at point of contact, in a petri dish), this is not, for most couples, the preferred manner of proceeding. Similarly, Christian community is best lived face-to-face, with real people, rather than virtually or at a distance. In turn, communication and reception of the Christian gospel seem likewise best suited to flesh-and-blood presence on the part of believers. Feminist perspectives in particular emphasize that preaching is an intrinsically embodied activity; the women whom Amy McCullough interviewed in the course of her ethnographic research "affirmed that the body is essential to preaching and that every preacher preaches in and through her body."[43]

Admittedly, the point may be moot for congregations that either consciously choose or are forced by circumstance to meet online: all that remains is to assess the strengths and weaknesses of virtual interaction. Building on the characteristics of Barth's threefold schema, Sunggu Yang proposes that digitalization entails seven key benefits: fluidity, usability,

---

41. Creamer, "Toward a Theology," 63 (emphasis original).

42. O'Donnell, *Broken Bodies*, 12.

43. McCullough, "Her Preaching Body," 5; further, McCullough, *Her Preaching Body*, *passim*.

cross-cultural ubiquity, connectivity, instant communication, holistic artistry, and shareability; different forms of online preaching emphasize one or another of these characteristics.[44] Such benefits depend, of course, on access to appropriate technological resources and infrastructure, which will not be the case in all parts of the world (or even in Western countries).[45] Yang acknowledges, in any event, that "the most challenging conflict is between immutability/reliability and fluidity/usability."[46] Although he upholds the traditional authority and immutability of Scripture, increased autonomy by virtue of online participation implies greater freedom of interpretation on the part of viewers.[47] Appropriately so, democratization facilitated by technology forces the question of whether homiletical authority is properly vested in the preacher, the preached word, or the living Word to whom both bear witness.

In his own assessment of the interface between preaching and technology, Luke A. Powery identifies significant advantages (enhanced cultural knowledge; addressing a wider range of learning styles; broader dissemination of the Christian message) as well as potential dangers inherent within electronic forms of communication.[48] First among the latter, as also proposed here, is the "loss of incarnational preaching." Given the precedent of Jesus's incarnation, which is "God's sermon in Jesus Christ . . . real human bodies, as opposed to virtual realities and bodies, are essential for the preaching ministry. . . . Jesus was the Word incarnate, a person, an enfleshed sermon, not a text."[49] More precisely, he writes, electronic media potentially entail "loss of humanity." Although Powery warns of digital "voyeurism without compassion," a more subtle dimension of this loss is failure to recognize that virtual representation is just that, and no more.[50] Either aspect represents a form of depersonalization, for the simple reason that in electronically mediated communication we are interacting with digital representations rather than real persons (however much the

44. Yang, "Word Digitalized," 78–89.
45. O'Lynn, "'Digital Jazz, Man,'" 25.
46. Yang, "Word Digitalized," 82.
47. Yang, "Word Digitalized," 78.
48. Powery, "Preaching and Technology," in Brown and Powery, *Ways of the Word*, 224–28; followed by O'Lynn, "'Digital Jazz, Man,'" 10–14.
49. Powery, "Preaching and Technology," in Brown and Powery, *Ways of the Word*, 215.
50. Powery, "Preaching and Technology," in Brown and Powery, *Ways of the Word*, 218.

technology encourages us to ignore this fact). Just as Baudrillard warns, visual representation replaces the (personally) real.

Here we may be more precise. On a personal level, electronic participation tends to foster self-consciousness, but at the expense of self-awareness. Most communication apps present an image of ourselves back at us even as we view the images of others. Thus, we are conscious of the image that we are projecting more keenly than might otherwise be the case. At the very least, un-self-consciousness seems more elusive, as we fret over the quality, fitness, or simple tidiness of the personal image that we project to others. Ironically, our electronic avatar is no more personally real than those of anyone else on the screen, but we obsess with it anyway. This is precisely the problem that McLuhan—and Baudrillard in his turn—identifies by appeal to Narcissus:[51] in practice, we are persuaded that the pixelated or virtual image is our most "presentable" self, an improvement on the complexities of everyday embodiment.

Apart from journalism or documentary research, it is in the nature of electronic media to present an edited, idealized image of human experience: meticulously timed, perfectly lit, with hardly a hair out of place. In one of his own sermons, Henry Mitchell describes our day as "an age of image projection and prophets cosmetically concealed and camera conscious."[52] Deep down, we know that neither television presenters nor television preachers really look that good in the flesh, yet precisely because they portray such an appealing image we aspire to emulate them, sharing what seems to be their flaw-free experience—including their experience of God. Recalling McLuhan's contrast between "hot" and "cool" media—so distinguished by the degree of epistemological labor required of the viewer—it is precisely the artificiality of the projected image that encourages us to invest it with greater value, thereby accelerating the replacement of the real by its idealized representation. Baudrillard allows us to see, especially with reference to theological identity (whether of God or human persons), that idealized (in this case, visual) representations in fact run counter to their concrete realization, distancing both ourselves and (in our eyes) God from the reality of each. To grant "virtual" identity a status equivalent to lived experience—live streaming as good as live—is in any event implicitly gnostic,

---

51. Baudrillard invokes Narcissus to introduce his discussion of holographic representation, which he takes to be an extension of "propaganda" into the visible realm (SS 105–9).

52. Mitchell, "Living Epistles," 17.

substituting knowledge about persons for persons themselves. Indeed, denial of the body amounts to what Hyung Rak Kim aptly terms "digital docetism," reinforcing dualist notions of human identity.[53] At either extreme, idealization and erasure alike are affronts to our common humanity.

Along the same lines, but in more directly pastoral terms, Powery warns that a third danger with overreliance on electronically mediated forms of communication is the loss of a sense of community: "Through technological means we may have the illusion of companionship or friendship but it is just that—an illusion." This premise entails two distinct concerns: a posture of (apparent) control on the part of the viewer or congregant, and the loss of intimacy, vulnerability, and mutuality to which it can lead: "Technology provides the illusion that we are sovereign, immutable gods in control of ourselves and others, which undercuts genuine dialogue in community."[54] By contrast, he insists, "A genuine homiletical community experiences mutual vulnerability in the presence of a God who became vulnerable for us."[55]

A fourth and final danger is "loss of spiritual growth and depth." "Technology," Powery explains, "has rewired our brains to such an extent that people are less capable of reading and reflecting beyond a shallow level"; the danger is that in an era of sound bites and quick answers, preachers and congregations alike become "skillful at superficiality."[56] Electronic media represent the "tyranny of the convenient": we use them because they demand so little of us, which is quite different from being guided or governed by the exigencies of virtue and grace. On this point, Powery's concluding observation is perhaps his most trenchant: "The Spirit is poured out on all flesh (Acts 2) and not all technology."[57]

---

53. Kim, "Study of Christian Metaverse," 41; Brown and Strawn, *Physical Nature*, 14–27.

54. Powery, "Preaching and Technology," in Brown and Powery, *Ways of the Word*, 219.

55. Powery, "Preaching and Technology," in Brown and Powery, *Ways of the Word*, 219.

56. Powery, "Preaching and Technology," in Brown and Powery, *Ways of the Word*, 223.

57. Powery, "Preaching and Technology," in Brown and Powery, *Ways of the Word*, 233.

PREACHING AND ELECTRONIC MEDIA: SOME POSSIBLE WAYS FORWARD

Although its benefits are undeniable, we should not imagine that the Western church will shed its addiction to technology or turn away from electronic media any time soon. But neither can we afford to ignore the theological challenge that technology presents. While electronically mediated preaching promotes the message and content of the gospel (by facilitating its dissemination), it also encourages subtle forms of idolatry, in three senses.[58] First, and most obviously, images (whether of the preacher and sermon, the congregational setting, or God) replace their intended referents (which is Baudrillard's key contention). Second, virtual viewing reiterates the audience's effective control over reception and interpretation of the message (as McLuhan insists). Third, the medium itself (rather than the preached word) becomes the vehicle of access to God, which constitutes idolatry in its most technical sense. Deliberative and practical responses to these concerns can be loosely grouped under the headings of identity, community, and spirituality.

Personal Identity

Whether from the perspective of the online preacher or her virtual viewers, we tend to overlook the fact (even in the case of prerecorded material) that the images we see on screen are not, most immediately, actual persons or situations, even though that is precisely what they appear to be. In other words, we too easily accept the sign as a sufficient representation of its referent, and in so doing overlook what is lost in the process. This calls for more conscious theological deliberation on the nature of Christian identity and the axiomatic role of interpersonal engagement. McLuhan's point about consumers being largely unaware of the effect that technology has on them is key. Preachers have a responsibility to stir up a kind of holy discontent with any form of understanding or interaction that fails to acknowledge—all the more so anything that obscures or impairs—the full (and fully embodied) humanity of their congregants. Given Jesus's validation of human identity in principle and his goal of providing "life abundant" (John 10:10) in particular, resistance to the dehumanizing

---

58. This key insight originates with Seán McGuire, to whom I am indebted for corrections to an earlier draft of this chapter.

implications of electronic avatars and simulacra has a theological and not merely anthropological ground.

The blurred boundaries of online representation highlight Baudrillard's concern for the difference between simulation and dissimulation, in whatever degree. Whereas the latter merely entails pretense (and is thus more easily unmasked), "simulation threatens the difference between the 'true' and the 'false,' the 'real' and the 'imaginary'" (SS 3). Once we concede the epistemological—or theological—sufficiency of virtual representation, we are faced with difficult decisions as to what constitutes the "real" as distinct from what is virtual or "hyperreal." As O'Leary notes, "the relationship between the physical sign and the spiritual signified . . . is the crux of the issue that will have to be debated and resolved by those who wish to lead a significant portion of their religious lives online."[59]

This observation is relevant both to preachers, insofar as electronic media and the entertainment industry encourage cults of personality, and to congregants, especially when negotiating online identity in iconic form.[60] Admitting a growing pessimism on this point, O'Leary contends that the boundaries between embodied and machine-mediated aspects of identity are sufficiently fluid "that we are all, in one way or another, becoming cyborgs."[61] Conversely, the anonymity afforded by online participation has the potential to moderate bias or prejudice occasioned by gender, ethnicity, economic status, and the like.[62]

Although this point is considerably more subtle and part of a much larger discussion, it is likewise critical for users of technology (pastors and preachers among them) to distinguish between construction of meaning on the part of the viewer and the priority of grace in determining Christian identity. Which aspects of personal identity are intrinsic to human experience (as a reflection of the created order) and which are negotiable is currently a matter of intense debate. But what is not negotiable for Christian faith is the priority of divine grace in the processes of salvation, whereby identity itself (and not merely our forensic status) is transformed by the work of God, both historically in the ministry of Christ and via the present agency of the Holy Spirit. As a subset of this concern (or included within it) are questions of revelation and illumination, both in the original

---

59. O'Leary, "Utopian and Dystopian Possibilities," 45.
60. Hutchings, "Dis/Embodied Church," 50–52.
61. O'Leary, "Utopian and Dystopian Possibilities," 38; cf. 47–48.
62. Dawson, "Religion," 80.

formulation of Scripture and in human experience today. If the priority of divine initiative is to be maintained, the appropriate posture for a viewer or reader is one of submission rather than epistemic autocracy, no matter how much technology encourages the latter stance. "For we are his [i.e., God's] workmanship," insists the letter to the Ephesians, "created in Christ Jesus for good works" (Eph 2:10 RSV). Rather than being left to fashion the images by which we know ourselves and make ourselves known, our task is to assume an identity already prepared for us; hence we are admonished to "*put on* the new nature, created after the likeness of God in true righteousness and holiness" (Eph 4:24 RSV).

Community

The danger of substituting words for divine encounter (that is, reducing encounter to the words themselves) or, at a further remove, of allowing electronic communication to replace personal communion, both seem particularly germane to classic Protestantism, with its heavy emphasis on verbal proclamation and doctrinal abstraction. Post-pandemic, intentionally reappropriating baptism and the Lord's Supper can help to counterbalance these more impersonal dimensions of our common life. A major thrust of the Protestant Reformation was on revalorizing sacramental signs that had been largely reduced to mechanisms of exchange.[63] Even though the Eucharist remains liable to a similar devaluation, a robust emphasis on personal communion (whether in terms of baptism, eucharistic participation, or in-person community) is needed to counteract the more depersonalizing effects of intermittent, if sometimes necessary, interaction in virtual form.[64]

Maintaining a theologically appropriate balance between individualist and collectivist constructions of identity is a separate concern. Hutchings observes that "the key shift made possible by new media is a centring of connective power on the individual, who gains new freedom to gather and shed resources, allegiances and relationships."[65] In global perspective, however,

---

63. As noted by Walters (*Baudrillard and Theology*, 72) in discussing appropriation of Baudrillard's categories by French sacramental theologian Louis-Marie Chauvet (b. 1942). Fittingly, Calvin's critique of transubstantiation was that it "destroys the analogy between the sign and the thing signified [*everti analogiam signi et rei signatae*]" (*Ioannis Calvini Opera* 9:231; ET Calvin, "Last Admonition," 467).

64. Potgieter, "Digitalisation and the Church," 569–71.

65. Hutchings, "Dis/Embodied Church," 45–46.

collectivist cultures may see this as a weakness rather than a strength, since Christian identity—the identity of a church "in Christ"—is more properly construed in corporate terms. Yet here, too, electronic representation poses a subtle challenge, at least in the sense that it reduces genuine community—complete with people whispering, babies crying, and the person in front blocking your view—to the *image* of a community. All the more so when the recording of a sermon, praise song, or worship service has been edited prior to posting, electronic media yield an intentionally idealized representation of experience. While there is no virtue in celebrating missed cues or other minor errors, neither can an electronic church be allowed to resemble the third-order machineries of entertainment and spectacle that Baudrillard dissects with such compelling insight, whether Disneyland, Enchanted Village, Marine World, or others of their kind. Each he terms "a space of the regeneration of the imaginary" (SS 13) that reflects back to us an image of the world as we wish it could be, thereby masking our failure to realize these very aspirations.[66] On the contrary, the threat of false idealization ("keeping up the image") should encourage congregations to embrace simplicity, imperfection, and repentance, contrary to the fascination with spectacle that is so characteristic of contemporary Western cultures.

Spirituality

Implicit within the whole of the foregoing discussion, and critical to it, are questions of spirituality and the Holy Spirit. There is no doubt that the Spirit of God can adopt even the most unusual instruments to communicate divine truth. That was the point of Barth's comment about blossoming shrubs and dead dogs. But these are outliers: embodied, *immediate*, verbal forms of communication remain a theologically mandated norm. To state the matter more finely: if, as McLuhan insists, Jesus "is the one case where we can say that the medium and the message are fully one and the same"[67]—if Jesus is the definitive medium of communication between God and humanity—there is no place for any other communicative intermediary. Other, that is, than the Holy Spirit who is also "the Spirit of Jesus Christ" (Phil 1:19). As Jesus himself says of the Paraclete in John 16:14, "He

---

66. Hence, "the imaginary of Disneyland is neither true nor false, it is a deterrence machine set up in order to rejuvenate the fiction of the real in the opposite camp"! (SS 13).

67. McLuhan, *Medium and the Light*, 103.

will take what is mine and declare it to you." Without getting too tangled in the details of Trinitarian theology, we may summarize by saying that in the eschatological interim, communication of Christian truth, whether in the mouths of preachers or by other means, relies absolutely on the agency of the Spirit of God.

Attention to pneumatology and Christian spirituality must therefore be at the forefront of the church's appropriation of technology in general and online forms of preaching in particular. This is not to suggest that the operations of the Holy Spirit obviate concern over "substituting the signs of the real for the real" (SS 2). On the contrary, personal reliance on the Spirit is necessary to forestall any such substitution and the attendant erasure of divine identity, even in their earliest stages. As the counterpoint to electronic narcissism, it is the Spirit who fashions us into the image of Christ (both individually and corporately), as Paul argues in 2 Corinthians 3:18.[68] But since the work of the Spirit is neither automatic nor autocratic, emancipation from the more deleterious effects of technology awaits a willing turn to the Paraclete on the part of preachers and congregants alike (so 1 Cor 3:6–7). In this regard, notwithstanding the limitations of the digital divide,[69] online connectivity can foster awareness of preaching in cultures other than our own, thereby reminding us of the global reach and diversity of the Spirit's work.[70] Conversely, overreliance on second- or third-hand representations of God—signs and simulacra in place of the divine (so Mark 8:11–12, etc.)—is clear evidence of failure to rely on the mediatorial immediacy of the Holy Spirit. Such a situation cannot be remedied simply by recalibrating media usage (which would merely reinscribe its pivotal role), but only by direct recourse to the Spirit, which is the essential purpose and domain of Christian spirituality itself.

There is no doubt that employing technology to make ourselves look good is considerably less hazardous and demanding than relying on the Holy Spirit to give our sermons life. Yet McLuhan and Baudrillard indicate that what is potentially at stake in our use of electronic media is nothing less than direct engagement with, and transformation by, the God who is the object of our faith. While the practical benefits of technology may well

---

68. "All of us . . . are being transformed into the same image from one degree of glory to another; for this comes from the Lord, the Spirit."

69. Aichele, "Electronic Culture," 16; O'Leary, "Utopian and Dystopian Possibilities," 46.

70. Matsen Neal, "Boundaries of Belonging," 10.

outweigh the risks, theological acuity must predominate over technological convenience, lest technology supplant theology, as McLuhan and Baudrillard both fear.

BIBLIOGRAPHY

Aichele, George. "Electronic Culture and the Future of the Canon of Scripture, or: The Hyperreal Bible." In *Redirected Travel: Alternative Journeys and Places in Biblical Studies*, edited by Roland Boer and Edgar W. Conrad, 8–23. Journal for the Study of the Old Testament Supplement Series 382. London: T&T Clark, 2003.

Augustine, Saint. *The City of God Against the Pagans III (Books VIII–XI)*. Loeb Classical Library 413. Trans. David S. Wiesen. Cambridge: Harvard University Press; London: Heinemann, 1968.

Barth, Karl. *Homiletics*. Translated by Geoffrey W. Bromiley and Donald E. Daniels. Louisville: Westminster John Knox, 1991.

———. *The Word of God and the Word of Man*. Translated by Douglas Horton. Boston: Pilgrim, 1928. Rpr. New York: Harper, 1957.

———. *Church Dogmatics* I.1. Edited by G. W. Bromiley and T. F. Torrance. Translated by G. W. Bromiley. Peabody, MA: Hendrickson, 2010.

Baudrillard, Jean. "Compte Rendu de Marshall McLuhan, *Understanding Media: The Extensions of Man*." *L'Homme et la société* 5 (1967) 227–30.

———. *L'Échange symbolique et la mort*. Paris: Gallimard, 1976.

———. *Impossible Exchange*. Translated by Chris Turner. London: Verso, 2001.

———. *Simulacra and Simulation*. Translated by Sheila Faria Glaser. The Body, In Theory: Histories of Cultural Materialism. Ann Arbor, MI: University of Michigan Press, 1994.

Borges, Jorge Luis. *Dreamtigers*. Translated by Mildred Boyer and Harold Morland. Austin: University of Texas Press, 1964.

———. *El hacedor*. Buenos Aires: Emecé, 1960.

Brown, Raymond E. *The Gospel According to John I–XII: A New Translation with Introduction and Commentary*. Anchor Bible 29. Garden City, NY: Doubleday, 1981.

Brown, Sally A., and Luke A. Powery. *Ways of the Word: Learning to Preach for Your Time and Place*. Minneapolis: Fortress, 2016.

Brown, Warren S., and Brad D. Strawn. *The Physical Nature of Christian Life: Neuroscience, Psychology, and the Church*. Cambridge: Cambridge University Press, 2012.

Calvin, John. *Institutes of the Christian Religion*. Translated by Ford Lewis Battles. Edited by John McNeill. Library of Christian Classics 21. Philadelphia: Westminster, 1960.

———. *Ioannis Calvini Opera Quae Supersunt Omnia*. Vol. 9. Edited by Wilhelm Baum, Eduard Cunitz and Eduard Reuss. Corpus Reformatorum 37. Brunswick: C. A. Schwetschke and Son, 1870.

———. *Joannis Calvini Opera Selecta*, Vol. V: *Institutionis Christianae Religionis 1559 Librum IV*. 2nd ed. Edited by Peter Barth and Wilhelm Niesel. Munich: Kaiser, 1974.

———. "Last Admonition to Joachim Westphal" [1557]. In *Tracts and Treatises on Doctrine and Worship of the Church*, translated by Henry Beveridge, 346–495. Grand Rapids: Eerdmans, 1958.

Creamer, Deborah. "Toward a Theology that Includes Human Experience of Disability." *Journal of Religion, Disability and Health* 7.3 (2008) 57–67.

Dawson, Lorne L. "Religion and the Quest for Virtual Community." In *Religion Online: Finding Faith on the Internet*, edited by Lorne L. Dawson and Douglas E. Cowan, 75–89. New York: Routledge, 2004.

Friesen, Norm. "Marshaling McLuhan for Media Theory." *English Studies in Canada* 36.2–3 (2010) 5–9.

Genosko, Gary. *McLuhan and Baudrillard: Masters of Implosion*. London: Routledge, 1999.

Gordon, W. Terrence. *McLuhan: A Guide for the Perplexed*. New York: Continuum, 2010.

Greenman, Jeffrey P., Read Mercer Schuchardt, and Noah J. Toly. *Understanding Jacques Ellul*. Eugene, OR: Cascade, 2012.

Hutchings, Tim. "The Dis/Embodied Church: Worship, New Media and the Body." In *Christianity in the Modern World: Changes and Controversies*, edited by Elijah Obinna et al., 37–57. London: Routledge, 2014.

Huyssen, Andreas. "In the Shadow of McLuhan: Jean Baudrillard's Theory of Simulation." *Assemblage* 10 (1989) 6–17.

Kim, Hyung-Rak. "A Study of Christian Metaverse Community and Worship." *Theology and Praxis* 76 (2021) 41–66 [Korean].

Kupp, David D. *Matthew's Emmanuel: Divine Presence and God's People in the First Gospel*. Society for New Testament Studies Monograph Series 90. Cambridge: Cambridge University Press, 1996.

Leder, Drew. *The Absent Body*. Chicago: University of Chicago Press 1990.

———. "A Tale of Two Bodies: The Cartesian Corpse and the Lived Body." In *The Body in Medical Thought and Practice*, edited by Drew Leder, 17–35. Philosophy and Medicine 43. Dordrecht: Kluwer Academic, 1992.

Levinson, Paul. *Digital McLuhan: A Guide to the Information Millennium*. London: Routledge, 1999.

Luther, Martin. *D. Martin Luthers Tischreden, 1531–46. Vierter Band: Tischreden aus den Jahren 1538–1540*. Weimar: H. Böhlaus, 1916. [= WA TR]

Marchessault, Janine. *Marshall Mcluhan: Cosmic Media*. London: Sage, 2005.

Margreiter, Reinhard. *Medienphilosophie: Eine Einführung*. Berlin: Parerga, 2006.

Matsen Neal, Jerusha. "Boundaries of Belonging: The Necessity of a Global Homiletic Conversation." *Homiletic* 43 (2018) 3–17.

McCullough, Amy P. "Her Preaching Body: Embodiment and the Female Preaching Body." *Practical Matters* 6 (2013) 1–8.

———. *Her Preaching Body: Conversations about Identity, Agency, and Embodiment Among Contemporary Female Preachers*. Eugene, OR: Cascade, 2018.

McLuhan, Marshall. *The Gutenberg Galaxy: The Making of Typographic Man*. Toronto: University of Toronto Press, 1962.

———. *The Medium and the Light: Reflections on Religion*. Edited by Eric McLuhan and Jacek Szklarek. Toronto: Stoddart, 1999. Rpr. Eugene, OR: Wipf & Stock, 2010.

———. *Understanding Media: The Extensions of Man*. Edited by W. Terrence Gordon. Corte Madera, CA: Gingko, 2003.

Mitchell, Henry H. "Living Epistles." In *Patterns of Preaching: A Sermon Sampler*, edited by Ronald J. Allen, 16–21. St. Louis: Chalice, 1998.

O'Donnell, Karen. *Broken Bodies: The Eucharist, Mary, and the Body in Trauma Theology*. London: SCM Research, 2018.

O'Leary, Stephen D. "Cyberspace as Sacred Space: Communicating Religion on Computer Networks." In *Religion Online: Finding Faith on the Internet*, edited by Lorne L. Dawson and Douglas E. Cowan, 37–58. New York: Routledge, 2004.

———. "Utopian and Dystopian Possibilities of Networked Religion in the New Millenium." In *Religion and Cyberspace*, edited by Morten Højsgaard and Margit Warburg, 38–49. New York: Routledge, 2005.

O'Lynn, Rob. "'Digital Jazz, Man': The Intersection of Preaching and Media in the Era of COVID (And After)." Academy of Homiletics 2021 Workgroup Papers and Abstracts (2021) 4–15. https://academyofhomiletics.app.neoncrm.com/neon/resource/academyofhomiletics/files/Academy%20of%20Homiletics%20Papers%202021(2).pdf.

Potgieter, Annette. "Digitalisation and the Church—A Corporeal Understanding of Church and the Influence of Technology." *Stellenbosch Theological Journal* 5 (2019) 561–76.

Walters, James. *Baudrillard and Theology*. New York: Continuum, 2012.

Wood, Arthur Skevington. *Captive to the Word: Martin Luther: Doctor of Sacred Scripture*. Grand Rapids: Eerdmans, 1969.

Yang, Sunggu A. "The Word Digitalized: A Techno-Theological Reflection on Online Preaching and Its Types." *Homiletic* 46 (2021) 75–90.

8

Resolution and Remote Real Presence

How Does Preaching Relate to the Eucharist in Remote Worship?

TIMOTHY A. LEITZKE

LITURGICAL PARTNERSHIP

Preaching and Eucharist are partners. Decades of liturgical renewal have pressed this claim. A key reform of Vatican II is that *Sacrosanctum Concilium* explicitly requires a homily at Mass.[1] From the protestant side, the push has been for more frequent celebration of Holy Communion. The movement has been toward the position of Martin Luther. As summarized by Theodore Bachmann, the sacraments "are not substitutes for the Word, instead they substantiate the Word and the intention of God," and "the sacrament is therefore not simply subordinate to the Word but it takes its place visibly on the same level as the preached Word. . . . The communion available in the Lord's Supper is given nowhere else in this same vivified way."[2]

    I write from the perspective of a preacher who counts on Eucharist. I experience Bachmann's assertion that Eucharist offers a "vivified" communion. To put it in terms of the title metaphor, proclamation without its partner, Eucharist, is waiting to resolve. The metaphor is musical, and I

---

1. Paul VI, *Sacrosanctum Concilium*, 52.
2. Bachmann, "Introduction," xiii and xvi.

apologize to those who do not hear. In Western music, there are chords that, to the ear, sound inconclusive. The listener does not have to know any music theory; they can tell that this chord is not the end of a song. Another chord will follow and will "resolve" the tension. This resolution need not be tidy; a piece might intentionally end in dissonance. The listener still knows that this is the ending, where the previous chord was not. With just the resolution, there is nothing to resolve and the listener wonders if the performer missed something. Preaching and Eucharist are, in this example, two chords together in the same piece of music. With just the chord of preaching, the piece is incomplete.

I count on the Eucharist in no small part because of the richness of symbol involved. I use the word symbol in the sense of multiple meanings "thrown together" and not in the colloquial sense of "mere symbolism." The prayer uttered at the table during Eucharist calls to mind a God acting through (and even before) history, the dominical institution of the meal on the night of Christ's arrest, memory of crucifixion, eschatological hope, God making all things holy including the grave—and that is not even getting to the contemporary humans who planted, harvested, baked, and fermented the food and drink on the table. I assume this complex of meanings when I use the word "Eucharist."

Remote worship poses challenges to this way of thinking. One might meditate on the mystery of God not only being in words but in words transmitted via radio, satellite, internet, etc. This is still a matter of words and not objects. What of the mystery of Christ's bodily presence? What of the mystery of a physical union with the saints of every time and place? What of the mystery of the Spirit present in something or someone not myself? What of the mystery of a meal shared in remembrance of Christ and anticipation of the reign of God?[3] What of the fact that these are beyond words, and that their being beyond words helps anchor proclamation both in the mundane world of food and drink and the absolutely alien world of a god beyond our comprehension? Alternatively, in terms of my title: am I left only to offer an unresolved chord when preaching remotely?

I believe the answer is no. I believe Eucharist in remote worship is not only possible but preferable. Remote Eucharist grounds remote proclamation at each location in which it is celebrated. Remote preaching calls out for remote Eucharist to embody the grace spoken in preaching. In what follows I will describe two prepandemic approaches to eucharistic and

---

3. World Council of Churches, "Baptism, Eucharist, and Ministry," 10–15.

homiletic partnership—one developed from the work of Jean-Luc Marion, the other from liturgical theologian Melinda Quivik. Then, I will show how this partnership has been ignored in conversations about remote worship since the start of the COVID-19 pandemic. In the course of this section, I will cover how churches have officially barred remote holy communion. Finally, with help from a sixteenth century theologian (Martin Luther) and a twenty-first century theologian (Jean-Luc Marion), I will show how remote eucharistic celebration and remote preaching as partners provide a way around the remote Eucharist impasse.

SACRAMENT AND WORD (BEFORE COVID)

In *Serving the Word*, Melinda Quivik asks us to ask the question: could Scripture's eucharistic narrative be telling us that we need more than words? Quivik opens with a modest claim that "proclamation of the Word in the sermon serves the whole of worship, just as the worship serves the preaching."[4] This claim rests on another, that "[t]he assembly does not grasp the meaning of God's word simply by cognitive means but by living within many modes of expression: verbal and nonverbal, spoken and silent, still and moving, through symbols presented and even through their absence."[5]

Quivik anchors her proposal in the Emmaus Road story in Luke 24. She makes an important—perhaps so obvious it is ignored—claim that Jesus interpreted scriptures as referring to himself. In Luke 24, Jesus "opens up the scriptures so that their interpretation brings light into darkness, hope into despair. This is preaching."[6] In other words, the first Christian sermon was preached by the risen Jesus Christ and consisted of his explanation that scripture refers to him, and this is a cause for hope. Quivik links the eucharistic meal closely with preaching. She asserts that we do not discern Jesus's identity on our own, but only in Jesus's interpretation, which culminates in the giving of his body; that the eucharistic meal makes "visible the otherwise invisible, audible Word of God"; and that the eucharistic meal visually represents the realm of God which should have been named (as a place of equality and grace) in the preaching.[7] Quivik does not indicate

---

4. Quivik, *Serving the Word*, 2.
5. Quivik, *Serving the Word*, 3.
6. Quivik, *Serving the Word*, 60.
7. Quivik, *Serving the Word*, 70–73.

the *necessity* of preaching alongside Eucharist, but does suggest this is the preferred order of things.

Having opened with a modest claim, Quivik closes with a more radical claim:

> The Emmaus story challenges us to think about the possibility that Scripture is telling us something about how we learn. This story does not say that the disciples understood the events in Jerusalem when the Scriptures were opened for them. No, it was only in the meal that they fully "got it." ... The very primal act of gathering around food, intending to feed on what will give us another day of life, tells us something about Jesus, the bread of life.[8]

Eucharist preaches in a way spoken words do not, a way that is resonant with how people learn. Word and Eucharist belong together.

My own work has resonated with Quivik, and at turns gone further than she. Where Quivik draws upon the previous generation's liturgical scholarship, I draw upon a(n evolving) reading of Jean-Luc Marion. Marion suggests the Eucharist (in Roman Catholic practice) is an example of God's "givenness." It is part of Marion's overall project to talk about God within a "phenomenology of givenness."

Briefly stated, a phenomenology of givenness contends that humans first experience a phenomenon as giving itself. Only after this do humans attach the quality of being to a phenomenon.[9] The concept of being might be too much or too little to attach to God. Such a God might function as a "god of the gaps" in our knowledge, or as the foundation of a system of thinking that otherwise has no justification, or even—as Levinas (a holocaust survivor) critiques Heidegger (his teacher turned Nazi)—as the justification for dominating (having more being than) others. The consequences of God-as-Being are not confined to classrooms and lecture halls. According to Levinas's critique, Western philosophy falsely presents Being as the origin, or *arkhe*, of all things. Postcolonial theologian HyeRan Kim-Cragg recounts how appeals to the *arkhe* or official (colonizers') archive functioned to replace indigenous knowledge with knowledge approved by the colonizers. (In Levinas's terms, colonizer knowledge *is* while the knowledge of the colonized *is* [presented as] *not*.) Following the performance studies of Diane Taylor, Kim-Cragg contrasts the *arkhe* or archive with the changing repertoire or *reperio* of the conquered. The repertoire gives lie to

---

8. Quivik, *Serving the Word*, 81.
9. Marion, *Being Given*, 321.

the claims of the archive.[10] A God who is Being and comes with his official archive is highly problematic. Yet people experience God. Thus, Marion argues, before we experience God as possessing Being, we experience God as giving of God's self.[11]

For my purposes, this comes into play in preaching and the Eucharist. Marion argues that, in the Eucharist, Christ gives himself. This giving is an interpretation. The key text, as with Quivik, is the Emmaus Road story in Luke 24. The disciples do not understand what has happened in the death (and rumored resurrection) of Christ, so Christ gives himself as an interpretation of Scripture, first verbally and then at the table. Likewise in the mass, the homily verbally executes an interpretation, and the meal "accomplishes" the interpretation. Or, expressed phenomenologically, worshippers experience the texts, then experience an interpretation. The first part of the interpretation is verbal—the homily. The second part of the same interpretation involves touching, smelling, tasting—the Eucharist.

Robyn Horner criticizes Marion's phenomenology as incomplete: "What we have, in fact, is a phenomenology that has recognized shortcomings and must be explicitly supplemented by hermeneutics."[12] Christina Gschwandtner critiques Marion's approach as individualistic and dependent upon the worshipper having the "proper" experience of Eucharist, an experience that Marion's approach cannot guarantee. Gschwandtner argues that the worshipping community plays a role in confirming each participant's hermeneutic. Furthermore, Marion places an unrealistic emphasis on the surprising nature of the eucharistic phenomenon. Gschwandtner rightly notes that the Eucharist "is deeply grounded in the larger liturgical context in which it occurs," such that it cannot really come as a surprise.[13] I agree with both critiques, and in *my* use of Marion, *I* assume a great deal of liturgical situatedness that he seems to pass over, and I read him *for* the hermeneutic he describes.

Marion provides a compelling example of Eucharist as givenness. More to my purposes, he binds Eucharist to preaching—the phenomenon

---

10. Kim-Cragg, "Postcolonial Practices," 79–80.

11. It bears mentioning that Marion does not explicitly root his project in anything resembling postcolonial theory, but rather that Marion shares many sources with it.

12. Horner, "Translator's Introduction," xiii.

13. Gschwandtner, *Degrees of Givenness*, 190.

to its indispensable hermeneutic. Preaching and the meal are two parts of the same act, incomplete without each other.[14]

The chief objection to such a claim is that preaching happens in the absence of the Eucharist all the time. However, this then leads us back to Quivik's observation that the act of gathering around food tells us something about Jesus, something we could not say only with words. The homily and the Eucharist together proclaim what they cannot proclaim separately. Thus, the Presbyterian Church USA states in the *Book of Order*: "The Lord's Supper enacts and seals what the Word proclaims."[15] Similarly, *Sacrosanctum Concilium* recognizes the homily as a necessary part of the Mass—an instruction for the faithful as they participate in the Eucharist.[16]

ENTER THE PANDEMIC

In mid-March of 2020, the COVID-19 pandemic began driving worshipping communities in the United States to worship exclusively online. Platforms varied, decisions were made on the fly, but even people such as myself—who had previously rejected online worship as invalid—were forced to admit that worship online was possible. Was remote worship "better than nothing"? Over the fourteen months that remote worship was the only available format for my parish, I came to the conclusion that remote worship was worship. Period. I cannot qualify it beyond saying that my personal preference is to gather in person, *and* that remote worship opened possibilities that are not available in person.

One point of contention in remote worship was the validity of Eucharist celebrated online. The relationship between Eucharist and preaching did not factor into debates about online Eucharist. On matters of digital worship, it was largely assumed that preaching was preaching, even if

---

14. Marion acknowledges that the transition in Luke 24, from Jesus's interpretation of Scripture to his breaking of bread, appears abrupt, and could lead the reader to conclude that we do not know what Jesus said "concerning himself"—that is, that we do not know what his "hermeneutic" was. Marion asks: why separate the actions, here? Why assume that verses 28 and 29—in which the disciples ask Jesus to stay with them—break up two essentially different actions, preaching and Eucharist? What if they don't? What if the four verses are narrating one complete action? Jesus preaches, the disciples respond by asking him to stay, and Jesus breaks bread. The entire preaching–prayer–Eucharist event is a single action. Marion, *God Without Being*, 150–52.

15. Office of the General Assembly, *Book of Order*, W.3.0409.

16. Paul VI, *Sacrosanctum Concilium*, 52, 48.

listened to remotely. Rather than discuss preaching in relation to Eucharist, the church approached Eucharist in terms of two categories, which I will call "transmissibility of grace" and "the validity of community."

By "transmissibility of grace," I mean whether the divine benefits of a rite can be carried over distance. In discussions of online worship, it is widely assumed that God can speak to a listener through a sermon that was recorded or telecast live. It might not be the same as being in the room with the preacher, but God's grace is transmitted whether present in person or not. Some might object that the term "transmissibility" itself suggests the preacher possesses some kind of magic. That is not intended. (I welcome a better term.) The point is that the benefits of the preacher's words can be obtained by someone not in the room with the preacher, receiving the words by means other than hearing them in person.

When it came to Eucharist online, transmissibility came into dispute. Thus, Quivik challenged the very notion of transmissibility of benefits into eucharistic elements, saying that this was assigning magic powers to the words of the presider.[17] Timothy Wengert and Gordon Lathrop argued that to hear preaching was necessary but to receive Holy Communion was not, since—for Luther—the Word itself is sacramental.[18] In other words, grace could travel through words (spoken over the internet) so there was no need to eat and drink anything. Deanna Thompson turned the argument around, arguing "[I]f God is *really present* through the Word . . . it is worth reflecting on the theological possibility of the real presence of the Word incarnate in, with, and through the experience of virtual communion."[19] The Roman Catholic archdiocese of New York encouraged its members to view remotely a priest celebrating Mass and to thereby participate in a "spiritual communion," an "ardent desire to receive Jesus in the Most Holy Sacrament" at a time when communion was not possible.[20] Something transmitted, but it wasn't the sacrament. Everyone agreed that the Word and its benefits could travel. The question was whether the Word could be bread and wine at multiple remote locations.

By "validity of community," I mean what constitutes a bona fide gathering. In discussions of online worship, it is a point of contention whether online gatherings are valid for the purpose of celebrating Eucharist. The

---

17. Schmit, "Holy Communion."
18. Wengert and Lathrop, "Holy Communion," 2.
19. Thompson, "Christ Is Really Present Virtually," para. 13.
20. Burridge, *Holy Communion*, 22.

validity of a gathering does not appear to be a factor in whether a sermon can transmit its benefits. What is debated is whether the benefits of Eucharist can "transmit" such that a valid community exists at multiple points connected through technology.

For Quivik, what makes the eucharistic meal so important is the gathering of people in physical proximity. This precludes any remote or online liturgy from being (what I call) valid for Eucharist.[21] At the opposite pole, Deanna Thompson argues from her prepandemic experience as a cancer patient in isolation that online community is real: "These virtual connections were not simply poor substitutes for real interaction; they filled my soul at a time of despair."[22] The Episcopal Church USA provides perhaps the sharpest statement on the matter. Presiding Bishop Michael Curry writes that sacraments are "communal actions," "physical and social realities that are not duplicable in the virtual world."[23]

The relation of Eucharist to preaching does not seem to have played a role in the conversation about remote Eucharist (except to say that preaching was sufficient in lieu of Eucharist) or, more to my purposes, about remote *preaching*. At no point is it suggested that remote preaching might be missing the table. The Roman Catholic homily is part of the Mass, but those worshipping remotely are encouraged to trust that the Mass is happening somewhere, just not where they are. In protestant expressions, the relation between Word and Eucharist is largely understood as one-directional, from preaching to meal. It is not suggested in any debates about online protestant worship that a remote meal might complete proclamation, or preach by other means. One statement that came close was by the Presbyterian Church USA (PCUSA). In March of 2020, the Office of the General Assembly issued an advisory opinion, noting that the PCUSA *Book of Order* contains provisions for a worshipping community's session—or local governing body—to authorize Holy Communion even for gatherings that are not in-person. The same general rubric ties proclamation to Eucharist: "At all such [non-in-person] events, the Word is to be read and proclaimed."[24]

While there are nuances to the debate, it comes down to some variation of the following two sides: one side saying there is sufficient grace in the spoken word and/or virtual community is invalid; and the other side

---

21. Schmit, "Holy Communion."
22. Thompson, "Christ Is Really Present Virtually," para. 3.
23. Burridge, *Holy Communion*, 21.
24. Office of the General Assembly, *Book of Order*, 97.

saying that virtual community is valid and/or if a sacramental word can travel over the internet, then it can get into bread and wine. To date, official teachings have not evolved since the early days of the pandemic. Richard Burridge's preliminary study reveals that the practice of online communion exists even though it is usually officially discouraged or forbidden.[25] As a result, some worshipping communities explicitly offer Eucharist to those worshipping online. Some tacitly permit it. Some assume viewers at home are not taking communion. Some expect remote worshippers to gather in online waiting rooms while those in person partake of the sacrament. I think that the relationship between preaching and Eucharist offers a way around the impasse. The route begins with Marion.

FORWARD WITH MARION

Marion's eucharistic hermeneutic presents preaching and Eucharist as two parts of a single action. In this action, bread and wine become the "real presence" of Christ.[26] Real presence is a concept used by Catholics, Lutherans, and others to confess how Christ is in the Eucharist. It means Christ is really there, "given for you." Theories such as transubstantiation are explanations of the more basic article of faith that Christ is in the meal as promised. Marion explains "real presence" from his phenomenology of givenness. Phenomena give themselves in different ways, most profoundly in the aspect of what Marion calls the "icon." A phenomenon is an icon in that "it no longer offers any spectacle to the gaze and tolerates no gaze from any spectator, but rather exerts its own gaze over that which meets it."[27] The Other is not so much seen as it sees. In the Eucharist, Christ is present "iconically." We see bread and wine; Jesus Christ, obfuscated from our gaze as bread and wine, sees us. In the Eucharist, "the Word in person, silently, speaks and blesses."[28] In a way that defies definitive explanation, in an incarnate manner that nonetheless is not flesh and blood except to faith, Christ is in Eucharist. As such, he is an Other, regarding us while not himself easily regarded. Bread and wine simply do not look like a human!

Following Marion and operating within a phenomenology of givenness, one could say that preaching is rooted in the proclamation of Christ

25. Burridge, *Holy Communion*, 1–25.
26. Marion, *God Without Being*, 176.
27. Marion, *Being Given*, 232.
28. Marion, *God Without Being*, 151.

himself who is present iconically in Eucharist. Christ the Eucharist preaches. The Eucharist is Christ interpreting himself, giving of himself nonverbally. This Christ who is really present is the source of proclamation. His presence communicates in a way that differs from hearing and comprehending. As Marion puts it, the community "hears the text, verbally passes through it in the direction of the referent Word, because the carnal Word comes to the community, and the community into him."[29]

Marion's position is Catholic; I believe there is something to that catholicity that helps us conceive of preaching and Eucharist remotely. Preaching happens, even remotely. But if preaching is grounded in the Eucharist, then it would follow that preaching remotely is possible *because of* the Eucharist. Instead of debating whether community is valid or whether grace can transmit online—and thereby approve or reject a remote Eucharist—I submit that the church should approach the matter from the other direction. We have proclamation because of Christ's real presence. We have proclamation in remote worship because of Christ's real presence. Eucharist clearly can happen because proclamation is happening, and preaching comes from Christ present in the Eucharist. Eucharist can happen *remotely* because proclamation is happening *remotely*, and proclamation comes from Christ present *remotely* in the Eucharist. Furthermore, preaching without Eucharist is still, in Marion's terms, a hermeneutic calling out for completion. The hermeneutic for a remote worshipper is not finished until the bread is eaten and the wine is drunk. The hermeneutic is "unresolved" until completed in the eucharistic meal. Therefore, not only is Christ present in remote worship, in a eucharistic manner, but Christ offers to complete our hermeneutic as food.

CONSEQUENCES

I anticipate a number of objections. I will address five which are, I believe, within the scope of this essay. This is not done in order to deny other objections. One objection: this is too Catholic a view of Holy Communion. This objection can be paired with another, which is that Roman Catholics are, as of this writing, not permitted to celebrate such remote Masses.

As to the first objection, it is true that my sacramental theology leans hard toward the Catholic end of the spectrum, at least compared to many Protestants. If we perceive Eucharist as more of a memorial than Christ's

---

29. Marion, *God Without Being*, 152.

presence, we are more likely to see the table as an extension of the Word. This, however, returns to Quivik's observation that Luke 24 "is telling us something about how we learn," and that "intending to feed on what will give us another day of life . . . tells us something about Jesus, the bread of life."[30] Surely eucharistic eating and drinking in remote worship could help worshippers know something about Christ in their worship location, maybe *especially* if they feel isolated.

Bread and wine would be more easily grasped as Christ present, even in remote worship, than would words alone. This claim finds an unlikely proponent in Martin Luther. Obviously, Luther was not describing worship via remote means, a technological impossibility in the 1500s. He did, however, describe how Christ was present. More specifically, Luther was insistent that the risen Jesus Christ was bodily present everywhere. This is Luther's doctrine of the ubiquity, a consequence of Christ's two natures as defined under the Council of Chalcedon. "If you can say, 'Here is God,' then you must also say, 'Christ the man is present too.'"[31] It is the linchpin of Luther's assertion that Christ is really present in Eucharist. In the course of his argument, Luther offers an illustration. A preacher speaks with one voice, which passes to an unlimited number of listeners while remaining one voice, present in so many listeners. Luther then asserts:

> My friend, if God can do this with a physical voice, why should he not be able to do it far more easily with the body of Christ, even if it were at a particular place, as they say, and yet at the same time be truly in the bread and wine at many places, as it were in two ears? For his body is much quicker and lighter than any voice, and all creation is more permeable to him than the air is to the voice, as he proved in the case of [Christ's] gravestone, inasmuch as no voice can pass through stone as easily as Christ's body does.[32]

In other words, Luther argues that it is easier to believe Christ is in bread and wine at multiple locations than it is to believe he is present in words. And, for Luther, Christ's presence in the Word is a given. The argument follows the same flow as mine: if Christ is present in preaching, then it follows that he is present eucharistically. And if it is easier to believe that Christ is bodily present in bread and wine than in words, then the Eucharist

---

30. Quivik, *Serving the Word*, 81.
31. Luther, "Confession Concerning Christ's Supper," 218.
32. Luther, "Confession Concerning Christ's Supper," 225.

makes sense as an aid to proclamation. I contend that Eucharist celebrated remotely is an aid to proclamation heard remotely.

I would be remiss in mentioning Quivik without mentioning her opposition to remote celebrations of Eucharist. Early in the pandemic, she declared that what "makes this meal so important, so sacred, so sacramental . . . is the gathering of the body of Christ." Quivik's position has not changed. In a paper presented at the 2023 North American Academy of Liturgy Annual Meeting, Quivik wrote, "Gordon Lathrop's *The Assembly* offers strong historical and theological considerations, setting the stage for the case to be made that gathering in person is required for sacramental integrity."[33] I have a hard time getting past the claim that human work (other than that of Christ) is required for something so broadly understood as a gift from Jesus to the church.

Indeed, this privileging of human work seems to underlie a whole range of objections to remote worship. An in-person gathering is suggested as preventing the commodification of the sacraments, as though in-person events such as concerts are not routinely commodified. An in-person gathering is also offered as a means to prevent making worship attendance too easy. Quivik writes, "When the church seeks to connect through virtual worship with those who are unchurched or absent for other reasons, the church accommodates those for whom absence is a convenience."[34] Heaven forbid going to church be too easy! This insistence on being present in person rather than church being too easy is simply and unabashedly exclusivist. Furthermore, it would seem that Quivik's own prepandemic argument is ignored. If Eucharist proclaims something that the words alone do not, it would make sense to include Eucharist in remote worship, to let Eucharist preach. Quivik now appears to reject any kind of remote worship action on the grounds that it is not an in-person gathering. It is not clear if this rejection includes preaching. If it does, this is one of the few cases of preaching being rejected unless you are within earshot (which raises all kinds of questions about sound systems, hearing loss, and preachers with poor diction!).

As to the second objection, I do think that I have raised a question that the current ban on remote Eucharist—in Catholic and Protestant settings—does not answer. It is the job of theology to deal with reality. If Eucharist is possible (already happening, and perhaps is preferable) remotely, then

33. Quivik, "Liturgical Questions for Discussion," 6.
34. Quivik, "Liturgical Questions for Discussion," 5.

theologies of consecration of elements, ordination, and ministry of priests, etc., might have to adjust. The question of archives and repertoire, raised by Kim-Cragg in terms of postcolonial knowledge, arises again, here. Is the celebrant the keeper of the archive or the leader of a repertoire? According to Kim-Cragg, the answer is "both." The act of celebrating Eucharist demonstrates its hybridity. "Even if we do it often, and repetitively, it is never the same. We can never totally and forever capture what it is in the same way. In Eucharist, there is alterity and irreducibility that liberates and reverses the status quo."[35] The very act of Eucharist calls into question limits that we would place on Eucharist.

The matter of eucharistic presidency brings me into direct confrontation with a third objection: the role of the bishop in Marion's eucharistic hermeneutic. Marion presents the eucharistic hermeneutic within the Roman Catholic ministry structure, complete with lifetime episcopal appointments. The bishop is, by presidency at the eucharistic site, the "theologian par excellence," for whom priests serve as stand-ins because the bishop cannot be everywhere at once.[36] The person of the bishop problematizes Marion's hermeneutic. Marion presents the bishop as the one who, by virtue of his eucharistic knowledge of the Word, cannot be contradicted by any teacher of theology who wishes to remain in a teaching position.[37] This is troublesome even in traditions with a high view of episcopacy. Marion ignores a hypothetical bishop who teaches contrary to the Eucharist, or aids and abets in criminal actions. Furthermore, he ignores the historical development of episcopacy and ministry, presuming a high view of contemporary Roman Catholic episcopal authority as the norm since that biblical eucharistic moment in Luke 24.

The matter of the bishop is an unnecessary step for Marion to take. Marion's goal in this hermeneutic is (or at least is stated as) an attempt to avoid construing the presence of Christ as some sort of presence in the consciousness of the worshippers, rather than a real presence. This presence in consciousness Marion says is idolatry. As John Macquarrie observes, associating Christ's presence "with the physical elements has the advantage of drawing the worshippers beyond themselves."[38] I believe Macquarrie is

---

35. Kim-Cragg, "Postcolonial Practices," 81.
36. Marion, *God Without Being*, 151–54.
37. Marion, *God Without Being*, 153.
38. Macquarrie, "Review," 99–101.

correct in identifying the Eucharist, rather than the presider, as the key to Marion's hermeneutic.

A fourth objection is that multiple breads at multiple locations undermines the unity of the sacrament and contradicts certain teachings. For example, Roman Catholic teaching discourages the use of any bread but hosts consecrated in the Mass at which they are being distributed.[39] Would not this preclude remote Mass? However, I am not suggesting the use of elements consecrated elsewhere. I am arguing that elements even at remote locations are the body and blood of Christ because preaching depends on that, and preaching is happening. Remote worship is worship. There is no reason to resort to "pre-consecrated" elements; Christ shows up anew. Nor does this practice undermine the sense of unity in the bread any more than the use of factory-made individual hosts or multiple loaves on a routine basis at in-person liturgies.

The fifth objection: does this not argue that Christ is present in private, thereby precluding any need for connecting to community? Certainly, those who reject online community as (what I call) invalid could contend that the scenario I describe is one of private, disconnected experience. The thrust of my argument is that Christ proves online community to exist by virtue of his being preached in it and through it. The act of preaching presumes an other. Someone besides me speaks. Such a community might be small, but it is community, not a lone individual.

CONCLUSIONS

For an essay ostensibly about *preaching*, this has dwelt a great deal on questions of eucharistic presence. What I have done, though, is to investigate the relationship between Word and Eucharist. I have argued that the two belong together. I have shown that, by and large, the church accepts that the Word is preached remotely, and officially opposes remote celebration of the Eucharist. I have argued that in doing so the church undercuts its understanding of the relationship between Word and Eucharist. Eucharist is part of one Word and Eucharist action. If the Word himself preaches from a Eucharist that is present for its recipient, and that is how we have preaching, then Christ is present eucharistically and the proof is in the preaching. In other words, the challenge before the church is not one of virtual representation, transmissibility, and validity; the challenge is that

---

39. *General Instruction of the Roman Missal*, no. 85.

preaching shows Christ to be present eucharisticially in remote worship and the church is arguing that Christ is not there.

Eucharist as a partner to preaching is already happening remotely. It is possible, because Christ is really present. It is preferable, because preaching and Eucharist are partners. And it is happening, despite the wide range of official statements disapproving it. The church has reached an "Acts 11" moment with remote Eucharist. In Acts 11, Peter tells the church in Jerusalem that in the course of his preaching to gentiles, the Holy Spirit fell upon them. "If then God gave them the same gift that he gave us when we believed in the Lord Jesus Christ, who was I that I could hinder God?" (Acts 11:17). One might respond that the church nonetheless imposed rules on the gentiles at the Council of Jerusalem in Acts 15. Yes, they did. Rules will have to exist. As for the rules imposed in Acts 15, I will note that most churches today do not forbid food served at civic events or social clubs (our closest corollary to sacrifices to idols) or rare steak. Clearly, even these rules can change. Remote preaching has been with us for some time, and it is not going away. *That this preaching is preaching is due to the presence of Christ in it.*

BIBLIOGRAPHY

Bachmann, E. Theodore, ed. "Introduction." In vol. 35 of *Luther's Works*, edited by E. Theodore Bachmann, xi–xvi. Philadelphia: Fortress, 1960.

Burridge, Richard A. *Holy Communion in Contagious Times: Celebrating the Eucharist in the Everyday and Online Worlds*. Eugene, OR: Cascade, 2022.

General Instruction of the Roman Missal. Washington, DC: United States Conference of Catholic Bishops, 2011. https://www.usccb.org/prayer-and-worship/the-mass/general-instruction-of-the-roman-missal.

Gschwandtner, Christina M. *Degrees of Givenness: On Saturation in Jean-Luc Marion*. Bloomington: Indiana University Press, 2014.

Horner, Robyn. "Translator's Introduction." In *In Excess: Studies of Saturated Phenomena*. Jean-Luc Marion. Translated by Robyn Horner and Vincent Berraud, ix–xx. New York: Fordham University Press, 2002.

Kim-Cragg, HyeRan. "Postcolonial Practices on Eucharist." In *Postcolonial Practice of Ministry: Leadership, Liturgy, and Interfaith Engagement*, edited by Kwok Pui-lan and Stephen Burns, 77–90. New York: Lexington, 2016.

Luther, Martin. "Confession Concerning Christ's Supper." In vol. 37 of *Luther's Works*, edited by Theodore Bachmann et al. Translated by Robert H. Fischer, 151–372. Philadelphia: Fortress, 1961.

Macquarrie, John. "Review of *God Without Being*, by Jean-Luc Marion." *Journal of Religion* 73 (1993) 99–101.

Marion, Jean-Luc. *Being Given: Toward a Phenomenology of Givenness*. Translated by Jeffrey L. Kossky. Stanford: Stanford University Press, 2002.

———. *God Without Being*. Translated by Thomas A. Carlson. Chicago: University of Chicago Press, 1991.

Office of the General Assembly (PCUSA). *Book of Order, 2019–2023*. Louisville: Office of the General Assembly, 2019.

Paul, Pope VI. *Sacrosanctum Concilium (Constitution on the Sacred Liturgy)*. Vatican, December 4, 1963. https://www.vatican.va/archive/hist_councils/ii_vatican_council/documents/vat-ii_const_19631204_sacrosanctum-concilium_en.html.

Quivik, Melinda. "Liturgical Questions for Discussion." Paper presented at the North American Academy of Liturgy Annual Meeting, Liturgical Hermeneutics Seminar. Toronto, January 2–5, 2023.

———. *Serving the Word*. Minneapolis: Fortress, 2009.

Schmit, Clayton. "Holy Communion in a Time of Isolation: A Theological Conversation." YouTube, April 9, 2020, 33:49. https://youtu.be/-bSvXFzA6Nk.

Thompson, Deanna. "Christ Is Really Present Virtually: A Proposal for Virtual Communion." St. Olaf College Lutheran Centre (blog), March 26, 2020. wp.stolaf.edu/luthercenter/2020/03/christ-is-really-present-virtually-a-proposal-for-virtual-communion/.

Wengert, Timothy, and Gordon Lathrop. "Holy Communion Under Quarantine." n.d. bishop.nesynod.org/Holy%20Communion%20under%20Quarantine.pdf.

World Council of Churches. "Baptism, Eucharist, and Ministry." Faith and Order Paper No. 111. Geneva, World Council of Churches, 1982.

Index

ANT/Actor-Network Theory, 24, 28n21, 29n24, 32n46, 29–35, 46–48
Absence, 43, 47, 99, 128, 140, 154, 175, 178, 184
Aichele, George, 125n3, 147n8, 169n69,
Analogical reasoning, 88
Analogical structure, 87–88
Appropriation, 89, 167n63, 169
Aristotle, 17, 101, 129n13, 131, 131n19, 131n20, 132, 132n25, 136n37, 137, 137n39, 137n40, 137n41, 145
Ashlin-Mayo, Bryce, 9, 9n33, 9n34, 12, 12n42, 14, 14n47, 17, 20, 135, 141
audience selection, 93–95
Augustine of Hippo, 100, 133, 133n28, 155, 155n31,
Authority, xv, 14, 15, 17, 54, 56, 57, 58, 59, 60, 62, 63, 63n36, 64, 64n37, 65, 66, 70, 71, 72, 76, 77, 78, 80, 81, 118n26, 121n30, 122, 129, 132, 139, 147, 162, 185
Autonomy, 60, 122, 162

Bail, Chris, 5n18, 15, 15n48
Barth, Karl, 13, 157, 157n36, 158, 158n37, 160, 160n39, 161, 168
Baudrillard, Jean, 4n13, 144, 146, 150n18, 150–54, 159–60, 163, 163n51, 165, 166, 167n63, 168, 169, 170
biblical reflections, 92, 94, 98
Blackbox/blackboxed, 29n25
Blackwood, Rick, 7, 8n24, 8n25, 17

Body, xi, 23, 24, 33, 45, 46, 46n56, 46n57, 46n58, 47, 47n60, 53, 73, 101, 108, 116, 119, 129, 138, 148, 149, 160, 160n40, 161, 161n43, 164, 175, 180, 183, 184, 186
Borges, Jorge Luis, 150, 150n19,
Brown, Raymond E., 155, 155n30
Brown, Sally A., 160n39, 162n48, 162n49, 162n50, 164n53, 164n54, 164n55, 164n56, 164n57
Burke, K., 126, 134, 134n31, 135, 135n32, 135n33, 136n37

caring media, 32–33, 41, 44
Calvin, John, 145, 145n2, 160, 160n63
Chan, Michael J., 14, 14n46
Chauvet, Louis-Marie, 167
Christianity, xv, 65, 65n14, 98, 154n28, 156n33, 160
Christology, 146, 160
Church of Fools, 112, 112n15, 112n16
Cicero, 128, 128n7, 131n18, 132, 133, 133n26, 139
Co-Preaching, 34n50, 54–85
communism, 160
community, 4, 8, 9, 10, 11, 15, 15n49, 15n50, 29n25, 43, 44, 47, 57, 49, 131, 138, 139, 148, 149, 155, 156, 161, 164, 165, 167–68, 177, 179, 180, 181, 182, 186
context, xi, xv, 4, 5, 11, 13, 18, 19, 24, 26, 28, 31, 53, 56, 56n13, 66, 68n45, 72, 74, 77, 79n54, 86, 108, 126, 127n6, 128, 133, 134, 135n35, 136n37, 137, 138, 140, 154, 156, 161, 177
core beliefs, 100

189

Index

Cornerstone Church, 113, 114, 114n20, 114n21
Cox, Richard H., 8, 8n26
Creamer, Deborah, 160, 161, 161n41
creativity, 1, 7, 8, 18, 19, 20, 33, 34, 39
cultural symbols, 86, 90–91, 103

Dawson, Lorne L., 166n62
democratization, xv, 162
depersonalization, 162
Derrida, J., 126, 126n3, 126n4, 141
digital
  age, 10, 16n51, 56, 64, 85, 87, 91, 100–103, 127n6
  Docetism, 164
  preaching, xii, 12, 13, 14, 15, 18, 105, 135n35
  storytelling, 109, 110, 110n11, 110n12, 111, 117–20, 122
  ecology, 16
  homiletics, 2, 16–19
  media, 1–22, 24–26, 28, 32–48, 54, 56, 57, 59, 64, 74, 79, 105, 105n1, 110, 111, 119, 121–22, 125, 125n1, 139
  rhetoric, 1, 3, 3n9, 4, 4nn11–12, 4n14, 5, 19–20
  spokesperson, 57, 59, 60, 72, 74, 76, 77, 78, 80
  strategist, 57, 58, 59, 66, 74, 80
digitalization, 63n36, 161
dignitas, 133, 139
discipleship, 7–10, 15, 17, 19, 103
discursive language, 90
Disneyland, 168, 168n66
distance, ix, x, 29, 63, 108, 120, 120n29, 126n2, 127n6, 125–29, 135n35, 138n43, 138n44, 134–40, 148, 155, 161, 179
divine action, 159
divine presence, 157
Dockterman, Eliana, 3n6

Ellul, Jacques, 153, 153n24
embodiment, 20, 31, 132, 139, 163
Emmaus, road to (story), 175, 176, 177
ethos, 1, 9, 14–20, 33, 39, 41–45, 101, 122, 126, 126n2, 128, 131–41
  of care, 42–45

of quantification, 33, 39, 41, 45
Eucharist, 31, 62, 160, 167, 174–87
  relation to preaching, 176, 184
  remote, 174, 175, 180, 182, 184, 187
Eyman, Douglas, 4–5, 4n12, 4n13, 6

Facebook ads, 87, 90, 91–103
Friesen, Norm, 146n5,
Funk, R., 129, 129nn10–12, 130n14

Genosko, Gary, 152n22
global village, 149
Gordon, W. Terrence, 149, 149n16
Grace, 17n54, 17n56, 75, 76, 157, 159, 164, 166, 174, 175, 179, 180, 182
Greenman, Jeffrey P., 153n24

Haas, Angela M., 5, 5n16, 5n19, 6, 6n20
Hanley, Dan W., 3n7
Hays, Ramona, 10–11, 11n37, 11n38, 18
Heba, Gary, 4, 4n15
Heidi Campbell, 26n13, 54, 54n10, 56, 56n15, 56n16, 57, 57n17, 57n18, 58, 58n21, 58n22, 58n23, 59, 59n24, 59n25, 60, 66, 76, 80, 133, 135n35, 138, 138n43, 138n44, 139, 139n45
Hogan, Lucy Lind, 17, 17n53
Holy Spirit, 78, 146, 166, 168, 169, 187
"hot" vs. "cool" media, 147n7, 163
Hudgins, Tripp, 12–13, 13n43
Hutchings, Tim, 166n60, 167, 1667n65
Huyssen, Andreas, 152, 152n21, 153n23
Hybels, Bill, 102
hyper-real, 151, 154, 166

iconoclasm, 151
idealization, 164, 168
identification, 126, 126n2, 127n6, 134n31, 136n37, 134–37, 140
identity, 4
idolatry, 149, 150n17, 151, 165, 185
implosion, 152, 152n22
Incarnation, 25, 47, 134n31, 155–56, 160–162
inhomination, 156

Index

interactive sharing, 103
intermediaries, 31, 47
interpretative reading, 89
Isocrates, 132, 132n23,

Kalas, J. Ellsworth, 8, 8n27
Kim, Hyung-Rak, 164, 164n53
Kim, Julius J., 8, 8n28, 17
Knowles, Michael P., 1, 1n2, 125
Kranzberg, Melvin, 15, 15n50
Kupp, David D., 156n34

Lagerkvist, Amanda, 24, 28, 32, 33, 33n47, 33n48, 33n49, 39, 39n54, 40, 41, 45, 45n55
Lamb, Lisa Washington, 17, 17n8
Lanham, Richard, 2, 2nn-5, 3, 3n8, 4, 6
Latour, Bruno, 29, 29n24, 30, 30n29, 30n33, 30n34, 31, 31n41, 32, 32n45, 37, 37n51,
Law, John, 29, 29n24, 30n28, 31, 31nn39–40, 31n42
Leder, Drew, 160n40
letter writing, 128, 129, 140
Levinson, Paul, 147n6, 147n7, 148n12
Life.Church, 113
limit situation, 32
Lindgren, Lena, 28, 28n21, 38, 38nn52–53, 39
Linn Sæbø Rystad, 52, 53, 53nn7–8, 62, 63, 63nn33–35, 66, 79
Listener-Oriented Preaching, 120
Logos, 90, 91, 100–101, 103, 131–32, 140, 155, 158
Luther, Martin, 46, 145, 173, 175, 179, 183, 183nn31–32,

Marchessault, Janine, 146n4, 148nn9–10, 148n14, 149n15
Margreiter, Reinhard, 146n5
Marion, Jean-Luc, 175–76, 176n9, 177, 177n11, 178, 178n14, 181, 181nn26–28, 182, 182n29, 185, 185nn36–37, 186
Marlene Ringgaard Lorensen, 61, 61n28, 62, 62n29, 62nn30–32, 66
McClure, John S., 16, 17, 17n55, 18n18, 19n64, 61, 64, 64n38, 77, 77n49, 121, 121n32

McCullough, Amy P., 161, 161n43
media-oriented, 24, 47
mediator, 30, 31, 31n38, 34, 36, 37, 37n51, 44, 157, 169
metric media, 32–33, 39, 41, 45
message-oriented, 24, 25, 47
metaverse preaching, 105–123
Mikhail Bakhtin, 53, 55, 61, 61n26, 62, 63, 66, 81
Mimesis, 28n21, 38n52, 39, 136, 136n38
mimetic/mimetic toolbox/mimetic visibility contest, 38, 38n52, 39, 40, 136, 137
Mitchell, Henry H., 163, 163n52
Mode of authenticity, 41, 42, 45–46

Narcissus, 149, 150, 163, 163n51
narcosis, 149
Neal, Jerusha Matsen, 5n17, 169n70
new creation, 159
nonhuman actor, 30, 32, 35, 37, 39, 42, 44, 46–48
Nouwen, Henri, 15, 16

online preaching, xii, 1, 24n2, 25, 105–7, 127, 140, 162
ontology of numbers, 33, 39, 41, 43, 45
ontology-oriented, 46
Overdorf, Daniel, 7, 7n22
O'Donnell, Karen, 161
O'Leary, Stephen D., 145n3, 166n59, 166n61, 169n69
O'Lynn, Rob, 162n45, 162n48

Palmer, Parker, 17
pandemic, ix, x, xii, xiin1, 1, 11–13, 15, 23, 24, 26, 30, 35, 37, 39, 41, 42, 43, 55, 57, 58, 59, 69, 71, 96, 105, 112, 113, 115, 127, 135, 167, 174, 175, 178, 180, 181, 184
Paul (apostle), 47, 89, 102, 128, 128n9, 129, 139, 158, 160,
Pawlett, William, 4n13
pedagogy, 17, 19, 125, 159
perception, 89, 146, 150, 153
Peterson, Jeffrey, 11, 12n40,
Plato, 132, 132n22, 133n27, 145, 145n1
pneumatology, 146, 156, 169

Index

polyphonic preaching, 54, 61–66, 77, 79, 80, 81
pornography, 149
Potgieter, Annette, 167n64
Powery, Luke A., 17, 17n59, 25, 25n10, 160n39, 162, 162nn48–50, 164, 164nn54–57
preaching event, 24, 25, 52–84, 112, 118, 121, 122
presence, 1, 9, 20, 25, 39, 42, 46, 57, 107, 125–42, 145, 148, 152, 154, 156–59, 161, 164, 174–88
printing press, 145
propaganda, 153, 153n24, 163n51
Protestantism, 93, 167

Quintilian, 132, 134n30
Quivik, Melinda, 175, 175n4, 175nn5–7, 176n8, 177, 178, 179, 180, 183, 183n30, 184, 184nn33–34

Reid, Robert Stephen, 17, 17n53, 131, 131n18, 132n21, 135, 135n34
Religious Digital Creative/RDC, 54, 56–59, 66–67, 69, 72, 74, 77–78, 80–81
Resner, Andre, 16, 16n52
resonance, 136, 136n37
revelation, 26, 64, 155, 156n33, 157, 158, 161, 166
Rhetorica ad Herennium, 126n2
Robinson, Dominique, 19, 19n65
Rouault, Georges, 147n6

sacrament, 7, 114, 139, 151, 153, 159, 167, 167n63, 173, 175, 179–81, 182, 184, 186
Sampson, Melva, 19, 19n66
Sancken, Joni S., 17, 17n60,
Schatzle, Joshua, 16, 16n51
Schuchardt, Read Mercer, 153n24
Schultze, Quentin J., 17, 17n54, 17n56
Sensing, Tim, xvii, 1, 1n1, 125–42
Seurat, Georges, 147n6
Sigmon, Casey Thornburg, 10, 10n35, 10n36, 15, 15n49, 15n50, 17, 17n57, 25, 25n9, 64, 64n39, 65, 65nn40–42, 66, 66n43, 80, 80n56

signs, 86, 150–52, 154, 160, 167, 169
simulacra, 144, 150n18, 151n20, 154, 166, 169
simulation, 144, 150–51, 152, 154, 159, 160, 166
social media, xv, xvi, 3, 3n10, 5n18, 7, 9, 13, 14, 15n48, 17, 25n7, 30, 34, 36, 38, 39, 40, 41, 45, 48, 45, 55, 56, 66, 68, 74, 75, 76, 77, 79, 81, 91, 140
sociomaterial, 23, 26, 28, 28n21, 29, 47, 48, 54
spirituality, 76, 165, 168, 169
Strawn, Brad D., 164n53

television, x, xi, xv, 42, 43, 108, 137, 147, 148, 152, 152n22, 163
testimony, 103, 157, 158
theological invention, 16, 18
Thompson, Deanna A., 24, 32, 45, 46, 46n56, 46n27, 46n57, 46n58, 47, 47n59, 47n60, 179, 179n19, 180, 180n22
Toly, Noah J., 153n24
Travis, Sarah, 17, 17n61
Troeger, Thomas H., 7, 7n21

user-oriented experience, 111, 120, 122

VR Church, 115–17, 117n25
Virtualization, 148
virtual reality, ix, xvi, 47, 106, 107, 113–15, 117
virtue, 5, 17, 131, 132, 147, 152, 160, 162, 164, 168, 185, 186
visibility contest, 34–35, 38, 40, 41, 42, 45, 46
Voelz, Richard W., 8, 8n29, 17;
vulnerability, 32, 33, 39, 40, 45, 46, 164,

Wagner, Kimberly R., 17, 17n62
Walters, James, 153n25, 154n26, 154n28, 167n63
Wiseman, Karyn L., 7, 7n23
Witte, Alison C., 8, 9, 9n31, 9n32, 16
Wood, Arthur Skevington, 145n1
Word of God, 24, 103, 125n1, 154, 156, 157n36, 158, 175

Index

Yang, Sunggu A., 12, 12n41, 13, 14, 14n45, 23n1, 105n1, 161–62, 162n44, 162n46, 162n47

Zappen, James P., 3, 3n9, 4, 4n11, 6

www.ingramcontent.com/pod-product-compliance
Lightning Source LLC
Chambersburg PA
CBHW031427150426
43191CB00006B/422